Trauma-Informed Law

A Primer for Lawyer Resilience and Healing

Helgi Maki, Marjorie Florestal, Myrna McCallum, and J. Kim Wright, Editors

AMERICAN**BAR**ASSOCIATION

Law Practice Division

Cover design by Jill Tedhams/ABA Design

Printed in the United States of America.

27 26 25 24 23   5 4 3 2

Library of Congress Cataloging-in-Publication Data

Names: Maki, Helgi, editor. | Florestal, Marjorie, editor. | McCallum, Myrna, editor. | Wright, J. Kim, editor.

Title: Trauma-informed law : a primer for lawyer resilience and healing / Helgi Maki, Marjorie Florestal, Myrna McCallum, and J. Kim Wright, editors.

Description: First edition. | Chicago : American Bar Association, [2023] | Includes bibliographical references and index. | Summary: "Our focus is on trauma as it impacts and applies to lawyers and clients in practice, legal education, courts and judges, and the legal system and profession as a whole. This book gives voice to only some of the many traumatic experiences that arise in all aspects of law. Unless we hear these voices, we cannot begin to address the many legal, ethical, moral, educational, juridical systems or other issues they raise even where we have tools to do so. The pursuit of justice means voices of trauma in the legal system deserve to be heard, individually and collectively, even when it's difficult to listen"—Provided by publisher.

Identifiers: LCCN 2023010933 (print) | LCCN 2023010934 (ebook) | ISBN 9781639052752 (paperback) | ISBN 9781639052769 (epub)

Subjects: LCSH: Lawyers—Mental health—United States. | Lawyers—United States—Discipline. | Psychic trauma—Patients—Rehabilitation. | Psychic trauma—Treatment. | Resilience. | Post-traumatic stress disorder.

Classification: LCC KF308 .T73 2023 (print) | LCC KF308 (ebook) | DDC 174/.30973—dc23/eng/20230524

LC record available at https://lccn.loc.gov/2023010933

LC ebook record available at https://lccn.loc.gov/2023010934

Discounts are available for books ordered in bulk. Special consideration is given to state bars, CLE programs, and other bar-related organizations. Inquire at Book Publishing, ABA Publishing, American Bar Association, 321 N. Clark Street, Chicago, Illinois 60654-7598.

www.shopABA.org

To each person who shared stories or insights about trauma and healing with us, whether in words or wordlessly, in the present or the past. We hope to honor what you shared in this book.

Contents

PART I   LAWYERS AND PRACTICES

PART II SYSTEMS, GROUPS (OR ORGANIZATIONS), AND LEGAL CULTURE

CHAPTER 6 Trauma and Healing in Legal Systems: Courts and Judges 155

CHAPTER 7 Legal Education and Trauma 171

Contributors

Acknowledgments

The idea for this book came from Brooke Deratany Goldfarb, a lawyer and social work student, who was looking for a resource. Brooke planted the seeds and we are grateful to her and all who have joined us along the way.

A Chorus of Voices

In addition to stories and contributions of the editors, we have included articles by a diverse chorus of voices who have something to say about trauma. They are lawyers, law professors, therapists, and space holders. Some hold multiple credentials; more than one of them can claim title to all the categories we just mentioned.

We acknowledge and thank everyone who trusted us in this book process and guided us with this important topic: every person who shared their story, perspective, or insight, those who entrusted us with a story anonymously or helped us by sending us information, connecting us to a network, or otherwise helping assist us in our journey.

We're grateful to the many who took time to answer our survey and to share their stories and ideas. We listened to all of you and we hope that is apparent in these pages.

We're especially grateful for the generous contributions of the authors for their work and all the guidance and assistance they have provided. Contributing authors' biographies are provided with their respective contributions.

Content Warning

The content of this book may be disturbing or triggering to some readers. Stories or information about trauma can trigger painful memories or evoke grief. If you experience discomfort of any kind, we encourage you to seek professional advice or help with your experience. Topics included that may be difficult to read, while not discussed in specific graphic detail, include but are not limited to mental health challenges, violence, death, sexual violence, child abuse, suicide, and genocide. These topics have been included with the aim of helping to create better tools to help lawyers and other legal professionals advocate more effectively and sustain their own well-being when working with people or situations impacted by trauma.

CHAPTER 1

Introduction to Trauma-Informed Lawyering

Overview of the Book

This book is intended as a primer on trauma-informed lawyering, and a starting point for resilience and even healing. It isn't a complete course on trauma and isn't intended to cover all aspects of a growing, evolving field of work. We discuss the many intersections of trauma and law where it is often denied, ignored, covered up, or avoided. It is a broad topic—even broader than we appreciated at the beginning of our journey. Some concepts are explored in depth. Others are merely mentioned, despite deserving entire books (or libraries) of their own. We had to make some hard decisions about what to include and what to leave out.

Our focus is on trauma as it impacts and applies to lawyers and clients in practice, legal education, courts and judges, and the legal system and profession as a whole. This book gives voice to only some of the many traumatic experiences that arise in all aspects of law. Unless we hear these voices, we cannot begin to address the many legal, ethical, moral, educational, juridical systems or other issues they raise even where we have tools to do so. The pursuit of justice means voices of trauma in the legal system deserve to be heard, individually and collectively, even when it's difficult to listen.

Generally, we view trauma as an event or situation that overwhelms or limits a person's capacity to freely respond at a physical, mental, emotional level (and with other human capacities, including the spiritual level). We have intentionally refrained from taking a medicalized view of trauma. Reacting to an upsetting or harmful situation is normal, not illness.

Because the legal system is so foundational to society, we will necessarily touch on diverse perspectives and areas of knowledge, including the biology of trauma, neuroscience, psychology, sociology, trauma studies, critical race theory, systems thinking, design thinking, history (including oral history), and social sciences.

This book is intended for lawyers, law students, legal educators, and judges. We intend that others—decision-makers, administrators, staff, and anyone impacted by the court—will find it helpful, too.

This book is intended as a collection of cases and situations with practice implications for other cases impacted by trauma, whether those cases and situations involve race, class, gender, different physical or mental abilities (or disability), sexual orientation, or other diverse factors including the impact of developmental health issues, substance use disorder (and/or addiction), poverty, access to opportunities, community safety or belonging, and more. Each scenario holds useful implications for both practice issues within the same area of law and even in other areas of law or the legal system.

Trauma-informed lawyering falls under the general umbrella of integrative law. It is a broader view of law, beyond the black-letter legal substance and addressing a more holistic perspective. It provides support for legal professionals and clients encountering trauma as it shows up at multiple levels in our legal ecosystem, including the individual, relationship, community, and system levels.

Our clients often don't come to us for happy reasons, whether it's an arrest, a divorce, the loss of a job and a constructive dismissal claim, a business dispute, or a human rights violation. Lawyers often work with people who are affected by adversity that rises to the level of trauma.

Generally, trauma-informed lawyering acknowledges the presence of trauma and its impact in the legal system, responds to indicators of trauma with human needs in mind, and seeks to prevent re-traumatization. Its benefits include increasing client and stakeholder (including lawyer) satisfaction with legal processes or outcomes, prioritizing well-being and increasing access to justice or legal services by removing barriers that may be created by trauma.

Trauma-informed law must be a relational practice, not a transactional one. Transactional practice (especially in communication) is the style of interaction we're often taught in law school. It's an approach to clients, colleagues, or ourselves where we want "just the facts please," or focus on goals, deliverables, and wins without much awareness of people or their needs, and people may feel like a means to an end. A relational approach (especially in communication) prioritizes continuously building a trusting relationship as the context in which legal activities and interactions take place.[1] Working relationally provides a double basis for working together— there is both the trusting relationship and the work. In a transactional approach, there are only the work aims without much else (perhaps even trust) to rely on.

---

[1] HELENA HARGADEN & WILLIAM F. CORNELL, EDS., THE EVOLUTION OF A RELATIONAL PARADIGM IN TRANSACTIONAL ANALYSIS: WHAT'S THE RELATIONSHIP GOT TO DO WITH IT? (London: Routledge, 2019).

As a framework, trauma-informed lawyering has four overall elements for working with clients, colleagues, students, and communities in a manner intended to avoid adding to the harm, injury, damages, or costs that have already been sustained:

1. Emotionally intelligent and psychologically informed approaches to legal work that often increase client satisfaction;
2. Client-focused service design strategies that meet core stakeholder needs;
3. Well-being supports that reflect the priorities in the ABA well-being pledge and related reports on lawyer well-being; and
4. Social impact, including improving or providing support for access to justice, access to legal services, and legal outcomes.

The book addresses trauma from both an analytical and experiential perspective. We provide cutting-edge information and analysis from experts in law, psychology, and allied fields. And we tend to the experiential perspective with evidence-based tools and practice recommendations.

About Us

Helgi Maki

I decided to become a lawyer when I was six years old, after sudden bad news from an unexpected phone call made me aware that "something terrible" happened in my family history. What I learned was awful enough that I stopped reading fairy tales in grade school and started reading murder mysteries and war stories because I found them more relatable. Becoming a lawyer felt like it promised to help me deal with formidable conflict—even shocking forms of criminality or violence I learned about from my family's history. But not much of law school seemed to help reduce the impact of conflict. So, when it was time to apply for jobs, I felt my best hope would be to work somewhere like Big Law where I assumed trauma would be unlikely to find me again. I advocated for better supports for people affected by sexual assault in my spare time.

Unfortunately, I discovered that Big Law was not exempt from trauma. While Big Law looked different on the surface than what I experienced, it had an eerily familiar backstory of toxic stress, invisible injuries, and sudden losses. I noticed too many lawyers affected by what were euphemistically called "nervous breakdowns," collapsing from burnout, suffering from chronic physical and mental health issues, experiencing addiction (including workaholism), struggling with broken relationships, or quietly dealing with the aftermath of suicide in the Big Law community, and silently warding off potential stigma about any of it. I personally related to the workaholics most of all.

I couldn't stop trauma from showing up at my office, where I attempted to achieve my way into only being seen for my professional accomplishments. One spring morning in 2006, while working in Big Law, a police officer came to my office to tell me that my mother, who was an intelligent and productive person, had died by suicide after years of experiencing violence (including sexual violence). My contribution to this book is to bridge personal and professional insights together with research about trauma.

Overall, I've heard both lawyers and clients say that the traditional legal system hurts more than it helps, or at least hurts more than it should. If we don't talk about and learn from trauma, it's simply deferred and transmitted for the next generation to deal with at the office, at home, or both. Finding new ways to work with trauma in the legal profession is a crucial alternative to conventional ways of working that lawyers are constantly trying to find new ways to leave.

Marjorie Florestal

The summer when I was nine years old my mother died, and that was when I decided to become a lawyer. I have friends who suffered a similar loss, but their stories end with the choice to become a doctor. For me, it wasn't my mother's disease I wanted to battle but the deep sense of injustice I felt at losing her. The only people I knew who fought injustice were civil rights lawyers. I wanted to be like them.

No one ever talks about the trauma these lawyers experienced in their quest to make the law live up to its ideals. What must it have been like to bear witness to the lynching of Emmett Till or the bombing death of those four little Black girls in the 16th Street Baptist church in Birmingham, Alabama? I was taught to think of these civil rights lawyers as heroes. It wasn't until I became a lawyer that I began to reflect on the price they paid for their heroism.

In law school I learned to "think like a lawyer," which I interpreted as a call to suppress emotion and favor logic. When I became a law professor, I passed the same lesson on to my students. One day, a student showed up at my office in tears, and all I could tell her was "let's talk about contract law." I knew then that something in me had to change. I needed to get in touch with the pain of my experiences, and not just the righteous indignation and the desire to fight for change.

It was a 25-year journey to get to this place—and because I am an academic in head and heart, part of the journey included getting advanced degrees in Jungian psychology and human development. My contribution to this book is my academic training in law and trauma as well as the lessons I learned on the journey. One of the most profound lessons is this: there is another way—a better way—to be a lawyer. And it does not require me to suppress any part of myself. I wish the same for you.

Myrna McCallum

I went to law school for a couple of reasons. I did not want to deal with emotions, and I did not want to have to console anyone or help anybody in the middle of an emotional break. I had experienced a lot of personal trauma in my life and if I could not be in touch with my own emotions, I knew I could not be there for others. I also wanted to serve Indigenous people, never contemplating for a moment, the collective and cultural trauma we experienced as a result of colonization. When I began to practice criminal law in Northern Saskatchewan, I found that the whole range of human suffering meets you in a courtroom. I was not prepared for the suffering I had to confront, in witnesses and, inevitably, in myself. I did not know how to deal with people in crisis who looked to me to rescue them and sometimes, pleading with me to do the impossible.

Our legal processes were never designed to be trauma-informed; in fact, I think they were designed to traumatize. No other outcome is possible when we are taught to treat people as nothing more than legal issues. Practicing law in this way creates a lot of harm in people who have already experienced significant harm in their lives. One day, upon meeting a little boy who had been sexually assaulted, I decided I could no longer recklessly contribute to the harm of others, in the name of justice. This little boy and the hundreds of survivors who followed over the course of my legal career, taught me what I now understand to be trauma-informed lawyering. My contribution to this book is my translation of the education they provided me, the education none of us received in law school—but should have.

J. Kim Wright

I've been a lawyer since 1989. In my early career, I was the director of a domestic violence program. (The deciding factor in getting the job was my own experience in a violent marriage.) Later, I was the associate director of a Restorative Justice agency and we worked with families of murder victims, bringing them together with those who killed their loved ones. I practiced family law, and my background drew clients from violent situations. One of my clients was killed by her estranged husband. I was a mother, stepmother, and foster mother to a blended, multiracial family.

I observed lawyers who seemed not to be impacted by events that shocked and traumatized me. They could tear families apart all day and then go home and have dinner with their own children. My heart couldn't stand that. I was compelled to explore options for more holistic, healing approaches for myself and my clients.

I soon discovered that I was not the broken one: the legal system was dysfunctional. There were baked-in, systemic and often toxic problems, and there were models and approaches that were healthier and more powerful for all the stakeholders. I studied those alternatives and I made it my mission to transform law.

For the last 25 years, I have been working in the field of integrative law. Integrative law addresses the holistic nature of the profession, from self to system. My role on the team was bolstered by having written two prior books about integrative law, published by the American Bar Association.

How We Included Other Perspectives in This Book

Of course, we brought our own life experiences with us, but we did a lot more. We conducted academic research and periodic literature reviews. We conducted surveys (and received approximately 50 responses). We published an RFP for contributions and we invited global participation. We interviewed people (formally and informally). We wrote academic and nonacademic articles, and spoke at law schools and with lawyers, judges, clients, witnesses, students, jury members, law clerks, transcriptionists, translators, legal innovators, as well as friends, neighbors, and community members affected by trauma. We connected with groups of trauma survivors and had one-on-one conversations with trauma survivors. We also listened to accused persons, offenders, and currently or previously incarcerated persons and the people who work with them, or their friends, families, and loved ones. We have included attributed and anonymous stories and insights from lawyers and law students affected by trauma. Above all, we sought to listen and include as many people and perspectives as we could.

From this listening, we heard that many people believe that this topic is an important one. We received and found a great number of resources, stories, and articles, and this book includes those we found both representative and that crossed our paths during research. We've distilled what we think is foundational.

This primer is a place to begin, and it cannot and does not include everything a lawyer may need to know about trauma-informed lawyering.

About Storytelling in This Book

Marjorie Florestal

Sometimes we need stories more than food to stay alive. If you have ever had a story touch something deep within you, then you understand the truth of this aphorism. Stories are powerful because they engage us through our emotions and give us permission to explore difficult, uncomfortable, and controversial topics. We look to stories as a way of making sense of our experiences, transforming them into something meaningful and transcendent, and passing on that knowledge to others.

In this book, we explore the stories of legal practitioners as a way to excavate the trauma embedded in the legal system, and to identify the paths we have taken to find our way back to wholeness. Our lived experience has convinced us of the power of story, but it just so happens that the literature supports our conclusion.

In neuroscience, Dr. Paul Zak was one of the first researchers to discover that the hormone oxytocin—sometimes called the "love hormone"—mediates our emotional response to narratives. In a series of experiments,[2] Zak asked participants to watch commercials on emotionally charged topics, including cancer, gun control,

---

[2] Paul J. Zak, *Why Inspiring Stories Make Us React: The Neuroscience of Narrative*, Cerebrum (Feb. 2, 2015). Available at https://www.ncbi.nlm.nih.gov/pmc/articles/PMC4445577/; *see also* Pei-Ying Lin, Naomi Sparks Grewal, Christophe Morin, Walter D. Johnson, and Paul J. Zak, *Oxytocin Increases the Influence of Public Service Advertisements*. PLoS ONE 8(2): e56934. Available at https://doi.org/10.1371/journal.pone.0056934.

and racism. When the commercials contained a strong narrative arc—a compelling story—participants saw an increase in their oxytocin and cortisol levels. The change in oxytocin had a positive correlation with participants' feelings of empathy, which in turn motivated them to take action; in this case, they donated money to charity without being solicited. In short, good stories are biologically transformative and motivate us to take action.

Narrative scholar Dr. Melanie C. Green explores why stories impact humans so profoundly. She posits a theory of narrative transportation, which is defined as the participant's "absorption in the story through the use of imagery, affect, and attentional focus."[3] Stories that immerse people in their narrative, transporting them into the story world, seem to have the capacity to change hearts and minds. In one study, Green found that individuals altered their real-world beliefs in response to experiences in the story world. Whether the story was labeled fact or fiction did not diminish this impact. While some argue that only positive narratives have such an effect, Dr. Green suggests otherwise. She maintains that in human history, the most powerful tales tend to be those involving negative aspects, such as dilemmas to be overcome or obstacles to be surmounted.[4]

Stories can also serve as a healing elixir for body and soul. Psychiatrist and narrative medicine storyteller Dr. Lewis Mehl-Madrona asserts that "by hearing stories about healing from people who seem like us, we become inspired to believe that our own healing is possible."[5] He offers a note of caution, however: it is not the stories that heal. What heals is transformation, which comes from "a reorganization of the elements of involved and participatory systems—organ, human, family, community."[6] Without this commitment to transformation nothing really changes.

Finally, the depth psychologists—building on the work of Jung and Freud—maintain that stories serve a developmental function by forcing us to ask fundamental questions as we advance through the life stages: Who am I? How am I to deal with the world's problems? What must I become? Psychologist Bruno Bettelheim concluded that the message of stories is "that a struggle against severe difficulties in life is unavoidable, is an intrinsic part of human existence . . . if one does not shy away, but steadfastly meets unexpected and often unjust hardships, one masters all obstacles and at the end emerges victorious."[7]

The stories in this book identify traumatic experiences we have encountered as legal professionals. But just as important, these stories offer a roadmap out of the dark and dangerous woods. We wish you safe passage.

---

[3] Melanie C. Green, Transportation into Narrative Worlds (2021). Available at DOI:10.1007/978-3-030-63614-2_6.

[4] Melanie C. Green, Jeffrey J. Strange, and Timothy C. Brock, Narrative Impact: Social and Cognitive Foundations (Hillsdale, NJ: Lawrence Erlbaum Associates Publishers: 2002).

[5] Lewis Mehl-Madrona, Coyote Wisdom: The Power of Story in Healing (Rochester, VT: Bear & Company, 2005), 1.

[6] Lewis Mehl-Madrona, Narrative Medicine: The Use of History and Story in the Healing Process (Rochester, VT: Bear & Company, 2007), 223.

[7] Bruno Bettelheim, The Uses of Enchantment: The Meaning and Importance of Fairy Tales (New York: Knopf, Seventh Printing ed. 1977).

About the Times in Which We Wrote

This book was created during a traumatic time in human history. For much of the time, we were in lockdown or impacted by the coronavirus pandemic, which killed more than a million Americans and millions of other people worldwide. We experienced racial strife, political unrest, and the renewal of the discovery of thousands of graves of Indigenous children and the renewed revelation that thousands of Indigenous children were murdered in government-mandated boarding schools. These events impacted people deeply, as we wrote a book about trauma. Many potential contributors just couldn't muster the resources to write.

Next, Myrna McCallum and Marjorie Florestal reflect on their experience of living and writing in these times.

The Indigenous Experience

Myrna McCallum

There were so many voices and lived experiences we wanted to include in this book, because there is so much yet to say. It was impossible however to reflect every perspective or intersection where trauma and law collide or where the law has been weaponized to inflict injury, suffering, and trauma onto Black, Indigenous, and People of Color (BIPOC) individuals or whole BIPOC communities.

Some unjust and traumatizing Indigenous experiences worthy of space in this book, or any book, immediately come to mind in the Canadian context: the murder of a young Cree man named Colten Boushie by a White farmer who was never held accountable by the courts due to a flawed investigation and prosecution fueled by racial bias; the thousands of missing and murdered Indigenous women and girls whose cases receive little to no investigation efforts; the racist and inhumane treatment of Cindy Gladue's remains, a murdered Métis mom and daughter, by the prosecution and an Alberta trial judge who allowed a portion of her preserved vagina to be admitted as evidence at the trial of her murderer; and, of course, the uninvestigated crimes against humanity committed by the church and the state in respect of the legalized kidnapping and detention of Indigenous children in Indian residential and boarding schools for decades and decades and decades, on both sides of our Canadian/U.S. border.

These events easily earn the central focus of a book on cultural trauma, collective trauma, generational trauma, racism in law, biased decision-making, or law as trauma for BIPOC community members. In fact, we hope these stories are centered in this way in various publications across many professional sectors and in law school courses all over the world. There is tremendous value in researching the examples just noted on your own, as each instance is an excellent illustration of how lawyers and judges have used the law to reveal their racist views and perpetuate harmful stereotypes while blatantly engaging in traumatizing conduct that causes lasting and irreparable harm to BIPOC individuals, groups, and communities.

We share this note with you, the reader, to let you know that we know there are many unspoken voices and perspectives missing from this book—and we wish we could include them all. But this book is only a primer, an introduction, a conversation starter—the beginning of a new exploration and awareness into the traumatizing aspects of our profession. We know there are more stories to share and lived experiences that must be reflected in legal education publications. We hope you will pick up where we leave off by lending your voice to this critical narrative.

Trauma and Re-membering

Marjorie Florestal

We have words to explain trauma in all of its complexity—from the single-event trauma of a car accident to the developmental traumas first introduced with our mother's milk. We understand the biological and physiological mechanisms at play. What remains ineffable is the *feeling* of trauma.

In the summer of 2020, America watched in horror as a Minneapolis police officer compressed the neck of George Floyd who gasped, "I can't breathe." As a Black woman I felt the heaviness in my own chest. The band of muscles surrounding my airways tightened, and sharp, wheezy puffs was all I could manage. "Asthma attack," my doctor said. But I knew better. I had been struck with George Floyd syndrome—or maybe it was Ahmaud Arbery disease. Sandra Bland's esophageal cancer? Breonna Taylorosis? So many Black lives lost. So many possibilities.

The world collectively cried out at the sight of George Floyd's life being drained out of him by a "peace officer," but what we know about trauma is that we were not all having the same experience. For some, serving as witness was uncomfortable, difficult, horrific—or, at most, an experience of vicarious trauma. For Black people, it was nothing short of dismemberment. This is how collective trauma works.

Collective trauma is a shared injury—"a blow to the basic tissues of social life"[8]—that causes psychological and somatic harm in those who identify with the in-group. In the age of social media, the potential for African Americans to experience collective trauma increases exponentially, and the impact on our collective health and well-being is staggering. In a study of 100 pregnant African Americans, researchers attributed an increase in depression among the studied population to highly publicized deadly encounters between police and African American boys.[9] In another, researchers found a causal relationship between police stop-and-

[8] Kai T. Erikson, Everything in Its Path (New York: Simon & Schuster, 1976), 153, 174.

[9] Fleda Mask Jackson, Sherman A. James, Tracy Curry Owens, and Alpha F. Bryan, *Anticipated Negative Police-Youth Encounters and Depressive Symptoms among Pregnant African American Women: A Brief Report*, Journal of Urban Health 94(2), pp. 259-265 (2017). Available at https://pubmed.ncbi.nlm.nih.gov/28283944/.

frisk policies and an increased prevalence of diabetes and high blood pressure in highly surveilled neighborhoods.[10] These risks were present even if one had had *no* personal confrontation with police. But collective trauma does not have a similar impact on out-groups. In a nationally representative study of police killings of unarmed African Americans, researchers found the adverse mental health effects the Black community suffered were not observed among White respondents.[11]

I reference these studies to tackle head-on the reality that some voices we would have liked to hear from are absent from this book. They are not absent because they are untouched by the trauma this book explores. In fact, just the opposite is true. The United States is a country born of trauma. It was conceived on stolen land; germinated on the corpses of Indigenous people; and nourished on the blood, sweat, and tears of enslaved Africans. Each step of the way, the law served as rationale, justification, and excuse to perpetuate violence on targeted groups. George Floyd is the tip of an enormous iceberg. Yet, in a book about the trauma of being a lawyer and practicing law, there are not nearly enough stories from the BIPOC legal community. Why? Because of dismemberment.

Why do I use the term *dismemberment*? The best way I can describe Black people's experience of dismemberment in the face of collective trauma is by way of a story. *The Descent of Inanna* is a Sumarian myth as relevant today as it was when recorded 3,000 years ago. Inanna, Queen of Heaven and Earth, descends to the underworld to attend a funeral. The underworld is a vast and uncharted territory smothered in darkness. Almost no one who arrives is allowed to leave again. At the entry gate stands a threshold guardian, a servant to Ereshkigal, ruler of the underworld. Before Inanna can enter the inner sanctum, she must pass through seven gates. At each gate, the guardian forces her to relinquish a part of her armor. Off comes Inanna's crown, her lapis beads, breastplate, gold jewelry, and even her royal robe. When she protests, the guardian replies: "Quiet, Inanna, the ways of the underworld are perfect. They may not be questioned." This is why Inanna arrives naked and bowed before Ereshkigal.

The goddess of the underworld shows no pity. She turns Inanna into a corpse, a piece of rotting meat, and hangs her from a hook on the wall. And all is lost . . . until the God of Wisdom sends down two beings, neither male nor female, to bring Inanna back. Ereshkigal cries out in pain and sorrow: "Oh my insides! Oh, my outsides! Oh, my liver! Oh, my heart!" The beings sigh and moan and commiserate with her. At long last, Ereshkigal, the goddess of darkness and shadow, is seen and

---

[10] Abigail A. Sewell and Kevin A. Jefferson, *Collateral Damage: The Health Effects of Invasive Police Encounters in New York City*. Journal of Urban Health, 93(S1), 42–67 (2016). Available at https://doi.org/10.1007/s11524-015-0016-7.

[11] There are many articles and research projects on this topic, including Jacob Bor, Atheendar S Venkataramani, David R Williams, and Alexander C Tsai, *Police Killings and Their Spillover Effects on the Mental Health of Black Americans: A Population-Based, Quasi-Experimental Study*. The Lancet, 392(10144), 302–310 (2018). Available at https://doi.org/10.1016/s0140-6736(18)31130-9.

witnessed. She promises the beings anything they want. They want only Inanna. They sprinkle the food and water of life on her lifeless corpse, and the Queen of Heaven and Earth is reborn.

There are voices missing from this book. They are not here because they are in the underworld, dismembered but not forgotten. Those of us who walk the topside world have an obligation to re-member them—and to help create a space for them to be reborn.

Outline of This Book

It is worth noting that we wrote each section with lawyers, law students *and* judges in mind. Lawyers, judges, and law students are all part of the same integrated system. Legal education does not end with law school. The concepts overlap so much that the section headings are guideposts, not silos.

The first section of this book (Chapters 1 and 2) introduces and explores trauma in the context of the legal system. What is it and why does it matter?

The second section (Chapters 3 through 5) explores lawyers' perspectives on trauma as it shows up in individuals and practices, and why we need trauma-informed lawyering practices. The second section explores several trauma-informed tools and lawyers' experiences with applying them. We have included a representative list of tools, practices and resources, and a reading list. Please use them. Have respect for any urge or instinct you may have to seek the support of a helping professional of your choosing. And it's important—even critical—to understand from a legal ethics perspective how trauma shows up in the culture of law itself, and how some specific practice areas are affected.

The third section (Chapters 7 and 8) focuses on how trauma can show up in systems, groups or organizations, and legal culture. Chapter 7 explains why we need trauma-informed judges and identifies key focus areas for jurists seeking to apply their growing awareness of direct and vicarious trauma in the courtroom. This section includes recommendations for legal system leaders who value the mental health and wellness of judges to identify, prevent, and possibly eliminate harms experienced, then perpetuated, by trial judges. Chapter 8 focuses on how trauma can show up in legal education. It explores how law professors and law students might create trauma-informed spaces that encourage more effective teaching and learning. The benefits of a trauma-informed legal pedagogy are likely to extend far beyond the law school classroom. Chapter 8 looks at trauma at the systemic rather than individual level, highlighting systemic challenges like racism and considering how systems change can help.

The book concludes with a call to action: what will we do now that we know? We know that lawyers are courageous professionals who want to provide better legal processes and outcomes for their clients, and better well-being options for students, colleagues, and themselves. This book presents a choice: to courageously acknowledge, remember, and turn toward trauma and the tools to address it, or to turn away. If we choose the latter, we must acknowledge that the next generation of students, lawyers, and clients would be fated to deal with these same cycles of trauma—and their voices would remain unheard or excluded. We invite you to turn to the hope, resilience, and renewal or even healing that trauma-informed legal practices would bring to all of us.

A Growing Topic

As we wrote this book, we noticed that the topic was mushrooming. Numerous leading lawyers and law schools around the world recognize the importance of addressing trauma in legal practice. It wasn't just our attention that had been piqued by the topic. Some voices had been raised in the past and many more were joining them. Myrna's podcast, *The Trauma-Informed Lawyer*, became increasingly popular and even mainstream legal periodicals increased their coverage of the topic. It has been hard to keep up, something we're both happy about and frustrated by, in writing about a moving target.

Many important or emerging trauma-informed activities didn't get featured in the book, a measure of how much is beginning to happen. Harvard Law School has incorporated trauma-informed approaches into its juvenile justice work; Stanford Law School has a Trauma and Mental Health Lab for its human rights work; Yale Law offers clinical law teaching materials on vicarious trauma; Columbia has had Dr. Katherine Porterfield, a contributor to this book, speak on working with traumatized clients; and NYU has included trauma-informed concepts in its clinical law work. As we neared our deadline, other practitioners, schools, and programs reached out to us to let us know that they, too, were becoming more trauma informed. This book was written in dialogue with many of the trauma resources used in these initiatives. Best practices for trauma-informed lawyering are still growing.

> We often think about trauma in terms of perpetrator and victim. However, we now know that trauma impacts not only the person on the delivering or receiving end, but also anyone who witnesses a traumatic act. Obviously, there are varying degrees of trauma, but like radiation, it can be cumulative, with small trauma piling up over the years and damaging our ability to care for ourselves and each other.
>
> Unacknowledged and untreated trauma is a silent epidemic in today's world that is calling out for healing at every level—individuals, families, communities, and nations. The first step in healing trauma is to acknowledge that it has taken place. If, as you read the stories in this book, you find yourself becoming uncomfortable, or "triggered," place your feet flat on the floor and squeeze your toes as you breathe deeply several times in and out through your nose,

directing your exhales down through your body into the Earth. This will help to stabilize your nervous system so that you can stay focused on the content of what you are reading.

Ken Homer[12]

* * *

How to Read This Book (and About Experiencing Our Own Trauma)

This is a book on trauma. Don't try to read it in one sitting.

We have considered each story's impact and have edited out details so as not to exploit the storyteller with sensationalism or unduly traumatize the reader. (And unless the writer has given us a specific release, we have also changed names and—in some cases—identifying information so as to preserve the anonymity of some of our contributors.) There will always be some discomfort when dealing with traumatic material, but the goal is to remain within your "window of tolerance" so that the information does not overwhelm your nervous system. We have edited our stories with these caveats in mind.

Still, we do not know your life experience. What might deeply impact one person may not affect another in the same way. It is important for you to monitor your reactions and determine how much you can tolerate in one sitting.

Some of our writers and survey respondents noted they did not realize how much they, or their colleagues or practices, were affected by trauma until they read the information we provide here.

You may find that the trauma doesn't bother you at first but that certain symptoms show up. You might find it hard to sleep or notice that you are crankier than usual. Or you may become irritated that some of the stories seem angry and you might wish that they were written from a more detached perspective. You might find yourself feeling angry and wishing that we weren't making such a big deal out of things. Anger often masks other feelings. Denial is actually a stage of grief, trauma's close cousin.

Maybe your lived experiences have been such that you've never experienced trauma, maybe you don't believe trauma shows up in your workplace or in your law firm, or that your experience of law school was far from traumatizing. We want you to know that such a lived experience without some type of trauma is rare—it is not the experience of the majority of people. Health studies since the 1990s indicate that the majority of people in North America, regardless of where they live or

---

[12] Ken Homer is a senior executive coach and founder of Collaborative Conversations, https://www.linkedin.com/in/kenhomer/details/experience/.

socioeconomic status, have experienced at least one type of trauma.[13] Maybe you really are in the lucky minority, but consider that perhaps you're not.

As you read this book, you may begin to see scenarios that mirror events that occurred in your life or in your practice. You may recognize some experiences as similar to those of people in your life. You may be quite surprised and shocked by how, in fact, trauma has played a role in this profession for you, either as you've experienced it or as you've witnessed it in others.

It is also worth noting that the question of whether or not trauma is present is most often a subjective experience (or both a subjective and objective experience)— that is, two people may experience the same event very differently.

You may question yourself about whether you have even been traumatized, especially if you do not remember being traumatized in the past. Author of *The Body Keeps the Score*, Bessel van der Kolk, MD, says that "Trauma comes back as a reaction, not a memory."[14]

David Bedrick,[15] a lawyer turned therapist, posted this on his Facebook page.

> Question from a Facebook Friend to David Bedrick: "What can I do to heal if I have suffered abuse or trauma but don't have specific memories?"
>
> My response: Memories needn't be clear in the mind; the body has great clarity about how the injured person feels and the psyche can generate a narrative that fits that.
>
> The narrative, for psychological and healing purposes, need not be precise. Working somatically, with dreams, and other current patterns (relational patterns, addictive tendencies, inner dynamics) can still proceed.
>
> I have had many clients over the years with this concern. I noted that the more focused they are on needing to remember, the less likely they are to trust themselves. It is as if they "need proof" in order to feel worthy of being believed.
>
> What can a person do?

---

[13] Susan D. Solomon & Jonathan R.T. Davidson, *Trauma: Prevalence, Impairment, Service Use and Cost*, 58(S9) J. Clin. Psych. 5–11 (1997). *See also* Elizabeth Crouch, et al., *Prevalence of Adverse Childhood Experiences (ACEs) among US Children*, 92 Child Abuse & Neglect, 209–18 (2019), https://doi.org/10.1016/j.chiabu.2019.04.010; Larke N. Huang, et al., SAMHSA's Concept of Trauma and Guidance for a Trauma-Informed Approach (Rockville: SAMHSA, 2014).

[14] *See* Bessel Van der Kolk, The Body Keeps the Score: Brain, Mind and Body in the Healing of Trauma (New York, New York: Penguin Books, 2015).

[15] David is a speaker, teacher, and attorney and author of the acclaimed *Talking Back to Dr. Phil: Alternatives to Mainstream Psychology and his new book Revisioning Activism: Bringing Depth, Dialogue, and Diversity to Individual and Social Change*. David spent eight years on the faculty of the University of Phoenix and has taught for the U.S. Navy, 3M, psychological associations, and small groups. He has received notable awards for teaching, employee development, and legal service to the community. David completed graduate work in psychology at the University of Minnesota and clinical training at the Process Work Institute, where he is a diplomate and adjunct faculty member as well as a member of the ethics committee and the advisory board for the master of arts program in conflict facilitation. As a practitioner of process-oriented psychology—a branch of Jungian psychology—he has worked with groups, couples, and individuals for more than 20 years.

◆   Work somatically; the body doesn't need outer stories to know itself.

◆   Tell stories you remember; many will be resonant with the un-recalled story.

◆   Connect with others who don't shame your reactions in the present.

◆   Learn to trust yourself and the triggered experiences you have.

◆   Connect current feelings with older stories you do remember.

◆   Follow your nighttime dreams.

◆   Play, play, play. Use puppets, crazy drawings, sing or dance freely—all of this will bring out what wants to be witnessed.

◆   Be creative: make art, write poems, write music.

◆   Work with internalized oppression and inner criticism (this almost always mirrors early conditioning arising from powerful experiences).

Come to know your heart's path in life and stay close to it, trying not to abandon what your life is meant to do. (This, the unfolding of the flower of your life, of your soul, of your true path, is perhaps the most important of all.)[16]

David Bedrick offers good advice. You can't think yourself out of trauma. An analytical response is insufficient. As lawyers and law students, we have been trained to learn only with our minds. But there are other epistemologies—other ways of knowing and interacting with the world. We suggest you digest this book with more than just the intellect.

Read this book with care for yourself, attending to your own responses at the physical, mental, emotional, and spiritual levels. Pause to notice any sections that may evoke discomfort, feel difficult to read or feel connected to (or disconnected from) your sense of values, meaning, community, or spirituality. Remember, the stories are past events. The writers are okay. Pause to make sure that you are, too.

The Trauma of Others: Witnessing Trauma

Trauma is a holistic experience. It happens to people in their bodies, minds, emotions, spirits, relationships, and whole selves. It happens to the people we encounter and in communities. It is personal and systemic. One of the experts contributing to this book, Kate Porterfield, describes trauma as a "biopsychosocial" experience. An experience that is biopsychosocial cannot be fully understood or met without a biopsychosocial response—it cannot be met with only the intellectual or cognitive response we are trained to focus on in law.

---

[16] David Bedrick, Facebook Friend: What Can I Do to Heal If I Have Suffered Abuse or Trauma but Don't Have Specific Memories? (Mar. 4, 2021), https://www.facebook.com/DBedrick/. Reprinted with permission.

A lot of our coping mechanisms for trauma are very personal. We must make note that self-care is the privilege of few and that while a self-care approach may help us individually, it will not shift the design of the legal system, its culture and values, or address the need for collective care. Systemic problems are complex. J. Kim Wright likes to compare systemic problems to a bowl of spaghetti. The strands are all twisted together and it is hard to see what is connected to what. You might think you are looking at one strand of the problem, only to pull it and figure out that the strand is actually on the other side of the bowl and not connected at all.

CHAPTER 2

Why It Matters: The Context for Trauma-Informed Lawyering

Whether individual or collective, trauma fragments and fractures, it disowns and silences. It creates denial and forgetting. To assist in its repair, we must choose to acknowledge, to witness, and to thereby feel together, what has actually occurred, even the most horrific details we would rather close our eyes to. Because to look away, to dismiss, deny, minimize, or willfully forget, is to uphold the institutions of inequality, of inhumanity, that created them.[1]

—From Healing Collective Trauma: A Process for Integrating Our Intergenerational and Cultural Wounds by Thomas Hubl

What's the Big Deal about Trauma in the Law?

The prevalence of trauma is so widespread that it has been called a "public health epidemic,"[2] with almost two-thirds of the general population of the United States experiencing at least one indicia of trauma in the course of childhood (such as

---

[1] T. Hubl, Healing Collective Trauma: A Process for Integrating our Intergenerational and Cultural Wounds (New York: Sounds True Inc., 2021).

[2] S.I. Rosenbaum, *The Age of Trauma*, Harv. Pub. Health Mag. (Oct. 10, 2021), https://www.hsph.harvard.edu/magazine/magazine_article/the-age-of-trauma/. *See also* K. M. Magruder, K. A. McLaughlin & D. L. Elmore Borbon, *Trauma Is a Public Health Issue*, 8(1) European J. Psychotraumatology 1375338 (2017), https://doi.org/10.1080/20008198.2017.1375338. *Also see* Bessel Van der Kolk, The Body Keeps the Score: Brain, Mind and Body in the Healing of Trauma (New York, New York: Penguin Books, 2015).

domestic violence or abuse).[3] Since the 1990s, research on the individual and collective experiences of and responses to trauma has rapidly increased, ranging from customized health and well-being support for the physical or mental–emotional impact of trauma to government policies and new legislation addressing trauma at the federal or regional level.

Lawyers are not exempt from the prevalence of trauma. Numerous studies and literature reviews on the topic of high trauma prevalence among lawyers and judges, which can be consulted by any reader interested in the specific data on trauma in the legal profession, have generally found that trauma is prevalent among lawyers, judges, and law students.[4] Trauma is prevalent in the legal community, just as it is in the general population, where trauma is estimated to affect at least the majority of the population over a lifetime, before accounting for regional or demographic variations, which can often increase that number.[5]

While trauma is sometimes described as being more to less episodic or chronic, sometimes referred to as "big T trauma" and "little t trauma,"[6] using the terms "big" and "little" may not be accurate, as a person's objective and subjective experiences of an overwhelming situation involving toxic stress are personal and can vary widely. Trauma is often described as direct (directly experienced by a person) or secondary or vicarious (indirectly experienced or witnessed by a person in the course of their professional or personal lives), and again a person's objective and subjective experiences of these subtypes of trauma can vary.[7]

---

[3] Courtney N. Baker, Steven M. Brown, Patricia D. Wilcox, Stacy Overstreet & Prerna Arora, *Development and Psychometric Evaluation of the Attitudes Related to Trauma-Informed Care (ARTIC) Scale*, 8(1) SCHOOL MENTAL HEALTH 61, Traumatic Stress Institute (2015), http://traumaticstressinstitute.org/wp-content/uploads/2016 /01/Baker-Brown-Wilcox-2015-FINAL.pdf.

[4] S. Iverson, https://www.tandfonline.com/doi/full/10.1080/13218719.2020.1855270?src=recsys; M.-J. Léonard, D. Saumier & A. Brunet, *When the Lawyer Becomes Traumatized: A Scoping Review*, SAGE OPEN (July 2020), doi:10.1177/2158244020957032. Colin James, *Towards Trauma-Informed Legal Practice: A Review*, 27(2) PSYCHIATRY, PSYCH. & LAW 275–99 (Feb. 11, 2020), https://www.tandfonline.com/doi/figure/10.1080/13218719.2020.1 719377?scroll=top&needAccess=true; M. Leclerc et al. *The Unseen Cost of Justice: Post-Traumatic Stress Symptoms in Canadian Lawyers*, 26(1) PSYCH., CRIME & LAW 1–21 (Apr. 25, 2019), https://www.tandfonline.com/doi/abs /10.1080/1068316X.2019.1611830.

[5] DAWN D'AMICO, TRAUMA AND WELL-BEING AMONG LEGAL PROFESSIONALS (Montana: Summerland Publishing, 2021); Stephanie Francis Ward, *As Lawyer Stress Escalates during Pandemic, LAP Agencies See Significant Increase in Calls*, A.B.A. J. (May 26, 2021), https://www.abajournal.com/web/article/as-lawyer-stress-escalates-during -pandemic-lap-agencies-see-significant-increase-in-calls; James, *supra* note 4; M.-J. Leonard et al., *Traumatic Stress in Canadian Lawyers: A Longitudinal Study*, APA PSYCNET (2021), https://doi.org/10.1037/tra0001177. Karen Oehme & Nat Stern, *Improving Lawyers' Health by Addressing the Impact of Adverse Childhood Experiences*, 53 U. RICH. L. REV. 1311 (2018–2019).

[6] Straussner & A.J. Calnan, *Trauma through the Life Cycle: A Review of Current Literature*, 42 CLIN. SOC. WORK J. 323–35 (2014), https://doi.org/10.1007/s10615-014-0496-z.

[7] Megan Zwisohn et al., *Vicarious Trauma in Public Service Lawyering: How Chronic Exposure to Trauma Affects the Brain and Body*, 22 RICH. PUB. INT. L. REV. 101 (2018–2019).

The impact of a traumatic event is best considered from the perspective of a person's own lived experience of that event and its effect on the person's ability to cope, solve problems, and engage fully with life.[8]

There are high costs to ignoring the impact of trauma on the legal system. These costs include tolerating legal services that may not support clients' best interests or even inadvertently harm them. Or the cost of neglecting to address a key lawyer well-being issue. Ignoring trauma often means it's allowed to persist as an obstacle to access to justice or legal services, and clients may not be persuaded to engage with a system that remains unaware of its potential to foist further harm upon them even as it works to help them.

To facilitate the growing practice of trauma-informed lawyering and the evolving nature of this information due to the continuing advancement of trauma studies, we have taken a "working definition" approach, defining trauma in public health terms rather than strictly clinical terms.

From a public health perspective and for the purposes of this book, trauma (or traumatic stress) is broadly defined as a person's response to a situation, whether an acute or chronic situation, that overwhelms the human ability to cope effectively.[9] And, as mentioned in the introduction, we view trauma as an event or situation that overwhelms or limits a person's capacity to freely respond at a physical, mental, emotional level (and with other human capacities, including the spiritual level).

An experience with adversity, whether acute or chronic, sudden or ongoing, will impact each person differently. Among lawyers, while particular practice areas can be more prone to trauma, very few areas of law, if any, appear to be completely unaffected by or immune to trauma exposure. Practice areas that impact the daily lives of clients personally, such as family law, criminal law, immigration law, and personal injury or health law are rife with stories of trauma shared behind the scenes. Trauma or toxic stress can be experienced in any area of law, including corporate law, known for the stressors of high economic stakes (or losses), intense conflicts (among others), extreme work demands, and high-pressure work cultures.[10] But to say that the nature of trauma experienced in the corporate or commercial

---

[8] PETER A. LEVINE, WAKING THE TIGER: HEALING TRAUMA—THE INNATE CAPACITY TO TRANSFORM OVERWHELMING EXPERIENCES (Berkeley, California: North Atlantic Books, 1997); B. VAN DER KOLK ET AL., TRAUMATIC STRESS: THE EFFECTS OF OVERWHELMING EXPERIENCE ON MIND, BODY AND SOCIETY (New York, London: The Guildford Press, 2007).

[9] JUDITH HERMAN, TRAUMA AND RECOVERY: THE AFTERMATH OF VIOLENCE – FROM DOMESTIC ABUSE TO POLITICAL TERROR 33 (New York: Basic Books 1992). In Judith Herman's words, traumatic events overwhelm the ordinary systems of care that give people a sense of control, connection, and meaning. . . . Traumatic events are extraordinary, not because they occur rarely, but rather because they overwhelm the ordinary human adaptations to life." *See also* Helgi Maki & C. Tess Sheldon, *Trauma-Informed Strategies in Public Interest Litigation: Avoiding Unintended Consequences Through Integrative Legal Perspectives,* (2019) 90:2, SUPREME CT. L. REV. 65. *See also* Rosenbaum, *supra* note 2.

[10] Joanna Litt, *"'BigLaw Killed My Husband": An Open Letter from a Sidley Partner's Widow,* THE AMERICAN LAWYER, Nov. 12, 2018, https://www.law.com/americanlawyer/2018/11/12/big-law-killed-my-husband-an-open-letter-from-a-sidley-partners-widow/?slreturn=20210301235028.

sphere is directly comparable to the trauma involved in practice areas where life and liberty are at stake, such as immigration or asylum cases, would be a false equivalence.

Our focus is on the information that is necessary for lawyers to begin understanding and adopting trauma-informed practices. Defining each type of trauma to a lawyer's satisfaction, including direct trauma, secondary (or indirect or vicarious) trauma, complex trauma, historical trauma, intergenerational trauma, post-traumatic stress disorder, developmental trauma, stress load, toxic stress, adverse childhood experiences (ACEs), positive childhood experiences (PACEs), burnout, or compassion fatigue, could be the subject of an entire book.[11]

A key concept for trauma-informed lawyering is the shift that has occurred, both in trauma-informed care and in psychological perspectives, which is generally referred to as the shift from "what's wrong with you?" to "what happened to you?"[12] The first question, "what's wrong with you?," pathologizes trauma when it can be an expected or even predictable response to an overwhelming situation.

The second question avoids what's called the "fundamental attribution error," which is a cognitive bias that causes people (including lawyers) to underestimate the impact of situational factors on a person's behavior and overemphasize the role of a person's perceived personality, character, or disposition.[13] With the fundamental attribution error, if a person experiences difficulty coping due to trauma impact, the people around them (colleagues, family, friends, and even lawyers) are likely to attribute such difficulties to a personal flaw rather than an environmental factor.[14]

The question "what happened to you?" or "what did you experience?" ensures that a person's lived experience, their situation, and their environment are specifically included when we consider the factors that influence behavior.

In writing this book, it seemed the fundamental attribution error, along with stigma, is alive and well, as we heard many lawyers say they hesitated to discuss trauma due to fear of how others might perceive them.

---

[11] While we have consulted many such resources, they are beyond the scope of this primer. Interested readers may consult the following website: https://www.traumainformedlaw.org/resources.

[12] *See also* NADINE BURKE-HARRIS, THE DEEPEST WELL: HEALING THE LONG-TERM EFFECTS OF CHILDHOOD ADVERSITY (Boston: Houghton Mifflin Harcourt, 2018); SANDRA BLOOM, RESTORING SANCTUARY: A NEW OPERATING SYSTEM FOR TRAUMA-INFORMED SYSTEMS OF CARE (London: Oxford University Press, 2013); Angela Sweeney et al. *A paradigm shift: relationships in trauma-informed mental health services*, 24(5) BJPSYCH ADVANCES 319–33 (2018), doi:10.1192/bja.2018.29.

[13] Gilad Hirschberger, *Collective Trauma and the Social Construction of Meaning*, FRONTIERS IN PSYCHOLOGY, 2018 (9), https://www.frontiersin.org/article/10.3389/fpsyg.2018.01441.

[14] Liz Wall, Daryl Higgins & Cathryn Hunter, Cathryn. Trauma-informed care in child/welfare services (CFCA Paper No. 37), 2016, https://www.researchgate.net/publication/294775580_Trauma-informed_care_in _childwelfare_services_CFCA_Paper_No_37.

Why Every Lawyer Can Use Trauma-Informed Lawyering

No matter what kind of law or where you practice, if one of your clients suddenly rushed into your office for a previously scheduled client meeting over an hour late and exclaimed, "I've just been in a car accident," your own humanity might prompt you to instinctively ask "What happened? Was anyone hurt? Are you ok?"

Even though you're not a medical professional or therapist, you might say to your client: "Do you need anything? Do you need to call someone? Or reschedule? Or sit down and catch your breath?"

You likely wouldn't plow ahead with your meeting as originally planned and completely disregard your client's state or situation despite their discomfort, or even the inconvenience to you the situation may bring.

You'd probably understand that the client's lateness in that situation wasn't a sign of disregard or lack of credibility. You likely wouldn't be surprised if:

◆ The client blurted out information about the accident even though it seems unrelated to their client file or work with you; or

◆ The client seemed too upset to proceed with the meeting as planned; or

◆ The client's thinking seemed scattered or social interactions with you were fragmented.

You might also take a moment to regroup yourself after your own initial shock, take a second look at your agenda, and pick up the broken pieces of your meeting to find another path forward with the client in light of the accident's impact.

What we aren't taught in law school, and many lawyers don't realize, is just how many clients will show up in our practices who've experienced an impact (or injury) of this kind from adversity—but often that injury will be invisible. The client may not be in a position to explain the situation to us or even be fully aware that it happened. The injury or the event that caused it may not be visible or easily verbalized by the client or anyone else. The injury might be from some other kind of adversity or conflict—including neglectful or broken relationships, violence, serious family health issues, losing a parent at a young age, poverty, or systemic discrimination.

The adverse event may even have happened years before, but its impact can persist years or even decades later. Trauma that comes from experiencing adversity might fragment more than a meeting agenda; it can shatter a person's sense of themselves as professionals and as people.

When we work with clients from a trauma-informed perspective, we engage our awareness of trauma's impact to assist the client (and ourselves) with navigating the uncomfortable and inconvenient issues that can become obstacles to the pursuit of justice. We might only know that trauma is impacting a situation from the client's response (or even our own response) to trauma: fear, grief, or anger or dysregulation like physical discomfort, mental or emotional suffering, or strained relationships.

While some lawyers receive training in working from a client-centered perspective, we rarely learn how to deal with trauma and its impact. We've usually been taught to exclude trauma, or at least not talk about it. Without trauma-informed lawyering, clients impacted by trauma risk being inadvertently deprived of justice by the very injuries that injustice such as violence, racism, poverty, discrimination, and other disasters (visible or seemingly invisible) caused in the first place.

Turning away from trauma risks diminishing the quality of legal services, undermining a client's experience with the legal system or even eroding our own well-being as lawyers. In this book we propose to turn toward trauma in clients, in systems, and in ourselves with the same humanity you would offer a fellow human who has experienced a visible injury.

How Trauma-Informed Lawyering Can Help Us Serve Clients' Best Interests

No matter which practice area or jurisdiction, perhaps the most important responsibility of a lawyer is to protect and pursue the best interests of the client. We're not so unlike doctors in the nature of our duty toward clients. Yet how do we know when we've missed the mark and misinterpreted the client's best interests, or our decisions might even work against their interests?

In writing this book, we frequently heard comments from both lawyers and clients about how often the legal system helps more than it hurts, or perpetuates harm that could be avoided by modifying aspects of the legal process that are within the control of lawyers or other legal system professionals. So why don't we decide to do just that? The original role of lawyers had a focus on helping clients and community, and even on healing. Myrna McCallum observes that Robert Benham, former Chief Justice of the Georgia Supreme Court, once noted that the first professions in society were the *clergy*, who healed the spirit; the *doctor*, who healed the body; and the *lawyer*, who healed the community.[15] Chief Justice Warren E. Burger, in his annual speech to the American Bar Association, said the public image of lawyers was "near the bottom of the barrel," along with the rating of journalists and in contrast to the high standing of doctors. Doctors, he said, are thought of as "healers. Should lawyers not be healers? Healers, not warriors? Healers, not procurers? Healers, not hired guns?"[16]

---

[15] Robert Benham as quoted by Patrick Andrews, "Lawyer as Healer," The Conscious Lawyer Magazine, November 2017, https://www.theconsciouslawyermagazine.com/lawyer-as-healer/.

[16] Chief Justice Warren Burger as quoted by Andrews, *supra* note 15.

Dan Ariely[17] is an expert on decision-making, including rational decision-making by working professionals. His views are informed by his own uniquely harrowing experience with effective decision-making. At 17, after an explosion during one of his high school activities burned 70 percent of his body, Dan spent three years in a hospital being bandaged and rebandaged in order to heal his third-degree burns. Burn treatment can be excruciatingly painful, and Dan was told by his medical team that the best way to remove the bandages was quickly. Without testing what might be best, and despite his begging that they explore less uncomfortable options, Dan was told that the medical team knew best and quick removal was necessary because while the pain was intense it minimized the duration.

Dan later became a renowned behavioral economist who helps leaders make more effective decisions through his work as a professor of psychology and behavioral economics at Duke University, his column for the *Wall Street Journal*, and his book *Predictably Irrational*.

After leaving the hospital, Dan started conducting experiments to simulate the bandaging methods and found that there were techniques that could be used to avoid unnecessary pain. These techniques, in trauma-informed care terms, are called "modifiable factors." Some modifiable factors that Dan tested to reduce pain included giving him control over parts of the process (such as speed), starting from more painful areas and moving to less painful ones to decrease the sense of discomfort over time, and providing periodic breaks to recover. Overall, Dan found that a more effective method of pain management would have used modifiable factors to reduce the intensity of pain instead of reducing the duration of treatment (as doubling the length of time of a painful experience didn't double the amount of pain).

How did the medical team systematically provide services that misinterpreted Dan's best interests? Dan found that instead of inquiring which factors might be modified, his health care providers went largely with their intuition, based on professional norms or training, to decide which option would be best. They didn't ask him or conduct tests. When he discussed his findings about effective pain management with his medical team, they were truly surprised. One nurse on his medical team said that discussions of pain management strategies should include the psychological pain practitioners encounter when their clients scream from pain, so shortening the duration may be a way of reducing the practitioner's own suffering.

Traditional legal education trains us to engage with our clients without inquiry or providing options. Do lawyers default to avoiding engagement on the topic of trauma to reduce our own exposure to suffering or discomfort?

---

[17] Dan Ariely, Predictably Irrational: The Hidden Forces That Shape Our Decisions (New York: Harper Perennial, 2010).

With trauma-informed lawyering, we explicitly seek to more closely under-stand a client's needs and therefore their best interests. Bryan Stevenson,[18] founder of the Equal Justice Initiative, uses the term "proximity" to refer to the understand-ing of a client that can be cultivated by getting closer to a client's unique situa-tion and background (which may be generally excluded, neglected, or disfavored). Gaining proximity aims to provide a basis for designing effective problem-solving strategies by inquiring into the nuances and details of a client's situation, including social context such as socioeconomic or unique historical, regional, cultural, group, or personal factors.

Stevenson observes that gaining proximity in the pursuit of justice can often be uncomfortable or inconvenient. But gaining proximity isn't intended to cause a lawyer to "cross boundaries" or step outside their role as a lawyer. Often clients are in situations or face pressures that we cannot understand unless we take inten-tional steps to gain insight into the client's experience. Failing to inquire about best interests from the perspective of the client can have unintended, harmful conse-quences that can undermine justice itself.

Trauma-informed lawyering provides tools that can enable lawyers to gain proximity or use modifiable factors when trauma is affecting a client. It can reduce the assumptions made about a client's best interests, and although not all aspects of a painful legal process can be modified by a lawyer, often we can reduce the prospect of avoidable harm.

A key skill for trauma-informed lawyering is the inclusion of missing vocabu-lary and concepts for intangible harm—in other words, suffering. In many other professions, there are tools (such as the pain scale in the medical profession) for dealing with subjective distress that may not otherwise be easy to address.[19]

In many traditional law schools and other legal settings, however, a law stu-dent may be taught to deal with a routine case, such as a real estate boundary dis-pute, in much the same way as a case impacted by trauma, such as a tragic and sudden personal injury. Lawyers often haven't learned a vocabulary that would assist them with gaining proximity to harm or suffering.

---

[18] K. Davis," *Bryan Stevenson Calls on Lawyers to Get Uncomfortable and Deepen Commitment to Justice*, ABA J., August 4, 2018, https://www.abajournal.com/news/article/bryan_stevenson_calls_on_lawyers_to_get _uncomfortable_and_deepen_commitment. *See also* Bryan Stevenson's ABA Medal acceptance speech of August 2018. "Social justice activist Bryan Stevenson receives ABA's highest honor," ABA News, August 4, 2018, https://www.americanbar.org/news/abanews/aba-news-archives/2018/08/social_justice_activ/.

[19] K. Wailoo, Pain: A Political History (Baltimore: Johns Hopkins University Press, 2014).

Trauma Myths and Lawyers

Mallika Kaur[20]

> . . . *lawyers cannot afford to buy the myth that trauma is an aberration in the profession of otherwise Teflon-coated lawyering machines. Negotiating trauma is perhaps as old as the profession, even though we may have never given that emotional labor nomenclature or visibility, to our detriment.*

> *I think a lot about the Peter Levine reading you assigned us, where he talked about how antelopes forget the trauma of being chased by a lion because they mostly experience trauma as a physiological response, and don't try to rationalize it. Part of me wishes I could do that. Part of me wonders what I would lose if I could.*
>
> –B.N.

Thus, had concluded one of my student's final reflection journals for the semester.

The science of trauma's physiological (and not only psychological) manifestations, which can be felt deep in our body, often sticks with many lawyers and law students after a training or class on the topic, because many of us have experienced these manifestations: scanning from head (ache) to foot (ache), you too may now be able to identify how your body reacts under stress, despite your brain's rational issue-spotting, problem-solving legal training.

Here, the student was specifically reflecting on our reading and discussion of Waking the Tiger, by trauma expert Dr. Peter Levine. We had discussed Dr. Levine's description of how trauma-induced energy is eventually released by an animal being preyed on by a larger predator. If it lives, the brave survivor literally gets up to "shake it off." The response of freezing—and thus retaining that energy—is distinctly human. Dr. Levine has gone on to design therapeutic methods for humans to experience "release," sometimes decades after accumulating trauma. But my student, a trauma survivor—before and during her legal education—was expressing that shaking it off was not entirely something she wished for either, despite the advice she had received from some supervisors and peers. Her traumas made her everyday life and work very heavy, but also charged her as a passionate legal advocate, and I am very certain, future attorney.

Most simply put, trauma is a deeply distressing or disturbing experience. The actual or perceived lack of control during a terrifying incident sends our

---

[20] Mallika Kaur is an author and attorney focusing on human rights, with a specialization in gender and minority issues. She received her JD from the UC Berkeley School of Law, where she currently teaches, including the course she created, "Negotiating Trauma, Emotions, and the Practice of Law."

brain from a regulated to dysregulated state. The brain does in fact "short-circuit," and picks neural pathways that may not be the most rational response. The "fight/flight/freeze" mode takes over: a video[21] I often share with students breaks it down for those who haven't taken Biology since high school.

Having gone through any traumatic experience isn't without consequence. The body keeps the score, as explained by a recent book[22] of the same name. The consequences of the same traumatic experience (such as private trauma like a car accident or assault; or public trauma like a forest fire or school shooting) differ for different individuals. Their past accumulated traumas, histories, backgrounds, and childhoods all factor into how exhausted their body already is and how fast it may be able to bounce back this time.[23]

---

[21] See video "The Fight Flight Freeze Response," Braive, https://www.youtube.com/watch?v=jEHwB1PG_-Q.

[22] Van der Kolk, *supra* note 2.

[23] Reprinted with permission, Mallika Kaur, *Negotiating Trauma & the Law: Maybe We Won't "Shake It Off"*, Calif. L. Rev. Online (Nov. 2020), https://www.californialawreview.org/negotiating-trauma-and-law.

PART I

Lawyers and Practices

When people affected by trauma show up in our work as lawyers, we're more likely than not to miss seeing the impact of trauma entirely or to misinterpret it. They don't walk in saying they've just been in a car accident, but the trauma may seem as immediate. Since we haven't been taught to understand the impact of trauma, common myths or outdated information from our training may prevail, and we can misconstrue trauma as a "problem" due to a perceived personal weakness, character issue, or credibility issue. Chapters 3 and 4 demystify the experience of trauma from a lawyer's perspective and how it shows up in practice and discusses principles for beginning to address trauma in legal practice. Chapter 5 provides an overview of tools that can be used in a trauma-informed lawyer's practice and discusses some representative examples of specific skills and techniques.

Overall, Chapters 3 through 5 examine why trauma is prevalent among lawyers and what can be done about it at an individual or practice level. Trauma expert Gabor Maté[1] has said that too often we don't ask the right questions about trauma. For instance, if someone is experiencing addiction, we ask "why the addiction?," when it would be more helpful to ask "why the pain?," because asking that deeper question is more likely to generate awareness of an underlying traumatic factor that led to the addiction (or other behavioral adaptation to trauma) in the first place. In this section of the book, we're asking "why the pain?" about lawyers in general and in specific practice areas. In the next section of this book, we'll move toward a collective perspective, asking "why the pain?" in legal systems, and what to begin to do about it in connection with judges and courts, legal education, and legal systems as a whole. In Part I, we will discuss how lawyers can understand and begin to address trauma response in clients, lawyers and themselves, as illustrated in the figure that follows.

---

[1] GABOR MATÉ, IN THE REALM OF HUNGRY GHOSTS: CLOSE ENCOUNTERS WITH ADDICTION (Toronto: Knopf Canada, 2008). *See also* GABOR MATÉ, WHEN THE BODY SAYS NO: THE COST OF HIDDEN STRESS (Toronto: A.A. Knopf Canada, 2003).

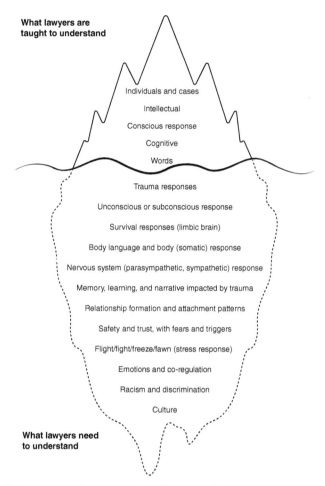

What lawyers are taught to understand

Individuals and cases

Intellectual

Conscious response

Cognitive

Words

Trauma responses

Unconscious or subconscious response

Survival responses (limbic brain)

Body language and body (somatic) response

Nervous system (parasympathetic, sympathetic) response

Memory, learning, and narrative impacted by trauma

Relationship formation and attachment patterns

Safety and trust, with fears and triggers

Flight/fight/freeze/fawn (stress response)

Emotions and co-regulation

Racism and discrimination

Culture

What lawyers need to understand

Understanding Trauma Response in Clients and Lawyers
Image credit: Helgi Maki

CHAPTER 3

Lawyers' Perspectives on Trauma: What Is Trauma in the Law and Lawyering?

Introduction

In this section, we discuss key trauma dynamics as they show up in practicing lawyers and judges (or their clients) and some pathways toward support or healing. For the purposes of this book, it is less important to understand the precise details of how trauma arises in our neurobiology or physiology than to become aware of its multilevel biopsychosocial nature and of resources for meeting trauma in clients, communities, and ourselves as it arises. Acknowledging the biopsychosocial impact of trauma on lawyering means becoming prepared to meet trauma not just with intellectual strategy or cognitive responses but to also consider how to include biologically calm, psychologically safe, and socially trustworthy approaches in our work as lawyers. However, it's important to know that trauma can fundamentally impact a person in a manner that isn't necessarily direct, since patterns of trauma embedded in families, society, cultures, or even workplaces can result in collective or intergenerational trauma where past events evoke a trauma response in the present.

More simply put, the deep distress of trauma disrupts our ability to engage all of our biological, psychological, and social skills and resources and puts us in survival mode. You have probably heard of the trauma responses of fight, flight, freeze, or fawn. Fight is the aggressive response; flight is running away; and freeze involves being incapable of making a choice or moving. The fourth, less commonly known response is called the fawn response. Fawning is a response often learned in childhood as a way of avoiding abuse. It involves trying to please someone to avoid conflict. These responses are survival methods that have developed over centuries of human evolution. They are embedded in human physiology and neurobiology. Instead of being able to rest and digest our food using the parasympathetic nervous system, we are in fight or flight mode with stress hormones provided by the sympathetic nervous system. When we might like to think we're free from fear with our prefrontal cortex, the limbic brain has been activated to ensure we survive. And even though it might make sense to connect with people who can help us navigate conflict, our relational approach to attachment with people may be anxious, avoidant, or disorganized instead of secure.

When many lawyers talk about trauma, what it is and how it might be relevant to their clients, colleagues, organizations, or themselves personally, they often say that they think of examples involving war or tragic violence. They may think of a veteran who is plagued by flashbacks. Or a child who lost a parent to sudden violence. Or police brutality. Or a woman attacked in a back alley by a rapist. These are all examples of traumatic events.

We also might have overhead stories about other lawyers being haunted by memories of a violent case, casually discussing murder in front of young children at the dinner table, keeping a small collection of keepsakes from a heartbreaking trial, or treating life like a law school exam by constantly warning their children about the risk of accident hidden in every possible activity.

We may see trauma affecting lawyers as being the exception, instead of something we can anticipate. However, trauma is more prevalent, subtler, and more chronically present than it may first appear. It can come from your own experience or from working with someone who has had a traumatic experience. It can be a one-time event or it can be a series of events over time, past, present, or anticipated in the future.

In traditional legal education, lawyers are rarely taught about how frequently trauma can affect clients, colleagues, students, communities, and ourselves. Our productivity may suffer. We may feel unmotivated. Some of us begin to play games on our computers or find escape in binging old television shows (or worse). Noticing that you are sending an email at 3 a.m. might be a sign that you are using work to escape. (Any similarity to the coping mechanisms of the editors is expressly admitted.)

In the growing literature about trauma in the legal profession, there has been some criticism that lawyers haven't yet distinguished clearly enough between the various types of trauma that can impact them and their clients. Direct trauma, secondary or vicarious trauma, complex trauma due to chronic traumatic events (or relationships) that often begin in childhood, historical trauma (or collective trauma affecting a community across generations), or other kinds of intergenerational trauma or collective trauma may each form part of a client's history or even a lawyer's experience. Work-related PTSD, or burnout or compassion fatigue, may emerge.[2] Clients may also experience retraumatization by aspects of the legal process. While it can be useful or necessary to distinguish between subtypes of trauma, each type has suffering in common. In the medical field and among therapists, there is a well-known quote by Dr. Rachel Remen about the impact of suffering on professionals: "The expectation that we can be immersed in suffering and loss daily and not be touched by it is as unrealistic as expecting to be able to walk through water without getting wet."[3] It's realistic to expect lawyers to be untouched by the mix of different types of trauma we encounter, together with clients, students, and other legal professionals.

Due to the high prevalence of trauma, lawyers and clients often don't have a choice about whether the situations in which they walk together contain traumatic material, but we can choose to anticipate and respond (or even prevent) appropriately. We can ensure that we and our clients do not walk through the challenging landscape of trauma without tools, practices, or resources to care for distress instead of ignoring it or putting all our resources into legal analysis alone. Actively preparing for this journey with trauma-informed law tools, practices, and resources is likely to create a more beneficial legal system experience for both clients and lawyers, and help lawyers find more sustainable ways of practicing effectively.

Client Trauma

For many lawyers, it may be easier to think about the impact of trauma on their work by considering the dynamics in client relationships. Consider that the so-called difficult client may actually be reacting to trauma. The impact of trauma can show up in responses and behavior that does not fit with the way legal processes are designed to work or may complicate our work.

Here are some examples that might occur across a variety of practice areas from real estate to civil litigation to family law. In each of these cases, instead of thinking of this situation as one in which it's appropriate to ask "what is wrong with you?" consider that the better question may actually be "what happened to you?"[4]

- ◆ The client who can't make a decision about their own case and responds repeatedly by asking you what you would do
- ◆ The client experiences so much grief when you talk about an aspect of their case that you find yourselves avoiding the subject or find it challenging to communicate about it with words rather than mostly silence or tears

[2] M.-J. Léonard, D. Saumier & A Brunet, *When the Lawyer Becomes Traumatized: A Scoping Review*, SAGE Open, July 2020, doi:10.1177/2158244020957032.

[3] RACHEL NAOMI REMEN, KITCHEN TABLE WISDOM: STORIES THAT HEAL (New York: Riverhead Books, 1996).

[4] OPRAH WINFREY & BRUCE D. PERRY, WHAT HAPPENED TO YOU? CONVERSATIONS ON TRAUMA, RESILIENCE AND HEALING (New York: Flatiron Books: An Oprah Book, 2021).

◆   The client returns blank forms or does not sign the documents necessary for their legal matter to succeed

◆   The client who, no matter what you ask them about their legal matter or case, appears unable to muster much of a response beyond yes or no answers and avoids participating in communications wherever possible

◆   The client who has been advised to settle their case but they want to keep pursuing it even though going to trial is not a sensible strategy

◆   The client whose story of events about their legal matter are out of order, and seem to shift or change despite writing down a timeline

◆   The client who appears to have difficulty maintaining focus in meetings with you, or loses track of dates or times even when it comes to important events like showing up in court

◆   The client who does not stand up for their own interests or otherwise tries to appease the person who they previously told you is at the center of their case

◆   The client who appears to become suspicious anytime you write any notes about their case

◆   The client who responds with extreme emotion or lack of emotion to a pivotal development in their case

◆   The client who tells the same story, over and over, often in great detail, looping around and retelling either particularly upsetting parts of the story or seemingly minor details

A lawyer is likely to receive a different response from a client if they ask in a thoughtful manner "what happened?" or "what happened to you?," instead of thinking (or asking some version of) "what's wrong with you?" or "what's your problem (or the problem)?"[5]

We might notice ourselves, colleagues, students, or community members exhibit those same signs of trauma response such as hypervigilance; dissociation; or all or part of a fight, flight, freeze, or fawn response; or other aspects of trauma response (such as withdrawal, lack of affect or emotion, disrupted memories or narratives).

Does that just about cover all your difficult clients and many of your colleagues when you perceive them as difficult? Or perhaps yourself, when you have your own moments of being a so-called difficult lawyer? Trauma is that pervasive. It is an epidemic with a psychobiological impact that can limit our capacity to advocate for the best interests of our clients, and for our clients to advocate for their own best interests. Lawyers are not traditionally taught to think about trauma in terms of its continuous impact on our capacity to advocate for the best interests of our clients, and to enable our clients to act in their own best interests.

---

[5] *Id.*

Lawyers also aren't taught to account for trauma response when analyzing the response of a "reasonable person" in a traumatic situation. The formation of memory, learning, behavior, and narrative can all be impacted by trauma, including developmental trauma (or how trauma impacts the development of brain functioning). The neurobiology of trauma underlying these responses is complex; however, it can be briefly summarized in general as follows:

The prefrontal cortex controls our attention, capacity to integrate memories into narrative, and our ability to plan and make decisions. Collectively, these are often referred to as "executive functions" of the prefrontal cortex. When trauma occurs, whether as a single event or a series of events, the human brain is wired to find a way to survive. Trauma is perceived as a threat by the brain, triggering a fear response. When the brain responds out of fear, the limbic brain rather than the prefrontal cortex is activated (specifically, the amygdala, which functions as an alarm system signaling the presence of danger, and the hippocampus, which facilitates the production of cortisol under stress, whereas without stress it facilitates memory formation). It's important to understand that the limbic brain functions more quickly than the prefrontal cortex to ensure survival, so it can rapidly take over or "hijack" cognitive functions. The limbic brain governs the functioning of emotions, memory encoding (i.e., how memories are stored), and survival responses. In order to defend against an extreme threat in which there is or appears to be little hope to escape or survive, the defensive responses of the limbic brain may cause a person to dissociate, or to become temporarily immobile or paralyzed (tonic immobility or collapsed immobility).[6] Under threat, human neurobiological processes become focused on survival instead of forming memory or narrative, since there is little use in remembering what we aren't likely to survive. As a result, memory or narrative may not be linear or chronological. In addition, the neurobiological impact of trauma can disrupt learning, particularly if neurobiological development occurred amid toxic stress or trauma.[7]

For further details on the neurobiology of trauma and other important trauma concepts, including the trauma of racism, we suggest the work of Dr. Alisha Moreland-Capuia.[8]

---

[6] L. Haskell & M. Randall, *The Impact of Trauma on Adult Sexual Assault Victims* (Department of Justice Canada, 2019), https://www.justice.gc.ca/eng/rp-pr/jr/trauma/trauma_eng.pdf.

[7] N. Burke-Harris, The Deepest Well: Healing the Long-Term Effects of Childhood Adversity (Mariner Books, 2018).

[8] A. Moreland-Capuia, Training for Change: Transforming Systems to be Trauma-Informed, Culturally Responsive and Neuroscientifically Focused (New York: Springer Press, 2019); A. Moreland-Capuia, The Trauma of Racism: Exploring the Systems and People Fear Built (New York: Springer Press, 2021).

Trauma Response or Sustainable Responses?

Table 3.1 summarizes patterns that may be observed when a person experiences a trauma response, which can overwhelm or override the human capacity to respond with all possible resources. Responses that allow for full or balanced engagement of human capacities is referred to here as a "sustainable response," as trauma responses are designed to allow us to survive a crisis rather than to sustain us continuously in our daily work or lives. It's important to note that it's normal for trauma responses to arise in overwhelming situations, alongside normal responses to loss such as grief, sadness, and other emotions. The focus of Table 3.1 is on imme- diate- or medium-term responses, and other chronic or long-term trauma response factors such as developmental trauma (in utero or otherwise), addiction or sub- stance use disorder, or other health factors (including mental health, community or public health, and historical trauma patterns) may be relevant to you or your clients and merit further specialized reading or consulting a qualified health professional.[9] The tools described in this book may help lawyers and clients activate the capac- ity to engage with aspects of sustainable responses as well as trauma responses in order to use all of their capacities to respond.

Table 3.1 Patterns of Trauma Responses and Sustainable Responses[10]

Aspect of Client or Self	Trauma Response ("Survival Mode")	Sustainable Response
Brain (memory, nar- rative, learning, and decision-making)	Executive function of the pre- frontal cortex disrupted by the brain's fear response. Limbic brain is activated instead of the prefrontal cortex. May have gaps in (or non- linear approach to) memory, narrative, learning, and decision-making.	Memory, narrative, learning, and decision-making done with the aid of executive function in the prefrontal cortex.
Nervous System	Fight/flight/freeze/ fawn. Hyperaroused or hypoaroused (overactive or underactive/collapsed). Sym- pathetic response.	Rest and digest. Able to mobilize in order to take considered action and/or respond in a calm manner. Parasympathetic response.

---

9   For some discussions of developmental health, addiction or substance use disorder and mental health, see MORELAND-CAPUIA, *supra* note 8.

10 Trauma responses listed here are discussed in MORELAND-CAPUIA, *supra* note 8. In addition, trauma responses are described extensively by many trauma experts including the following: JUDITH HERMAN, TRAUMA AND RECOVERY: THE AFTERMATH OF VIOLENCE – FROM DOMESTIC ABUSE TO POLITICAL TERROR (New York: Basic Books 1992); VAN DER KOLK, *supra* note 2; PETER A. LEVINE, WAKING THE TIGER: HEALING TRAUMA (Berkeley, California: North Atlantic Books, 1997); PAT OGDEN, JANINA FISHER ET AL., SENSORIMOTOR PSYCHOTHERAPY: INTERVENTIONS FOR TRAUMA AND ATTACHMENT, (New York: WW Norton & Company, 2015).

Aspect of Client or Self	Trauma Response ("Survival Mode")	Sustainable Response
Psychology and Mental Health	Fearful thoughts and moods, anticipating disaster, or giving up. Hypervigilant or hopeless. Grieving may not be accessible.	Non-fear thoughts and moods, possible to feel hope. Able to grieve.
Emotions	Lack of emotion, extreme emotion, or numb. May not be able to feel or identify emotions. Emotions may shift rapidly or remain stuck in constant patterns.	Able to feel, identify, and express a wide range of emotions and experience emotional shifts.
Communication	Withdraw or inundate with communication (too far or too close in interactions, not enough or too much information in communications).	Social engagement (give and take pattern of communication, responsive and relational communication).
Learning or Dealing with Change	Already outside the window of tolerance for new information or experiences. Challenging to learn new things or respond to questions.	Window of tolerance or capacity for learning and change has room. Possible to tolerate change, and even grow in tolerance.
Body	Painful, tense, or numb. Rigid or collapsed. Sleep, digestion, and other key functions disrupted (too much, too little, or irregular).	Sleep and digestion are mostly functional. Flexibility possible, able to respond to physical stressors.
Social / Relationships	Feeling unsafe and unable to trust, and anxious, insecure, or disorganized attachment patterns in relationships more likely. Capacity to attune or co-regulate with other people less available.	Psychological safety and trust, secure attachment patterns in relationships a possibility. Capacity to attune or co-regulate with other people is more available.
Community Connections	Systems intended to protect or help may not feel safe, may not engage with community even to seek or receive help. Capacity to feel belonging less available even in a safe or welcoming situation.	Capacity to engage with community, to seek or receive help, to connect and experience belonging.

Figure 3.1[11] illustrates some signs that may assist you with beginning to notice the states of being that clients, colleagues, and we lawyers ourselves can experience in connection with toxic stress and trauma. The diagram lists some signs that lawyers can notice in the course of their work when people are affected by toxic stress or trauma, such as breath, eye contact, posture, or approaches to communication, and is based on a collection of similar diagrams from trauma experts like Janina Fisher and Stephen Porges, illustrating the states of being involved in a trauma response. It is normal for a person dealing with toxic stress or trauma to experience any of the responses shown in Figure 3.1. It's important to understand that when the human nervous system is activated (or overactivated) a person may be in the hyperarousal (fight/flight/fawn) zone in order to mobilize a response to a perceived threat, and when it is further overactivated that person may move into the hypoarousal (freeze) zone in order to shut down and survive a perceived threat. In Figure 3.1, nervous system activation levels are represented by the bell curve. A person may have more capacity to solve problems, make decisions, learn, answer questions, and engage with others in a grounded and connected manner when they perceive themselves to be in a safe situation rather than perceiving a threat to safety. For details on nervous system activation in connection with toxic stress and trauma, including sympathetic and parasympathetic nervous system activation, please refer to the contributions in this book by Dr. Amar Dhall and Dr. Stephanie Shorter. For further reading on trauma and the nervous system, you may wish to consult the work of Peter Levine, Janina Fisher, and/or Stephen Porges.[12]

---

[11] Figure 3.1 focuses on language and concepts relevant to lawyers in connection with nervous system activation and states of being (flight/fight/freeze and fawn) that may be experienced by clients. This diagram draws upon diagrams by trauma experts Stephen Porges and Janina Fisher. *See* STEPHEN PORGES, THE POCKET GUIDE TO THE POLYVAGAL THEORY: THE TRANSFORMATIVE POWER OF FEELING SAFE (New York: WW Norton, 2017). *See also* PAT OGDEN, JANINA FISHER ET AL., SENSORIMOTOR PSYCHOTHERAPY: INTERVENTIONS FOR TRAUMA AND ATTACHMENT (New York: WW Norton, 2015); PETER A. LEVINE, TRAUMA AND MEMORY: BRAIN AND BODY IN A SEARCH FOR THE LIVING PAST (Berkeley, California: North Atlantic Books, 2015).

[12] Note that Stephen Porges is an expert on "polyvagal theory," which explains the fear response in people affected by trauma (and related patterns of social interaction) based on the levels of activation and/or tone of the vagus nerve, which is a cranial nerve. *See* STEPHEN PORGES, THE POCKET GUIDE TO THE POLYVAGAL THEORY: THE TRANSFORMATIVE POWER OF FEELING SAFE (New York: WW Norton, 2017). *See also* Ogden & Fisher et al., *supra* note 8; LEVINE, *supra* note 8.

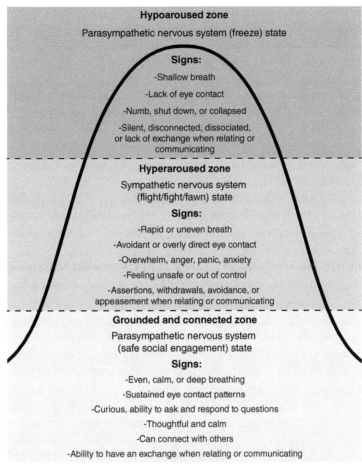

Note: Signs included on this chart are biological/physical, mental, emotional, or social indicators that can be noticed in the course of legal work. Bell curve indicates level of nervous system arousal.

Figure 3.1 Human Response Zones and Trauma
Image credit: Helgi Maki

Lawyers' Perspectives on Trauma

The following stories and contributions provide different angles on trauma in the legal system.

Built into the System

K.G. has been a personal injury lawyer for 20 years. He shared these thoughts about trauma.

Trauma is built into the tort law system. The more trauma I can prove, the better result I can get for my clients, and the more money I make. Sometimes bad things happen, and traumas get inflicted, because people can be bad, mean, even evil—criminal law and family law can involve impossible human dynamics. Generational trauma. Physical and verbal abuse. Passionate rage and revenge. But personal injury law is often an impersonal trauma. Not to downplay what I do, I have a noble, interesting, and even fun profession, but for the most part and in most cases (with, of course, many exceptions) the trauma of a personal injury is less traumatic and less personal than you might find in criminal or family law. Sometimes people just make simple absent-minded mistakes and don't apply the brakes in time to avoid a rear-end accident. My job is to extract as much money as I can in exchange for my client signing away his or her rights to go any further. Or to weave the story well enough that a jury gives a good award. I guess what I am saying is I am a little jolted and jaded by this assignment.

I spent the first few years of my legal career helping to develop a cutting-edge organization couched in the what was then radical premise that lawyering can be a healing profession, that lawyers can find satisfaction and joy in the practice of law, that creative and innovative modalities for solving problems have a place in the legal system. Then I started actually practicing and have held down a mainstream career as a personal injury plaintiff's attorney for almost two decades now. I don't actually know what "Trauma Informed Practice" is, which is the subject or theme of the story I was asked to tell. I can guess. I googled it and learned a little. But I don't really know. Yes, sure, of course, I am aware when my clients need support from other professionals outside of the legal system within the context of my representation, and I am studied in interpersonal communications such that I don't exacerbate my clients' traumas myself, and perhaps sometimes my presence is healing. After many years of misery, I eventually succeeded in finding joy and health in my own practice, and I am sure my clients are financially and emotionally better off because of that. I have represented thousands of people in which I needed to be informed about, from and with a multifaceted facility with the role trauma plays, in order to be capable of ethical quality lawyering. And I am sure I could tell hundreds of stories.

But oddly, the memory that comes up for this story is not about any of the thousands of cases I have handled but about Judge Fakename.

I appeared in front of Judge Fakename when I used to practice in the southwest at the beginning of my career. Judge Fakename enjoyed getting to know the lawyers presenting in his courtroom. During my first and only jury trial in front of him, when I was a very young trial lawyer, he spent part of a break Q&A-ing opposing counsel and me about our lives. When he learned that I had been a professional juggler in my past, he gathered three pieces of fruit, two apples and an orange, and ordered me to perform for opposing counsel, the courtroom personnel from whom he had gathered the produce, and himself for a moment of good-natured courtroom whimsy. This was all out of the presence of the parties and jury, in the middle of a trial involving varying levels of trauma amongst the parties. The frivolity did not blur lines into the trial itself, the traumas that were the subject of the case received their respectful due process, and my own vulnerable young professional

CHAPTER 3   Lawyers' Perspectives on Trauma

psyche was given a boost rather than a traumatic bite from a judge who brought humanity to his courtroom.

But . . . and . . . the main other memory I have of Judge Fakename is that he has three courtroom rules he gives to both attorneys. I would assume he only gives these instructions when both attorneys are men. At the end of the pretrial conference before jury selection begins, he instructs:

1. If I like your tie better than mine, you have to swap ties for the day with me. We will swap back before we recess for the evening.
2. Do your best and try your case with honor. I will respect you and you will respect the best interests of your respective clients at all times in my courtroom.
3. You have reasonable leeway to pick a jury, but you have to leave at least one good-looking piece of eye candy on the jury.

Three things can be true at the same time: judge was friendly, fun, and misogynistic.

Multidisciplinary Lenses

The following contributors each bring a different lens to the topic of trauma-informed lawyering. Each perspective offers us an opportunity to consider another aspect of what trauma is and how it relates to the law. Our first contribution points out that lawyers often see their own human needs through the lens of the skills they are taught to value: risk analysis and judgment instead of compassion or nonjudgement.

A Lawyer Therapist's Reflections on Trauma

Doron Gold[13]

The following are the observations of one trauma therapist and should not be taken as a definitive elucidation of a profoundly complex problem. Everyone's lived experience is unique. If you are struggling with distress borne of traumatic experiences, I encourage you to seek help from a therapist trained in working with trauma.

---

[13] Doron Gold is a registered social worker, certified professional coach, and psychotherapist, as well as having previously practiced law for ten years, primarily as a family and civil litigator. Since 2006, Doron has assisted lawyers, paralegals, law students, judges, and their immediate family members with personal and professional issues such as addiction, depression, anxiety, and career stress. Doron has written and been quoted extensively in publications such as *Lawyers' Weekly, Law Times, Canadian Lawyer* and *LawPro Magazine* on various topics related to lawyer distress and wellness. He is the co-author of the Canadian Bar Association's "Mental Health and Wellness in the Legal Profession" online course and is the recipient of the 2016 CBA Wellness Forum Award of Excellence. Doron can be reached at www.thelawyertherapist.ca or www.dorongold .com and can be found on Twitter at @DoronJGold.

Countless academics and commentators have observed certain unique traits possessed by the majority of legal professionals—including law students—which include intelligence, persistence, autonomy, perfectionism, and pessimism, among many others. They are more thinkers than feelers, and when facing mental distress, they seek rational solutions to emotional problems, ignoring or burying feelings that seem uncontrollable, unwieldy, and potentially intolerably painful. When their preferred strategy of pursuing logical analysis fails them in this effort, they isolate, unleashing upon themselves the full force of their unrelenting and unsparing self-judgment. Psychologically distressed lawyers retreat inward, donning a proverbial mask for colleagues, judges, clients, friends, and even family members, hoping nobody will notice their pain and judge them as harshly for it as they judge themselves. When lawyers are alone with their critical thoughts, unencumbered by concepts like compassion or kindness, their ample brainpower creates airtight narratives about their own failings and shamefulness. As a result, despite empirical data demonstrating that lawyers suffer with depression, anxiety, and addiction at three to four times the rate found in the general population, they are, at the same time, much less likely to ask for help to alleviate these conditions.[14]

Many of the mental health difficulties to which I refer arise from the unique demands of law practice, including the stresses of often oppressive time demands (work and billing), managing client and firm expectations, imposter syndrome, which is most often experienced by new lawyers finding their way in the profession, working in an area of law one is not suited to or interested in, incivility inside firms and offices as well as between opposing counsel, and, fear of making a mistake that may lead to a negligence claim or regulatory complaint. However, for many, compounding the considerable but common types of lawyer distress is trauma. Previous or even ongoing traumatic experiences and their impact on the individual can become the prism through which they view all of their other stresses, invariably magnifying and deepening them beyond how a non-traumatized or minimally traumatized person might experience those same stresses.

While traumatic events can leave these types of psychological scars on some, they do not necessarily affect everyone in the same way. Different people experiencing the same traumatic event may be affected by it differently. One feels what one feels and one experiences trauma the singular way that one individually experiences it, not measurable or judged against the way others experience it.

At the same time, legal professionals like frames of reference and comparables, measurements, and metrics. They are notorious for comparing themselves to, for instance, law school classmates, to determine their relative strength, success, value, and future prospects. They presume to know what others are truly

---

[14] Patrick R. Krill, Ryan Johnson & Linda Albert, *The Prevalence of Substance Use and Other Mental Health Concerns Among American Attorneys*, 10(1) MSSW J. ADDICTION MEDICINE 46–52 (January/February 2016).

feeling and how they are coping with their unique stresses, and they constantly judge themselves as falling short of the proverbial bar set by their colleagues. Therefore, if a lawyer or law student is feeling that they are not coping well, are struggling to function, and are in emotional distress, their assumption is likely to be that they are uniquely weak and failing.

As a psychotherapist, I see hope beyond all of the sadness and distress. Human beings are resilient beyond our own comprehension. We have a fire within us that presses us forward and keeps pushing us toward something better, even when we cannot comprehend what better looks like. There is a great deal that a traumatized person can do to improve their lives, both with the help of a therapist and otherwise. In therapy, one can gain perspective on one's life experiences and on one's self-image and one can begin to create a new, more compassionate narrative about oneself and one's place in the world.

That narrative can also include an awareness of the protective factors that assist them in avoiding the danger that their trauma taught them to fear. These can include an awareness of the way one's inner critic affects one's behavior and self-esteem.

Another of the protective factors is an awareness that who one is today is not who one was before, including at the time of, for instance, childhood trauma. The adult survivor has a fully formed brain, life experience, judgment, and power that the child never had. They can set boundaries to keep out toxic people or forces, a tool the child never had available to them. For lawyers, this can include firing abusive clients, leaving toxic workplaces, and avoiding work that retraumatizes them, such as a victim of domestic violence feeling compelled to help other victims by prosecuting alleged offenders but realizing that this work, while rewarding, can also be harmful to them.

Additional tools include developing social support systems to help them through difficult periods, a tool that the child likely did not have access to. They can identify the people in their lives that they actually felt safe with, to ground them in the knowledge that such safe attachments are possible.

Another powerful tool for building self-compassion is to employ an external observer or witness. One hones the skill of having a part of their awareness outside of themselves observing them from outside of their proverbial storm. The observer is nonjudgmental and curious. It wants to learn about the person but never criticizes or judges. This tool offers the individual the opportunity to gain perspective in the moment. Mindfulness practices are particularly effective in overcoming traumatic experiences.

Learning to put perfectionism aside and find one's good enough is a powerful tool in alleviating the self-defeating cycle of pursuing unattainable goals and the feelings of failure that inevitably result. Young lawyers often have no idea how much enough is. Many lawyers feel that they got where they are in their careers because they were perfectionists. Still others strongly resist the label altogether. The perfectionist born of trauma pursues unattainable perfection as a proxy for safety. The traumatized adult can come to understand that safety does not come from being perfect, it comes from self-compassion and self-love. In any event, the pursuit of excellence is not synonymous with the pursuit of perfection. Balance is the key to health, both physical and mental.

In my work as a psychotherapist working with lawyers, I have witnessed countless examples of legal professionals and law students gaining previously inconceivable recovery and peace. It is truly inspiring and moving. Lawyers may deem themselves fixers, not to be themselves assisted with their own challenges, but everyone deserves relief from the effects of trauma, and no one is a failure for having been affected by these experiences. We're just vulnerable human beings trying to get through. Some days it can be hard. But the effort and the journey are worth it. You're worth it.

A Neuro-Somatic Approach to Trauma-Informed Lawyering: From Survival of the Fittest to Fittest for Survival

Dr. Amar Dhall[15]

The Six Steps from Survival of the Fittest to Fittest for Survival

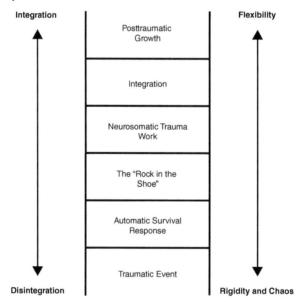

Figure 3.2: The journey from traumatic event to embodied coherence.
Image credit: Sandy Farac

---

[15] Dr. Amar Dhall empowers high-performing individuals, teams, and organizations to find trauma-informed and emotionally intelligent solutions to complex problems. He is a speaker, coach, and facilitator and a former International Headman for the Mankind Project. He holds a PhD from University of Canberra examining the intersection of legal philosophy, quantum mechanics, and human rights.

1.   Ground Zero: The Traumatic Event

The etymology of the word "trauma" is the Greek word for "wound." The essence of trauma is that the experiencer encounters an event that they cannot integrate into their body-mind (e.g., they experience a disintegration), which leads to some form of either rigidity or chaos. Trauma-forming events are not just big occurrences like vicarious trauma, accidents, live combat, abuse, assault, betrayal, death, divorce, bankruptcy, and the like (although these experiences often do produce trauma). Implicit traumas are many and in this present discussion widens the ordinary psychological definition of trauma of childhood trauma, to include any trauma the lawyer acquired outside their practice. In this sense, the causes of trauma responses are very diverse.

One of the most common misunderstandings about trauma is the erroneous belief that the experience of the event itself is the trauma. In point of fact trauma is the body-mind's response to the event, not the event itself. In this way, people's thoughts can become a trauma trigger. This is why one important aspect of being a trauma-informed practitioner is to understand that all trauma work is performed in the present, and why (as a corollary) sharing presence and mindful attention with traumatized clients is an appropriate way to work, because it will help them to ground themselves in the present.

2.   Automatic Survival Response

All complex animals (of which homo sapiens is one) move through the world with their nervous systems scanning the world with one priority question at the fore: "Am I safe?" When our body-mind finds a threat to safety or experiences pain, then a cascade of biological responses is triggered.

In such circumstances, our bodies become ready for action through the operation of our autonomic nervous system. If there is activation of our sympathetic nervous system, we prepare for fight or flight (hyperarousal), or if there is activation of our parasympathetic nervous system, then there is a decrease or crash in the amount of energy in our system and either we freeze or collapse in an overwhelmed state (hypoarousal). The particular pathway chosen by someone's autonomic nervous system is not in their conscious control in a trauma response; the choice is made by our brains scanning our emotion-toned memories, our cognitive analysis of the situation, and even by epigenetic factors.

These heightened energetic and emotional states are usually not fully expressed, as we often must hold back our most primal responses, perhaps because of fear of legal, relational, professional, or cultural repercussions. It is this kind of frustration of our natural biological responses that leads to the creation of trauma. The circumstances surrounding the event will frequently be imprinted by our hypothalamus as an emotion-toned memory. This is because big emotional experiences enhance our brain's capacity to make and store "flash-bulb" memories. Emotion-toned memories will trigger another trauma response in similar circumstances, as our bodies try to give us the energy best matched to the circumstances, because our bodies generate the response it "believes" will give us the best chance of survival. The more often we experience such events, the more frequent trauma responses become, until they are imprinted into our default mode network and become habitual behaviors.

Trauma responses are triggered from very early childhood onward. Because these responses endure (unless metabolized), many people erroneously believe that they are actually part of their personality. This is not the case. What was learned by our nervous systems can be unlearned. Being a trauma-informed lawyer means, inter alia, understanding that trauma responses (including our own) are initially created through the healthy functioning of our nervous systems.

3.   The "Rock in the Shoe"

One of the first steps in trauma work is for the person to realize that there is a way to live life beyond accepting and/or managing their symptoms. The first step to regaining a healthy life is acknowledging that trauma may be the driving force behind behaviors thought to be unrelated; these may vary from addiction to skin conditions and anxiety to conflict in one's personal relationships. Excavating these signs will in all probability require professional help, as trauma shapes the most fundamental building blocks of our perception—our autonomic nervous system. The key behavior for the trauma-informed lawyer at this stage is to acknowledge the signs of trauma when they are present in yourself or your clients, and to commit to doing something about it.

4.   Neuro-Somatic Trauma Work

Neuro-somatic trauma work supports lawyers to resolve their traumas of all kinds by building their interoceptive capability. Interoception is regarded as our eighth sensory system; we have now moved beyond considering ourselves as having five senses—touch, taste, sight, smell and sound—to include three additional "hidden" senses (Mahler 2015, 1):[16]

1.   Vestibular: our sense of head movement and balance
2.   Proprioception: our sense of our muscles and joints
3.   Interoception: our sense of feeling our internal organs and skin, which gives us the information about our internal state or condition of our bodies.

Building up our interoceptive awareness leads to the thickening of our insula cortex and increasing synaptic connections between it and our prefrontal cortex (PFC), which is the executive command center of our brains. The result is that neuro-somatic trauma work resolves trauma and brings with it a swathe of other benefits, including increased emotional intelligence. Although the phrase

---

[16] Kelly Mahler, *Interoception: The Eighth Sensory System*, AAPC Publishing, Kansas (2015).

"increased emotional intelligence" may sound a little nebulous, several specific benefits for lawyers have been identified by Muir (2017).[17] They include enhanced intelligence; better decision making; and building stronger practices, firms and departments. Additionally, there comes a heightened understanding of norm violations as well as improvements to many other aspects of life (Mahler 2015, 9).[18]

5. Integration

In stage one of the model, it was noted that trauma responses are built upon an experience that was unable to be metabolized and integrated into the experiencer's body-mind. Once someone has reached this stage (e.g., stage five) in their journey and engaged with a neuro-somatic approach, integration of the trauma-forming experience begins to occur at a deep level. As interoceptive awareness is deepening, there is a parallel heightened ability to integrate our "gut instinct" into our cognitive intelligence.

A 2016 Cambridge University study[19] showed that there is a proportional relationship between share trader performance on the trading floor and their interoceptive awareness. The results included both profit-making and longevity. The practice of law has many commonalities with trading; high pressure decisions (e.g., decisions with numerous complex considerations carrying grave consequences for errors) that need to be made in small timescales.

6. Posttraumatic Growth

Posttraumatic growth is an entire area of study that has shown that trauma is not a death sentence, and can ultimately lead people to living fuller and richer lives. Calhoun and Tedeschi (2013: 7–14)[20] found that it is possible for survivors of trauma to find empowered ways of being by working through their experiences. Confrontation with suffering and difficulty changes people and their sense of self. They found that survivors often connect with and increase their capacity for both vulnerability and resilience. This renewed sense of resilience helps them to navigate subsequent challenges more easily. Improvement to relationships have been reported as has the emergence of a renewed philosophy of life, greater empathy and compassion, and, of most relevance here, a changed sense of priorities and meaningful changes in the existential aspects of their life.

Lawyers identifying, metabolizing, and integrating their trauma does not mean that they create a pain-free life. It means that they cultivate greater resilience, and

---

[17] Ronda Muir, *Beyond Smart, Lawyering with Emotional Intelligence*, ABA (2017).

[18] Mahler, *supra* note 16, at 9.

[19] Kandasamy, N., Garfinkel, S., Page, L. et al., "Interoceptive Ability Predicts Survival on a London Trading Floor." *Sci Rep 6*, 32986 (2016). https://doi.org/10.1038/srep32986).

[20] Lawrence Calhoun and Richard Tedeschi, *Posttraumatic Growth in Clinical Practice*, Routledge, East Sussex (2013).

become smarter, happier, and more productive and ethical. Given the critical role that lawyers play in modern society, this can only be a good thing.

Looking at Law and Trauma through a Philosophical Lens: Zooming Out from One Victim to a Community of Actors

Susanne van der Meer[21]

Lawyers think in terms of cause and effect, problem and remedy. When applying this thinking model to trauma, the spotlight is on perpetrators as the cause and victims as the effect. When no clear individual cause or perpetrator can be identified, the spotlight narrows to the dimension of all victims, and eventually to the individual victim. The individual can be a litigant, a client, a citizen, an attorney, a judge, or any other participant in the legal system.

I find this focus on the individual problematic, because it isolates the individual from the collective complexity of trauma in the legal domain. Instead of zooming in on the individual, I argue for the opposite direction by expanding the scope of the critical conversation from the individual and singular to the universal and collective. I would like to bring attention to various philosophical perspectives to inspire big picture thinking:

Feminist critique. The slogan "the personal is political" has evolved from the women's rights movement into a broader critical framework. When personal problems are taken out of the domestic space into the public domain, they are open for a more political analysis. A grouping of individual experiences can expose the commonalities. One example can result in identifying a pattern or set of rules on how power is distributed.

Practically, this means moving from one person's traumatic story to a group of stories with a mindset of critical curiosity. Questions to ask are: What is happening here? What else is going on here? Who else is here? How did we get here? So now what?

A personal practice for trauma-resiliency becomes a public practice for trauma advocacy.

From singular to multiplicity. Gilles Deleuze developed the idea of "rhizomatic thinking," based on the ecological concept of the rhizome: a pattern of growing and developing that is nonlinear and a-central. Crabgrass and ginger roots grow as rhizomes, in contrast to a tree that starts from the roots and rises up through the trunk and the branches. Applied to organizational thinking,

---

[21] Susanne van der Meer is a practical philosopher, legal information designer, and visual facilitator. She worked for the Colorado Courts as a self-represented litigant coordinator. She can be reached at TryPhilosophy.com and Siftvisuals.com.

"tree thinking" looks at hierarchical organogram, whereas rhizome thinking looks at networks of actors.

Legal thinking, by searching for cause and effect, is a form of tree thinking. It might identify domestic violence as causes of trauma for the immediate victims, resulting in vicarious trauma for legal professionals, making them "vicarious victims."

Rhizome thinking can find any entry point, without looking for a beginning or end. It might explore what other factors may have influenced or mitigated the trauma, when, where, and how? Who has the power or influence: who benefits, who wins, who pays the price? Are there offshoots in the system that thrive better than others? How is this possible? It's a more heterogenic approach to assessing a situation, and in recognizing solutions.

This approach could be developed as a form of cartography: creating the trauma map of a certain area of the legal field, a certain process, a certain organization.

Subjectivity and power. Individualizing trauma overlooks the ethical and political dimensions that belong to a relational force field. The individual does not decide what is qualifying as traumatic and what is not. As a form of "zooming out," philosopher Michel Foucault's work explains that there is a public, historic domain of discourse and power that shapes how much agency this individual has to identify their own trauma, to tell their story, and to be an advocate for themselves and others. These power relations define what experiences are normal or deviant and what the individual's range of possible action looks like.

Judith Butler, furthering Foucault's work, has developed theories on subjectivity and vulnerability. To be a person, to claim any status as a subject, implies a corporeal state of being open to injury. In order to claim asylum in a legal process, for example, one has to inevitably identify as a subject, a foreign subject, a subject with a certain gender, a certain trauma history. Such a single conceptual move, in itself, exposes one to additional risk of trauma.

When trauma-informed practices are centered around the individual, this increases the individual's vulnerability as a subject. Awareness of this fundamental vulnerability is critical for ethical, political, and efficacy reasons. A less subject-oriented approach deserves further exploration and research in the legal community through questions such as: How can practices and policies zoom out from the individual to the relational field of other actors, norms, and factors of influence? To what extent can *they* take the vulnerable center stage? Can the legal community envision and enact the move from self-resilience to systems resilience, from self-improvement to collective improvement?

The Relationship between Burnout and Trauma

Jens Näsström[22]

While very real, both burnout and trauma are what the pioneering German sociologist Max Weber would call "ideal types" or "pure types." They are conceptualizations that constitute meaningful categories of specific empirical observations. They are also not absolutely distinct from each other, and share many commonalities. It may also be noted that there are several different forms of burnout and trauma respectively, with varying definitions.

Being related, the relationship between the two can be viewed in several ways. One can place them on a spectrum, quantitatively, ranging from low burnout levels to severe trauma. Burnout can indeed lead to trauma-like states and symptoms. However, one can also consider the qualitative differences between the two; trauma tends to be induced by different, more immediate, overwhelming, exceptional, and violent experiences—in any sphere of one's life. Burnout, in contrast, typically stems from slowly accumulated emotional stress in everyday life. The leading causes of burnout are in most models limited to work life, and consequences tend to be described in terms of impact on professional functioning. Nonetheless, the overlap of symptoms of burnout and criteria for PTSD has been confirmed in empirical studies as well.

While burnout certainly is less severe than trauma, it is of great importance in discussing trauma in lawyers because of its prevalence in the legal sector. It is relevant, front and center, not only because of the sheer number of lawyers experiencing varying degrees of burnout but also because it may lead to actual trauma.

Drivers of Burnout in Lawyers

General work-related stressors, such as quantitative and qualitative workload, low level of control, little or no social support at the workplace, have been validated as contributing factors in burnouts.[23] Incidentally, all of these are often present in various forms of legal practice.

The strongest precursor found in my research is overcommitment, which can be described as a lack of boundaries between work and leisure. Lawyers often work during non-office hours, that is, evenings and weekends, partly because of the significant workload and partly to meet expectations (real, or imagined) of availability. This minimizes rest and recovery and generates a mental twilight zone in which body and mind cannot recognize leisure.

---

[22] Swedish occupational psychologist Jens Näsström has specialized in researching, training, and consulting lawyers and law firms since 2005. He integrates genuine passion for his work with curiosity, science, boldness, and creativity.

[23] C. MASLACH, S.E. JACKSON & M.P. LEITER, MASLACH'S BURNOUT INVENTORY (3d. ed.) (Palo Alto, California: Consulting Psychologist's Press, 1996).

However, the most powerful driving factor in burnout, which is also the most characteristic, is working with vulnerable or difficult people, who may exert draining emotional demands and needs on those who work with them. These can stem from a psychological edge state, a precarious living situation, personality disorder, or any number of complicating background factors—or several of them in an intense combination.

Social welfare workers and health care providers are *helping professions*, which constitute both a definite and defining risk factor. Whether being a lawyer is a helping profession depends on the type of practice. Criminal, family, immigration, and health insurance law are all examples of legal areas in which lawyering de facto often is a helping profession. Psychologically, the everyday legal work in those types of practices contains factors sufficient to develop classical burnout: personal contact with vulnerable individuals, which is emotionally taxing due to heavy demands on empathy and complex interpersonal interactions. Interestingly, although this is not commonly discussed in the profession, there is an implicit understanding of this dimension of lawyering.

However, there is one factor that seems to overshadow all others. Gender. One of the most consistent findings in research on stress is that women are more stressed than men. This pattern is also very much present in lawyering (Weinberg & Tittle, 1987).[24]

Furthermore, female lawyers report specific gender-related stress factors such as sexual harassment and workplace discrimination.[25]

Maslach and Zimbardo[26] demonstrated gender differences in burnout. In one study of Swedish lawyers, however, women reported substantially higher levels of emotional exhaustion (M = 2.43 respectively 2.00), but very close to the men for cynicism (M = 1.72, respectively 1.66).[27]

The causes and conditions that would fully account for the gender discrepancies are important. They are also very complex and, in some instances, difficult to research.

What then are the signs of someone, such as a colleague, who is developing burnout?

---

[24] A. Elwork & A.D. Benjamin, *Lawyers in Distress*, 23 PSYCHIATRY & LAW 205–29 (1995); ANLEU, LAW AND SOCIAL CHANGE (2010); D. GALLIGAN, LAW IN A MODERN SOCIETY; S. L. Roach Anleu, *The Legal Profession in the United States and Australia: Deprofessionalization or Reorganisation?*, 19(2) WORK & OCCUPATIONS 184–204 (1992); P. MacCorquodale & G. Jensen, *Women in Law: Partners or Tokens?*, 7 GENDER & SOC'Y 582–93 (1993); J. Rosenberg, H. Perlstadt & W.R. Phillips, *Now that We Are Here: Discrimination, Disparagement, and Harassment at Work and the Experience of Women Lawyers*, 7(3) GENDER & SOC'Y 415–33 (1993); (Weinberg & Tittle, 1987). *See also* Weinberg, S. L., & Tittle, C. K. *Congruence of real and ideal job characteristics: A focus on sex, parenthood status, and extrinsic characteristics.* Journal of Vocational Behavior, 30(3), 227–239 (1987).

[25] Elwork & Benjamin, *supra* note 24.

[26] C. MASLACH & P.G. ZIMBARDO, BURNOUT: THE COST OF CARING (New Jersey: Prentice-Hall, 1982).

[27] Näsström, J. & Mesick, T. *Undersökning av svenska advokaters arbetssituation.* Master's thesis, University of Stockholm (2006).

1. Struggle to manage their work on their own

While needing support and help, individuals typically are unable or unwilling to receive help in their everyday work. Instead, they "centralize" and delegate insufficiently, and often become more rigid in their perfectionism. If you work for them, micromanagement may become more pronounced. All of this is of course making them even less effective.

2. Increased instancing and isolation

They typically show signs of depressive withdrawal; socially, psychologically, and physically. Patience runs very short; tempers may flare and there might be free-floating anger that can strike like lightning at whoever is around them.

3. Great efforts at reaching unattainable goals

The individual's unrealistic ambitions form the basis for an untenable lifestyle. The individual is unable to prioritize, and *everything* is important. The truth that time and energy are scarce resources that cannot sustain all the things the individual is trying to do does not strike home. In the final analysis, only so many things in life are truly important—especially when your health is hanging in the balance.

How Burnout in the Legal Sector Can Be Prevented

Burnout is strongly correlated with some of the legal sector's main challenges: intense working conditions and subsequent stress, underdeveloped leadership (Rhode 2013),[28] gender inequality, insufficient soft skills training, and possible weaknesses in the common recruiting protocol in terms of psychological traits correlating with resilience.

By far, the most blatantly overlooked reality of burnout in the lawyering profession is the challenge of working with vulnerable clients. This is evident by the almost complete absence of relevant training, that is, client psychology. In addition to skills in client psychology, lawyers can be trained to supervise each other and provide reflection, feedback, and time to process cases and clients that are particularly taxing and challenging psychologically.

In many parts of the world, client confidentiality does not extend to other lawyers in the same firm. Another method, which has good empirical support, can be utilized by solo lawyers and without threatening to breach confidentiality, that is, expressive writing. Developed by social psychologist James Pennebaker, expressive writing is a scientifically validated method to process difficult experiences, emotions, and thoughts.

Another method that is effective for preventing, reducing, and recovering from burnout is mindfulness. I have evaluated the impact of mindfulness

---

[28] Rhode, D. L. *Lawyers as Leaders*. Oxford University Press (2013).

training in law firms, and have measured reduction of emotional exhaustion of up to 15 percent and lowering of overcommitment (a powerful predictor of burnout) up to 22 percent. In the last few years, mindfulness has been fortified by training in compassion and self-compassion, which holds great promise for lawyers.

Burnout can be prevented at every stage of the talent management cycle; from recruiting to training to leadership. Indeed, the challenge is comprehensive and serious enough to demand attention to every phase of a lawyer's career, regardless of type of practice. When we add the gender factor to the equation, it becomes clear that substantial progress will necessitate the commitment of all parties in the legal system: lawyers, HR managers, managing partners, bar associations, law schools, CLE/CPD providers, and others can reduce burnout—and sometimes trauma—in lawyers.

Lawyering with Shared Humanity

S.L.

As I sit here thinking trauma-informed law, I'm noticing tightness in my chest, my heart beats heavy, and my stomach gurgles and constricts. Deep breaths lift and expand my belly, giving me clarity and more space between my thoughts.

My own personal story of trauma begins with my childhood. When I was a baby, I was sexually abused by a neighbor. I have little to no conscious memories of the abuse since I was preverbal. Almost all of my memories from the abuse are somatic, lodged in my body. On the worst days, they manifest as chronic pain in my anus. Depending on my perspective and spiritual condition, the pain is either debilitating or transforming, often a combination of both.

For most of my teenage years, I dissociated and played the role of the "nice guy," which I've learned is another response on the fight or flight or freeze or fawn continuum. When I felt triggered by threats (real or imagined), I'd feel a sharp, stabbing pain in my anus. Unconscious to my abuse as a baby, I always chalked it up to growing pains.

This unresolved trauma had left me stuck in a state mixed with terror, isolation, and shame. During college, I indulged in alcohol, sex, and crack cocaine to numb the pain into oblivion. Then, one night as I was coming down off a high, I was flooded by fleeting images of my abuser that I remembered seeing in old home movies. I kicked the floorboard of the car, screamed, cried, and released a torrent of 20-year pent-up emotion.

Soon after, I was arrested for my second DUI in Orange County, North Carolina. Facing a mandatory sentence of two weeks in jail, I stumbled into drug and alcohol treatment not fully realizing that I was starting on a road to recovery.

In treatment, I began to learn that men could be sexually abused. By some statistics, at least one in six men have been sexually abused or assaulted. I learned about PTSD, the limbic brain, fight or flight responses, and the many ways that humans cope with life's traumas. My own chronic pain had taught me that the body literally keeps the score.

As part of my recovery, I started working the 12 steps of Alcoholics Anonymous. The fourth step is a personal inventory that includes an accounting of all of our resentments toward anyone in our lives who has harmed us. Using a deeply thorough approach to the fourth step invented by some AA members in Massachusetts in the late 1980s, I started on the process called the "turnarounds."

After listing all of my resentments, I began the "turnaround," where I looked at my part in each of these resentments. The Big Book [used as the guidebook for recovery in Alcoholics Anonymous (AA)] asks us where were we to blame in each of these situations. Where had we been selfish, dishonest, self-seeking, and frightened?

I dutifully made each and every turnaround on all of my resentments until I got to my oldest resentment: the person who had sexually abused me. The thought that I had a part, no matter how remote, in being sexually abused as a baby was, at first, inconceivable. I literally couldn't imagine how I, as a baby, had a part in being sexually abused.

Then, it occurred to me, a "moment of clarity" in AA parlance. My "part" didn't involve anything that I had done as an infant but rather how I, as a 25-year-old adult, was relating to my abuser right now in my current life.

For me, this awareness was liberating because I realized that my part was my power. My response to being sexually abused was now my choice. Although I had no control over what happened to me as a child, I had complete control over what to do with it. Inspired by the writings of Victor Frankl, I sensed that our psychological reactions were not solely the result of life's conditions. Our freedom of choice was present even in severe suffering.

Each day I have a choice between victimhood and empowerment. Each day I have an opportunity to lovingly notice how I either react or respond to life's circumstances. My fiercest enemy can be my greatest teacher if I choose to see my own reactions, triggers, projections, and fears, and use them for greater awareness, growth, and compassion.

In my personal healing, I've embraced Peter Levine's form of therapy called somatic experiencing, where the client focuses on perceived bodily sensations or somatic experiences. When I'm flooded with past memories, old patterns of thoughts, or chronic pain, I try to lean into them. I try to engage with my body and my breath in the present moment. Through breath and awareness, I slowly feel more space inside of myself and greater clarity, creativity, and calm. I've learned to hold the infant part of myself with love and relate to him with the same compassion that I would feel for my own children.

In my practice as an attorney, I often counsel clients in crisis suffering from loss, resentment, anger, and bitterness. One particular guardianship case involved a woman fighting over custody of her 23-year-old son diagnosed with Down syndrome. During our meetings, she described being abused by her son's father over many years. Her anger, rage, hate, and resentment were visibly palpable.

As we sat together in mediation, she was consumed by these feelings to the point where it blinded her from considering any other outcome except complete control and full custody of her son. After listening intently for several hours, I gently offered understanding and affirmation of her past experience and her current emotions.

After honoring her pain and memories of abuse, I started to relate some of my own story as an abuse survivor, sharing enough detail for context and focusing on my own feelings of helplessness, rage, collapse, and resentment. After connecting with her emotionally, I put my hand on my heart and shared the Nelson Mandela quote that resentment is like taking poison and waiting for the other person to die.

Taking a deep breath, I lovingly asked her if and/or how these feelings were serving her. I asked her whether she wanted to be free of this resentment and anger toward her ex-husband. After she gently nodded, I began to share my own experience of letting go of resentment. Forgiveness was a gift that I gave to myself. Forgiveness was a change in my perspective and a choice to see how life's sufferings were happening for me rather than to me. I asked her if she could imagine any gifts inside of the pain? I shared how my pain and suffering have allowed me to be more human. I shared how the pain of being sexually abused has enriched my life.

Through deep breaths and my gentle questions, she softened. Her victimhood receded. Slowly, she considered other possibilities to full custody of her son, and his best interests became paramount. Looking back, the ultimate result of the case was less important than the healing process itself.

This case along with others have given me a chance to use my experience as a sexual abuse survivor to serve others. By helping others find a way through their pain, I've turned my own shadow into gold. By loving the wounded parts of myself, I've discovered greater compassion for others and greater purpose in my own life.

The Wounded Healer

Susan Daicoff[29]

My good friend, the late Brigham A. Fordham, Esq., coined the phrase "Lawyers Solve Problems." Yet lawyers often revel in conflict and hostility.

Psychologist Alfred Adler believed we choose our careers based on conscious or unconscious desires to rise above and conquer traumatic situations in our past. He chose to become a medical doctor because, as a child, he had a medical emergency that left him feeling helpless. I watched my parents divorce when I was nine and decided conflict was intolerable. I vowed to be part of the solution rather than part of the problem, which drove me to become a mediator decades later. When parties in mediation reach agreement, that nine-year-old inside me rejoices, saying, "see, people *can* agree to disagree and live together harmoniously!" And when my nine-year-old self pushes parties too hard to settle, trauma has overcome reason and wisdom in my professional practice.

When I watched my mother, in 1972, face discrimination as a single divorced woman in the deep South, I decided I would never allow myself to be as vulnerable in society as she was. She went from being a Mrs., a doctor's wife with all the credibility, social status, and financial credit one could ever want, to being a Ms., a divorced nobody, who couldn't get a credit card at even the smallest of stores in my hometown. She was furious at the store managers and the system—and so was I. But my response, rather than anger, was to go to law school and become a lawyer, so "the system" would never have me at its mercy. Living in the deep South, I witnessed racism on a level the rest of the country never sees, well into the 21st century. Those indelible experiences drove me to achieve and succeed, in school and in the profession, so that I'd never be victimized. When I find myself pushing too hard on behalf of a client I feel was treated unfairly, particularly a person of color, I ask "am I defending them, or am I defending myself, my mother, or my classmates again?"

In the 1980s, during law school and the early years of my work, I experienced sexual harassment in the workplace. At the time, I simply blamed myself or thought it was "par for the course." I acknowledged my own contribution to fostering these situations. It wasn't until 2020 that I reexamined those situations and acknowledged that I had experienced trauma as a result of them. When predatory behavior was aimed at me, with unequal bargaining power, by someone with power and control over my very career, I became sour on the legal profession. It drove me into graduate school in clinical psychology, work in trauma recovery, and a focus on legal ethics, professionalism, and

---

[29] Susan Daicoff is an experienced lawyer, professor, author, speaker, mediator, and administrator. Formerly the director of the Volunteer Lawyers Program of Southern Arizona Legal Aid, Inc., she also previously served as a court administrator and judge pro tem for limited jurisdiction courts in Maricopa County, Arizona. Before that, she was a tenured doctrinal professor of law for 23 years in three ABA-accredited law schools, the last four years of which she served as director of Clinical Programs. Her primary scholarship and speaking expertise focus on what she calls the "comprehensive law movement," or the practice of law as a healing profession.

compassionate lawyering. It also affected my representation of defendants in sexual harassment claims. Did I push the plaintiff too hard to settle, secretly believing "they were partly at fault for the inappropriate relationship" or did I push the client too hard to acknowledge, admit, and apologize for the employee's bad behavior?

However, in these cases, my work was also successful. I could help the plaintiff and defendant settle cases with healing, compassion, resolution, and some level of satisfaction all round, precisely because of my understanding of the dynamics at work in the traumatic situation.

First, I try to identify when my desire for justice for my own old wounds drives my actions and when it's an appropriate motivator and lender of compassion and understanding in a difficult situation. Second, when I'm self-aware and actively working to resolve and forgive my personal wounds, I can be an effective lawyer and mediator. I can resonate with others' pain and not overly identify to a point of blinded countertransference.

Lawyers can't successfully and permanently operate from a position of woundedness. When our clients share our wounds—domestic violence, sexual abuse, employment discrimination, criminal injustice—we can overdo, act compulsively, and fail unless we find ways to separate, compartmentalize their pain and ours, acknowledge and honor our pain and theirs, and grieve and resolve our own wounds. Then, we can champion clients' causes with true compassion and without the driven, compulsive behavior that stems from unresolved wounds. Our strength comes from digging down and unwrapping our own pain and trauma, so we can face others' trauma with courage, wisdom, forgiveness, and understanding.

I may have chosen my career in law as a very young person out of a place of trauma and woundedness, but I found myself re-choosing and remaking my career in law as a more mature person out of an intentional desire to heal others, using the law. Recently, I realized lawyers not only solve problems, as Brigham said; we actually heal people's lives with words alone. Some words harm, but our words can heal. Life as a healing lawyer is the most satisfying vocation I could have.

We Need to Talk about Trauma: The Personal and Professional Impact of an Oppressive Environment

Dr. Fernanda Guerra[30]

Every day, those who work in law see themselves as actors on the courtroom stage. This space is provided for representation, and although it is supposed

---

[30] Fernanda is a lawyer certified in the Conscious Contracts® model and facilitator of dialogues. She is the creator and co-founder of SER, a consultancy which guides lawyers to be constructors of consensus in conflicting relationships. She is the founder of Fernanda Guerra Advocacia in Rio de Janeiro, Brazil.

to be impartial, it fails to acknowledge that its actions can result in trauma for clients, members of the judiciary, and the attorneys themselves.

For a long time, I felt like a tree that was being carefully pruned to keep it in the right ornamental shape for a formal garden. This restricted my ability to express myself and discouraged me from developing any individuality.

And as we are all individuals, I brought this feeling home with me. I noticed how I reacted in a similar way in my private life. I felt like a mediocre lawyer, because, although I had originally wanted to, when I became a lawyer, I couldn't deal with my clients holistically. The suffering from having incomplete relationships, of only being able to care halfway, left me worrying about my own self-worth and I felt less of a person.

The variation of physical and psychological responses to stress is not only linked to its severity, nature, and how often someone is exposed but also to the person's individual characteristics, occupation, and even the social support they feel they have. Not infrequently, there is a desire to get away. In their eagerness to escape reality, there are those who resort to alcohol or medication or they develop ways to compensate.

If you look at trauma carefully and understand that it is something corrosive, where the harm can multiply, it is vital to reconsider the working environment and what is needed to change the situation. The solution, moreover, must include looking again at how we educate children, teenagers, and, eventually, young university students. Most educational systems use the concept of education that was created in the 19th century as their basis. When society began to focus on factories rather than agriculture, teaching was required to provide workers. As a result, education was shaped by repetitive and strictly disciplined factory environments.

Children were thrown into groups instead of taught individually, with designated places to sit. Knowledge was split into subjects to make teaching easier. In that way, the classrooms became a portrait of the manufacturing society, which had little interest in whether the student could adapt to the system.

What we have today is little better than an educational production line. Education should not be about providing information and plying students with tests. What we need to do is teach people how to use their abilities, and give them the skills to interpret and understand the world.

And the same goes for law courses, where technical qualifications are still needed to enter the profession, based on a system that does not change and perpetuates the cycle of trauma.

How to Deal with the Suffering Caused by Relationship Limitations

I grew up believing that conflict is best avoided, just like it is not polite to ask and showing your feelings is a sign of weakness. Brought up in this cultural paradigm, I lived my life realizing that most people around me also followed the same code of conduct.

However, throughout my career, I could see that this was not enough. I would use my legal tools first, as fighting or avoiding conflict seemed to me the best way to create harmony. I thought that the absence of conflict was the same as peace.

In some way, trying to eliminate conflict has brought me some professional success. However, I was failing to achieve what I felt in my soul was necessary, by using this approach, and I realized that my clients were only getting a superficial solution. It was not a transformative or regenerative experience, just a break.

Litigation gives an illusory feeling of being proactive, when you have to deal with a seemingly unsolvable problem. It is like summoning an arbitrator or a judge to provide a solution, it provides some parental-like support, when you have a difficult issue to deal with, like conflict.

Conflict, in itself, is not an essentially bad thing. On the contrary, it is a chance to review agreements and reconsider our roles within the relevant social dynamics, and it can be a driving force behind growth. The problem lies in the fact that we reduce conflict to a matter of whether we are right or not, which takes away the opportunity to work on something as essential and important as relationships.

The answer is simple and without any downsides: dialogue. Dialogue allows us to use our cultural skills to connect with each other; a communication process based on feelings, which requires presence, commitment, truth, and the ability to be receptive.

It is an opportunity to allow ourselves to listen and understand the nature of ourselves, through others, and, as a result, create greater empathy and compassion, thereby creating a genuine, collaborative relationship that can break down the aggressiveness and superficiality of conflict.

During my experience of over two decades in law, I have come to realize that my greatest achievements were not the cases I won but those where a consensus was achieved between the parties, without involving the "hammer" of the courts. When I was able to look after the relationships involved, I felt fulfilled as a lawyer.

Adverse Childhood Experiences: Research and Controversy

Trauma studies is an integrative field, combining neuroscience, public health, psychology, sociology, and other disciplines. Some trauma research, including the adverse childhood experiences (ACEs) studies about childhood adversity and its prevalence from a public health perspective, which are referenced in the following contribution, have been controversial for a number of reasons. In particular, the original ACEs study of 1995–1997 by the CDC and Kaiser[31]—which found a significant relationship between levels of exposure to childhood trauma and adverse health symptoms, disorders, and outcomes in adulthood—and the related ACEs questionnaire intended to measure levels of exposure to childhood adversity did not include several important aspects of trauma, including the impact of racism and other forms of discrimination, poverty, living in foster care, exposure to community violence, being bullied, and other factors that may apply in an urban versus suburban or rural social context. The original ACEs questionnaire focused largely on indicia of abuse, neglect, and mental health or addiction in a child's family before the age of 18. Subsequent studies, like the Philadelphia ACE Survey, have sought to include racism, poverty, and more as traumatic experiences.[32] Research on ACEs continues to evolve.

The ACE Controversy

Lorenn Walker[33]

"Do I count myself as being in jail?" I wonder while taking the Adverse Childhood Experiences (ACE) ten-questionnaire assessment. At 16, I was incarcerated, so I decide to count it as a "yes." My ACEs score becomes six, including affirmative answers about sexual abuse and a parent suffering mental illness. Five decades since experiencing my adverse childhood experiences (ACEs), this assessment disturbs me. It's too simplistic and excludes consideration of an individual's resiliency, which can protect them from being traumatized by adversity.

Trauma is not a fixed state that all individuals experience when facing adversity. Adversity is most often "converted by the survivor into a growth-producing stren."[34] Hollister, 1967, invented the word *stren* after Margret Mead told him in 1947:

> We have the word "trauma" to designate an unfortunate blow that injures the personality, but as yet we have no word that describes an experience that is fortunate, that strengthens the personality. The closest thing we come to this is to say, "It's a blessing." Counting our blessings does not

[31] *About the CDC-Kaiser ACE Study*, Apr. 6, 2021, https://www.cdc.gov/violenceprevention/aces/about.html?CDC_AA_refVal=https%3A%2F%2Fwww.cdc.gov%2Fviolenceprevention%2Facestudy%2Fabout.html.

[32] *See The Philadelphia ACE Project*, Philadelphia ACE Survey, https://www.philadelphiaaces.org/philadelphia-ace-survey.

[33] Lorenn Walker, JD, MPH, is a professor of practice and lecturer in law for the University of Hawai'i at Manoa, and the director of Hawai'i Friends of Restorative Justice.

[34] Jocelyn Proulx, Catherine Koverola, Anne Fedorowicz & Michael Kral, *Coping Strategies as Predictors of Distress in Survivors of Single and Multiple Sexual Victimization and Nonvictimized Controls*, 25(16) J. Applied Soc. Psych. 1464–83 (Aug. 1995), https://onlinelibrary.wiley.com/doi/abs/10.1111/j.1559-1816.1995.tb02627.x.

really meet our need for a collective noun directly opposite in meaning to "trauma."[35]

Individuals are mostly resilient and not traumatized by loss and violence.[36] "[A]n experience that is fortunate, that strengthens the personality" can result from adversity.[37] My research and life experiences confirm this.

I have studied resiliency for 25 years, which is driven by my personal experiences. My childhood family was troubled. My mother experienced unipolar depression, had six kids, and had not completed high school. She and my father, her second husband, had serious conflicts. There was screaming, fear, and apprehension in our home. They divorced when I was ten (the year I finally learned to read), but she had kept the divorce a secret from my two younger siblings and me. It was two years later, when I was 12 and my beloved 17-year-old brother was dying in the hospital, that she finally told us about the divorce. Our father, too, had kept up the charade, writing us letters inferring he was coming home any day now. It was astonishing to learn he wasn't coming home, and it was devastating for my family to lose my brother. By 14, I had moved out to live with a variety of single women who needed childcare. My mother allowed me to leave home with the admonition that "If you get into any trouble you'll be put into foster care." I earned room and board from babysitting, but anything else I needed was obtained through theft and selling LSD and marijuana. By 15, I dropped out of school. When I was 16, I was arrested for possession of marijuana in Seward, Nebraska. I'd been with two older men there looking for wild hemp to pick and sell in California. We had some smoking stash, and one of them got me to hold it, so I was charged with possession. The police gave me Miranda warnings, which I took seriously. I stayed silent despite the cops' threats: "You're going away to reform school until you're 18 if you don't tell us the truth about those guys." (I didn't, and the men were released while I stayed in jail for a week.) The experience motivated me to completely desist from crime. I had also convinced one of the men I was with to marry me. He had a job, and survival sex with him got me through the next few years. At 17, the sweet dog I loved got run over, and I decided to have a baby. By 18, I'd heard about this amazing school called Montessori. I asked my father, who I had no relationship with, to pay for a Montessori teacher training correspondence course from England. With that support, I was able to complete the course, and by the time I was 20 I had a job teaching preschool and kindergarten. I could support myself and my three-year-old daughter. At 21, I was able to leave my husband. By 23,

[35] W.G. Hollister, *The Concept of Sterns in Education: A Challenge to Curriculum Development*, in BEHAVIORAL SCIENCE FRONTIERS IN EDUCATION 197 (E.M. Bower & W.G. Hollister, eds., NY: John Wiley & Sons, 1967).

[36] G.A. Bonanno, *Loss, Trauma, and Human Resilience: Have We Underestimated the Human Capacity to Thrive After Extremely Aversive Events?*, 59(1) AM. PSYCH. 20–28 (2004), https://doi.org/10.1037/0003-066X.59.1.20.

[37] Hollister, *supra* note 35, at 197.

I'd become bored teaching preschool and moved to Kaua'i, where I waitressed. When I was 24, I was assaulted by a stranger. It was an attempted rape that turned into an attempted murder. I needed surgery and was hospitalized. After being released, I saw a therapist who helped me through the depression I was experiencing. He also convinced me to try college, despite my protests that I was "not college material."

Hawai'i allows anyone over age 18 to attend community college with or without a high school diploma. I did not expect to remain in college, but within days I found myself thriving at Kaua'i Community College. A year later I wanted to become a lawyer. I saw another therapist when I transferred to the University of Hawai'i on O'ahu. Both therapists helped me process the adversity and abuse I experienced in my youth. They both helped me believe I was intelligent, creative, and had a hardy disposition. Importantly, too, they each helped me see that I was not damaged by my experiences but made stronger and more resilient because of them.

I took the Hawai'i state bar examination at the same hotel where the police and ambulance had rescued me seven years earlier when I had been attacked. I clerked for judges and became a deputy attorney general for the state of Hawai'i. Besides becoming a lawyer, I married a great man my age. We had two more children, and we sent my first child to college. When she graduated from the University of California, she gave me her bachelor's degree on Mother's Day. It is framed in my office today. Having her was the best decision of my life, despite making it when I was a 17-year-old high school dropout needing someone to love.

While studying for my master's degree in public health, I studied and wrote my thesis on conflict and resiliency. I wrote about the Kaua'i Study where that island's whole 1955 birth cohort was studied until they reached their fifties. The study found that some of the cohort who faced tremendous adversity became more resilient than their peers who had more fortunate families. "With few exceptions, the resilient children grew into competent, confident, and caring adults whose educational and vocational accomplishments were equal to or exceeded those of the low-risk children in the cohort who had grown up in more affluent, secure, and stable environments."[38]

To date I have written a couple books and roughly 50 papers. One of my first papers was about how restorative justice practices promote resiliency.[39] When I took the ACEs test, I had second thoughts about my resiliency: "Maybe

---

[38] Emmy Werner & Rut Smith, Overcoming the Odds: High Risk Children from Birth to Adulthood 192 (New York: Cornell University Press, 1992).

[39] Lorenn Walker, *Second International Conference on Conferencing and Circles: Restorative Practice in Action*, in Restorative Practice in Action: Selective Papers (Bethlehem, PA: IIRP, 2000), https://www.iirp.edu /news/conferencing-a-group-process-that-promotes-resiliency?highlight=WyJsb3Jlbm4iLCJsb3Jlbm4ncyIsInd hbGtlciIsIndhbGtlcidzIiwibG9yZW5uIHdhbGtlciJd.

my sleeping trouble is because of the trauma I suffered?" But I have always been a light sleeper. No, it was the ten-question ACEs test that caused me to question my mental stability and coping skills.

ACEs caused me the "unintended consequences that can influence practices and programs to the detriment of the very individuals they intend to serve."[40] I experienced firsthand how individuals can be harmed from ACEs. I realized quickly that if that could happen to me, what would happen to the many people I work with and represent who might take the ACEs questionnaire and lack my understanding of resiliency and conflict?

"Re-traumatization" has been documented in service providers and social work students.[41] Leitch lists "[o]ver-attention to the negative," it brings up "[e] thical issues," and is known for "[g]enerating and reinforcing dysregulation" as serious concerns with ACEs and trauma-informed care.[42] George Bonanno, Columbia University clinical psychology professor, whose career has focused on studying how people deal with loss and tragedy, believes ACEs measurements are "more or less useless."[43]

From my many years of work with children in foster care, families in child welfare cases, people harmed by crime and social injustice, including incarcerated people, I know very well that many suffer from trauma and systemic biases. An ACEs questionnaire might help identify society's structural problems, but for individuals it is not reliable and can be harmful. Kelly-Irving and Delpierre argue that ACEs research should only be used

> for population-level or structural policies, it is an insufficient and ill-adapted tool for implementation by social workers, medical practitioners, child protection workers, and likely to stigmatize families and children. . . . The individualized use of the original ACEs questionnaire poses many potential ethical questions. What can an individual do with this information? Will they fear for their health, or even their lives even though the majority of exposed people will not develop any ACE-related problems?"[44]

---

[40] Laurie L. Leitch, *Action Steps Using ACEs and Trauma-Informed Care: A Resilience Model*, 5(1) Health Just. 5 (Apr. 28, 2017), https://healthandjusticejournal.biomedcentral.com/articles/10.1186/s40352-017-0050-5#citeas.

[41] *See* Francis J. Turner, Social Work Treatment: Interlocking Theoretical Approaches (Oxford: Oxford University Press, 2017); and L.D. Butler, J. Carello & E. Maguin, *Trauma, Stress, and Self-Care in Clinical Training: Predictors of Burnout, Decline in Health Status, Secondary Traumatic Stress Symptoms, and Compassion Satisfaction*, 9(4) Psych. Trauma. 416–24 (July 2017), doi: 10.1037/tra0000187. Epub 2016 Sep 12. PMID: 27617660.

[42] Leitch, *supra* note 40, at 4–5.

[43] George Bonanno, personal communication to author, Feb. 26, 2021.

[44] Michelle Kelly-Irving & Cyrille Delpierre, *A Critique of the Adverse Childhood Experiences Frame- work in Epidemiology and Public Health: Uses and Misuses*, *in* Social Policy and Society 11 (Cambridge University Press, 2019), https://hal.archives-ouvertes.fr/hal-02088653/document.

Kelly-Irving and Delpierre also argue the original ACEs researchers, Felitti, et al., 1997, promoted its use for "structural change" and not for "identifying people."[45] Focusing on individuals' deficits is unhelpful, while acknowledging their strengths and how they have managed to cope with past hardships is.[46]

ACE's "limitation of recall bias (relying on the memory of adults)" is also problematic.[47] A meta-analysis of prospective and retrospective studies measuring childhood maltreatment shows measurements like ACE are not as reliable as interviews and reports when the adversity happened.[48] Other researchers recommend the ACEs ten-question assessment should "not be used in clinical practice or for research surveys."[49]

All individuals who have suffered abuse and adversity need access to health care and services. Some people will suffer trauma, but not all will, and we should not create assessments that infer that they will. Some Indigenous people have said: "We are not to be defined by HT [historical trauma] . . . [c]olonizers would like us to be 'victims' to be 'saved, fixed, etc,' and colonial dependency that the Nation state requires can creep into helping systems relationship (good client, medicalization of HT)."[50]

Suggesting to someone they have suffered trauma can create a "self-fulfilling prophecy."[51] "Everyone does the best they can with what they have," my teacher and mentor Insoo Kim Berg taught me. Let's work to give people more by being solution-focused. Let's notice strengths, goals, and how amazing the disadvantaged people we work with manage to cope with hardship. Let's stop assuming and suggesting everyone who faces adversity has suffered a deficit and is traumatized.

---

[45] *Id.* at 12.

[46] Fredrike Bannink, *Posttraumatic Success: Solution-Focused Brief Therapy, in* Therapy, Training, Coaching, and Mediation Practice 1–11 (2008), https://www.fredrikebannink.com/bannink/wp-ontent/uploads/2011/03/Art_Posttraumatic_success.pdf.

[47] Zimmerman, Woolf & Haley, (2015). *Understanding the Relationship Between Education and Health: A Review of the Evidence and an Examination of Community Perspectives, in* Population Health: Behavioral and Social Science Insights 347–84, 364 (Rockville, MD: National Institutes of Health, 2015), https://www.ahrq.gov/sites/default/files/publications/files/population-health.pdf.

[48] J. Baldwin, A. Reuben, J. Newbury & A. Danese, *Agreement between Prospective and Retrospective Measures of Childhood Maltreatment: A Systematic Review and Meta-analysis*, 76(6) JAMA Psych. 584–93 (2019).

[49] John D. McLennan, Harriet L. Macmillan & Tracie O. Afifi, *Questioning the Use of Adverse Childhood Experiences (ACEs) Questionnaires*, 101(104331) Child Abuse & Neglect 3 (2020), doi:10.1016/j.chiabu.2019.104331.

[50] Karina Walters, *Imaiyachi (to Overcome) Living the Dreams of Our Ancestors: Transcending Historical Trauma*, YouTube Video, 45:16. https://www.youtube.com/watch?v=dtHZOKLG5xI.

[51] Kelly-Irving & Delpierre, *supra* note 44, at 15.

CHAPTER 4

Legal Practice and Trauma

Introduction

Helyi Maki

This section explores why trauma-informed lawyering and its principles can be considered important or even critical from a legal ethics perspective and how trauma can show up in the practice of law itself, and it includes a deeper dive into how some specific practice areas are affected by trauma. For some of these practices, we include representative stories or scenarios involving trauma, and in others proposals for change are presented.

Lawyers working with trauma will often need to reframe how they work in order to meet the client (and themselves) where they are at, in an emotionally intelligent and psychologically informed way. Often, the tools and frameworks involved in trauma-informed practices focus on cultivating trust and psychological safety with clients with relational communication practices and client-focused service design, anticipating and responding to client needs. An understanding of trauma is embedded in these practices, enabling us to work with clients in a biopsychosocial manner instead of only intellectually or cognitively, as we are often traditionally taught to do in law schools. The principles of trauma-informed lawyering are evolving, and various approaches have been proposed by lawyers, clinics, law schools, trauma experts, and government agencies. Trauma-informed care principles originate in the field of public health, and have been described as including a focus on trauma awareness, building safety, offering clients opportunities to control and using a strengths-based instead of deficit-oriented approach.[1] As trauma-informed lawyering is a "lens-based" practice, with a focus on how we communicate and engage in legal work, we suggest you read this section with the following principles

---

[1] E.K. Hopper, E.L. Bassuk & Jeffrey Olivet, *Shelter from the Storm: Trauma-Informed Care in Homelessness Services Settings*, 3 THE OPEN HEALTH SERVS. & POL'Y J. 80–100 (2010), https://benthamopen.com/contents/pdf/TOHSPJ/TOHSPJ-3-80.pdf.

in mind and reflect upon legal culture, the role of values and supports that might be useful in each practice area.

Many of these trauma-informed principles reflect the exhortations of Nuremberg prosecutor Benjamin Ferencz who said of the trials that "the trauma was indelible and will remain with me forever," and subsequently advocated for "developing new ways of thinking and new institutions that can create a more lawful and humane international society."[2]

Key Principles of Trauma-Informed Lawyering

Table 4.1 summarizes some of the key principles of trauma-informed lawyering discussed in numerous legal publications. Utilizing these principles can act as a meaningful support for clients and also for lawyers, allowing them to experience the legal process as more helpful or characterized by dignity. These principles can be used at any level of the legal process, with clients, within organizations or communities, in systems such as courts or schools, or even by lawyers in their own practices.

Table 4.1 Principles of Trauma-Informed Lawyering[3]

Principle	Description
1. A lens-based practice	Trauma-informed practice is about both what we say and do in our work and how we do it, rather than a checklist approach.[4]
2. "Do no harm" (harm prevention and reduction)	Anticipating that the legal process may be experienced as negative or harmful by a client, and seeking to prevent unnecessary harm wherever it can be avoided.

---

[2] Benjamin Ferencz, *A Prosecutor's Personal Account: From Nuremberg to Rome*, 52(2) J. Int'l Affairs (Spring 1999) [Note: Copyright: The Trustees of Columbia University in the City of New York.]

[3] The principles in this table for lawyers are drawn from the following sources: Myrna McCallum, *Trauma-Informed Legal Practice Toolkit*, Golden Eagle Rising Soc'y, 2020. H. Maki & C. Tess Sheldon, *Trauma-Informed Strategies in Public Interest Litigation: Avoiding Unintended Consequences Through Integrative Legal Perspectives*, 20(2d Series) Sup. Ct. L. Rev. (2019). Substance Abuse & Mental Health Servs. Admin., *Essential Components (White Paper) of Trauma-Informed Judicial Practice* (2013), online: National Association of State Mental Health Program Directors, https://www.nasmhpd.org/sites/default/files/JudgesEssential_5%201%202013final draft.pdf. *See also* Sarah Katz & Deeya Halder, *The Pedagogy of Trauma-Informed Lawyering*, 22 Clinical L. Rev. 359–93 (2016).

[4] The principles of trauma-informed care, first established in the public health (and mental health) context, have been adopted in other professional service contexts and have been articulated by a number of different authors and organizations. Many organizations establish their own version of these principles and related concepts. This table draws upon those principles and puts them into the legal context, using language that is relevant to lawyers and their clients. *See* Huang, Larke N., Rebecca Flatow, Tenly Biggs, Sara Afayee, Kelley Smith, Thomas Clark & Mary Blake, SAMHSA's Concept of Trauma and Guidance for a Trauma-Informed Approach (Rockville: SAMHSA, 2014). *See also* NCTSN Bench Card for the Trauma-Informed Judge (Los Angeles: NCTSN, 2013), https://www.nctsn.org/resources/nctsn-bench-cards-trauma-informed-judge.

Principle	Description
3. Awareness of trauma and trauma responses	Cultivating awareness of trauma responses in psychobiological terms, which may be complex, counterintuitive, or at first appear to be (or be misperceived as) so-called difficult behavior.
4. Psychological safety and dignity	A nonjudgmental approach to communication, providing time and space to discuss needs and preferences. Prioritizing client autonomy, control and consent wherever possible.
5. Lawyers are not therapists (and do not need to be)	We do not seek to act as therapists with the capacity to heal trauma, and we refer to or include appropriate experts on a case-by-case basis (as we would with any other expertise). We don't need to be therapists to be trauma informed, yet must adhere to the scope of our practice.
6. Inquiry instead of assumptions	Replace judgmental assumptions with nonjudgmental open-ended questions. Asking (or thinking) "what's your problem?" assumes there's a problem. Instead, we seek to ask "what did you experience?" or "what happened to you?"
7. Strengths-based communications that offer control	Acknowledging skills and capacities (client autonomy). Emphasis on what the client can do, their skills, capacities, consent, and opportunities for them to provide instructions, have control, or make decisions.
8. Transparency and accountability	Clear and open communication. Preparing and respectfully educating clients. Giving advance notice or providing learning materials in advance. Clearly articulating what to expect next in the process; giving an overview. Reliable and doing what we say we'll do.
9. Relational practice	Communicating with genuine curiosity and empathy to establish trust within the lawyer–client relationship. Communicating considerately, allowing for relationship formation instead of goal-oriented, transactional communications only.
10. Empathy and compassion	Considering what the client is feeling and seeking to understand how it feels to be in their shoes in order to respond with care.
11. Cultural humility	The guiding principles of cultural humility according to Tervalon and Murray-Garcia include recognizing and changing power imbalances and institutional accountability, alongside lifelong learning, self-reflection, and self-critique.[5]

---

[5] M. Tervalon & J. Murray-Garcia, *Cultural Humility Versus Cultural Competence: A Critical Distinction in Defining Physician Training Outcomes in Multicultural Education*, 0(2) J. Health Care for the Poor & Underserved 117–25 (May 1998), https://muse.jhu.edu/article/268076/summary.

Principle	Description
12. Self-reflection, including awareness of vicarious trauma	Openly asking ourselves what happened to us and what we have experienced, believed, or assumed. Understanding vicarious trauma (or secondary trauma) and related concepts like burnout or compassion fatigue. A continuous process.
13. Accommodation and support	Considering what the client needs at each step in the process (including time), with awareness that for many clients the legal process is stressful and requires learning. Allowing for needs and beyond cognitive processing and words. Actively engaging with or referring to professional supports (therapist, etc.) as needed. Allowing for needs in clients, colleagues, communities, organizations, and ourselves.

The following story provides a poignant example of why these principles are needed, and the gaps one lawyer identified in how her friend and colleague was treated.

When Unawareness Increases Pain: Why Probate Attorneys and Staff Need Trauma Training

Kelly McGrath[6]

I got a message this morning from a dear friend, one who's on a journey no one wants to be on: the loss of a spouse by suicide. She relays her experience with her probate attorney and staff.

"I gathered my heart together this morning to have a scheduled first call with the probate attorney, and at five minutes past the time (after I sent a query text), her assistant texts that she is 'running late' and thanks me for my patience. . . . She'll call me as soon as she can. Apparently, she doesn't get that one cannot hold the heart together indefinitely waiting by the phone for this kind of conversation."

"Forty-two minutes past the time—a second text, 'Our office apologizes for the inconvenience. She is running behind in her appointment.'"

My friend replied back, "Two months ago, my husband committed suicide. I have pulled myself together to prepare for this call and be able to do it with rational calm. Waiting more than 30 minutes without anything other than

---

[6] Kelly McGrath guides people through the most challenging conversations of their lives so they can stay out of court. As a mediator and peacebuilding lawyer, she facilitates divorces, elder care issues, business disputes, and serious harm cases. Kelly uses her skills in nonviolent communication and restorative justice to help her clients talk about their feelings and needs, what happened, and how to make things as right as possible. She's the founder of the Florida Restorative Justice Association and has a professional certificate in trauma & resilience through Florida State University. Her firm, Kelly McGrath Mediation, helps clients not only get through their legal issue without the court battle but also repair relationships, find peace through the challenge, and get back into alignment with their values.

"thank you for your patience" is difficult and my calm is dissolving into tears. Also difficult is the idea that we may have to reschedule, and I must again wait for the day to arrive and then go through this emotional juggernaut again."

An hour later the attorney called and explained she was on a call with the court. I'm glad my friend was able to express to the attorney how it landed for her when no one showed compassion or understanding around what my friend was experiencing. My friend's heart and world had just been shattered and she needed care in that moment.

Here's how I wanted my friend to be treated:

The attorney is running late. Staff understand the ways this deep hurt may show up for their clients after the loss of a loved one and is able to show empathy and care.

The legal assistant calls my friend, "Hello, Client, it's Legal Assistant from Attorney's Probate Firm. I know you were coming in about Name of Spouse's will. How are you doing right now?" (Lets her express and lets her know she's been heard without judging, evaluating, advising, minimizing, etc.)

"I'm so sorry to delay this, but the attorney is in court and it's run over and we're not exactly sure how long this is going to drag on. I'm guessing it took a lot to get here today and we want to make this as easy on you as possible so here are three options: x, y, z. What do you think would be best for you right now? Or, if you want to think about it and get back to me that's fine, too. Again, I'm so sorry we're having to make you wait in this moment. Is there anything we haven't thought of that would make this easier?"

A personal call right away, a check in to show care, and a few options that my friend could pick. These three things could have given this hard experience more warmth and care.

Most people see attorneys during the hardest parts of their lives. . . . But of all of the law practices out there, probate attorneys' clients have experienced the ultimate loss—the loss of a loved one. They are shattered, their worlds upended and loss palatable, the wound fresh.

Some people describe this time as being in a bubble of pain by themselves— looking out at the world as it moves on. Probate attorneys and their staff must be trained in trauma and responses that are helpful, not fall to their uncomfortable, inappropriate responses or, worse, no response at all.

The training must include empathy training and appropriate responses, anticipating and understanding how the client may show up, understanding trauma and its effects, and putting systems in place to deal with unanticipated delays or other emergencies to structure a response that tenderly wraps the client in compassion and love.

To end this story, frustratingly, my friend went to the attorney's office to drop off the will and another lawyer asked her name and said, "Oh yes, it's about the paperwork, right?" No! Handling the will for her husband who died by suicide is not about the paperwork. And in probate law, it never is about the paperwork—it's about the client's loss and needing a deeply compassionate legal guide through unknown and heartbreaking terrain.

This story identifies missing elements of communication that are part of trauma-informed practice. The following contribution provides a general framework for communicating with clients, regardless of practice area, and serves as a "lens" through which to view the suggestions, gaps, and missing pieces described in the remainder of this section.

Communication Strategies and Ethics

Trauma-Informed Client Communication Strategies for Lawyers

Katherine Porterfield, PhD[7]

Legal education over the last several decades has evolved to include teaching and training around effective approaches to client communication. Client-centered legal work requires a recognition from the lawyer that the person in front of him/her/them, seeking or utilizing their services, has an entire life history and an array of reactions and feelings that may impact that person's ability to work with the attorney. For example, the experience of sitting in front of a lawyer can evoke intense anxiety and vulnerability. Most people who find themselves needing legal services are under stress, and, in some cases, severe and life-altering events have taken place to bring the person in front of a lawyer. Outcomes of legal problems can have far-reaching consequences in a person's life. Additionally, the power differential that exists between lawyer and client can lead clients to have difficulty communicating their needs.

The Benefits of a Frame

A trauma-informed frame (or framework) for communicating with a client provides attorneys with a conceptual approach to their interactions with clients who may have suffered trauma or adversity and with concrete skills for communicating effectively. This frame has developed from the author's work over

[7] Katherine Porterfield is a consulting psychologist at the Bellevue Program for Survivors of Torture. Dr. Porterfield has provided clinical care to adults and children who have experienced war and refugee trauma and torture for over 25 years. She regularly consults on issues pertaining to trauma, including in cases at the Guantanamo Bay Detention Center, in U.S. Federal Courts, and at the International Criminal Court, as well as with journalists and human rights organizations. Dr. Porterfield is a founding staff member of the Journalist Trauma Support Network, an initiative at the Dart Center for Journalism and Trauma at Columbia University.

the last two decades working with survivors of severe trauma, including with incarcerated and detained individuals.

The framework presented here recognizes that survivors of trauma who are engaged in legal matters may suffer from symptoms that make it difficult for them to fully utilize their lawyer's knowledge, skills, and services. Lawyers who recognize this and who craft legal communications so as to maximize clients' sense of control and safety lay the groundwork for a more effective lawyer–client working relationship.

Figure 4.1 provides a representation of the trauma-informed frame proposed in this chapter. The interaction with the trauma-affected client is conceptualized as involving four principles—safety, control, reflection, and closure. These principles are operationalized with specific communication strategies that will be discussed later. First, each principle will be elaborated in relation to a trauma-informed approach, and then specific communication strategies will be described.

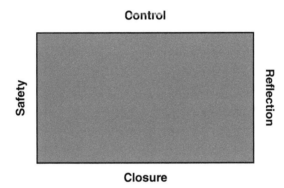

Figure 4.1 Trauma-Informed Frame for Communication with a Client
Image credit: Katherine Porterfield

Safety

Trauma is a biopsychosocial experience that leaves an imprint on the physiological, cognitive/emotional, and interpersonal functioning of humans. Trauma shatters the most basic human need for physical and psychic safety. Bodily reactions to trauma such as fight or flight arousal can be reactivated easily in the aftermath of trauma. Psychological constructs—thoughts and feelings about the traumatic events—take shape as people make meaning about what happened to them and why. And, social bonds can be frayed or ruptured due to the experience of interpersonal violence or coercion.

Individuals who have had their fundamental sense of safety and security challenged or erased due to trauma often operate in the world as if they are still in danger. This perception of ongoing threat emanates from both physiological messages coming from their nervous system that signal impending danger (i.e., hyperarousal), as well as conscious appraisals of the world as a dangerous place due to posttraumatic meaning-making. Additionally, for some survivors, the experience of lack of safety leads to a "shut-down" (i.e., dissociative) response where they have difficulty perceiving and acting in the world. For example, the victim of childhood sexual abuse who received no therapy or treatment and who now, in adulthood, sits across from an attorney, facing a criminal charge, may be suffering from conscious and unconscious experiences of threat that deeply affect her ability to process information with the lawyer, as well as plan for her defense. She may become silent, withdrawn, and flat in her responses, seemingly signaling apathy, while actually experiencing intense distress. Without recognizing this, a lawyer may "push" the client to answer, inadvertently exacerbating the client's sense of danger and threat, thereby derailing their communication.

Trauma-informed communication with a client, then, begins with the primacy of safety in the interaction. This priority on safety shapes the attorney's approach in everything from the physical layout of the meeting space to the way topics are introduced and anticipated. Creating a safe environment for a client lays the foundation for communication to proceed in a constructive way.

Next, three recommendations are provided for safety-enhancing communication.

1. *Acknowledge the physical space.* Client meetings with lawyers can take place in a number of highly restrictive spaces, including prisons, detention centers, holding cells, police stations, and a variety of offices, many of which can be intimidating and imposing. Telephone or video calls in which deeply personal information must be discussed are common for attorneys and clients. Representatives of those who can be perceived by the clients as adversaries (corrections officers, police, prosecutors, opposing attorneys, etc.) may be present or nearby, thus increasing clients' threat perception. Telling a client they can speak freely may be inadequate for them to overcome the physiological hyperarousal emanating from the nervous system. It is recommended that lawyers explicitly begin by asking if the client is comfortable in the current meeting conditions. A variety of questions can signal to the client that his comfort and safety is a priority to the lawyer, even within a challenging setting:

   ◆ "Is this an ok place for us to speak?"
   ◆ "How do you feel in this space as we speak?"
   ◆ "It's important that you feel safe speaking to me here. Do you feel able to talk?"

These questions, while simple, signal that the client's experience of the meeting is critical to the attorney. If the client says that she is not safe to proceed, there may be limits to what the lawyer can do, but it is essential that this be acknowledged. For example, if the client says, "I don't feel like I can talk here," in a detention setting, the lawyer may be able to ask a guard to move slightly farther away, ask to close a door further, move the client's chair so it is not facing the door, or ask the client what else would help. If the situation cannot be improved, the lawyer should acknowledge the difficulty and ask how the client would like to proceed.

2. *Anticipate what will happen in the meeting.* Individuals who have suffered trauma have often experienced severe helplessness and unpredictability in their environments. Thus, providing a client with a clear sense of what is happening can enhance a sense of safety and decrease uncertainty. There are a variety of ways to help a client anticipate what is happening next:

   ◆ "I'd like to share with you how I thought we could use the time together today."
   ◆ "Here is how I thought we could work together today."
   ◆ "I was hoping we could work on this today. How would you like to begin?"

Here, the lawyer signals to the client what the time together will entail. It is essential to also give the client agency over how he/she/they would like to use the time, as well. Thus, after sharing the intended goals of the meeting, the attorney should also elicit what the client would like to achieve.

3. *Explain your role in detail.* The legal profession provides multiple roles for lawyers, depending on the context. Some legal teams may have multiple lawyers and non-lawyers who will come in contact with the client. An overwhelmed client may have trouble processing the various professionals with whom he is having contact and may misconstrue people's roles. Thus, clarifying one's role is essential for the client's ability to utilize team members appropriately and feel secure in whom he is communicating with. For example, clarifying team members' roles can be done as follows:

   ◆ "I want to explain to you the members of your team, so you understand who you're talking with and why the person might be focusing on certain issues with you."
   ◆ "I'm the lead lawyer on your team. That means that you and I will always discuss the major decisions about your case. The other team members may work with you on different parts of your case. We all work together, but we each might have a different focus."

Control

If safety involves solidifying the client's orientation to what is happening to him and around him, then control involves enhancing his ability to be an active part of the legal process. For a survivor, the loss of control that occurred during the trauma can easily be recapitulated in dynamics with others. For example, a person who was tortured during interrogations may be easily triggered back into a state of learned helplessness (a state of passive acquiescence) as someone begins to question him. This can prevent the client from taking in and participating in even the most basic legal communication.

Next, two examples of ways to enhance control are described:

1. *Ask permission and ask for feedback throughout a meeting.* Since they perceive themselves as responsible for handling the case, lawyers frequently set the agenda for the client's meetings and legal process, and move through the issues that they believe are important. For a traumatized client, this barrage of questions can feel overwhelming and can lead to a defensive reaction of shutting down. Lawyers can minimize this by signaling that the client has shared control of the meeting. Examples of this include:

    ◆ "What would you like to achieve today?"
    ◆ "May I share with you my goals for today?"
    ◆ "I'd like to move on to this topic now—is that ok with you?"

2. *Talk about talking.* Lawyers need to elicit information from clients about the events that are related to their cases. This often means asking about profoundly distressing life experiences that evoke horror, physiological fear reactions, shame, sadness, and self-attack. In response to these distressing bodily and emotional states, survivors often want to avoid and deny these memories. The memories themselves can be fractured and distorted due to states of dissociation that clients suffered in the moments of trauma. Clients will even avoid talking about details that could assist in their cases, such as a client refusing to discuss childhood trauma that is central to mitigation.

    When attorneys are broaching difficult topics with clients, then, it is essential that they recognize that avoidance is an adaptive reaction, designed to protect the survivor's psychic and bodily integrity. If lawyers recognize this avoidance as a survival mechanism, rather than see it as a conscious obfuscation, they can work with the survivor to open up the topic in a safe, functional way. The concept of "talking about talking" then allows the lawyer to broach traumatic material in a way that allows the client to articulate impediments to talking.

    Specifically, this approach requires that topics that are perceived as threatening to the client's safety are raised first in the abstract. A lawyer using this technique first raises the *idea* of talking and asks the client how it would feel to proceed. Examples of this approach are:

◆ "I'd like to talk about what happened when you were arrested. How would it be to talk about that right now?"
◆ "It would be helpful for me to understand what happened when you were hurt by the people who were interrogating you. Would you be able to talk with me about those events?"
◆ "You are telling me that you don't want to tell me what happened when the soldiers came to your village. Do you think you can help me understand why that is something you don't want to describe?"

Lawyers who use this approach may find that simply surfacing the difficulty of certain topics allows a client to proceed with her narrative. If not, the client may be able to explain why they cannot talk about it. Asking "What are you worried will happen if we talk about these events?" may create opportunities for the client to describe her fears of becoming overwhelmed, feeling distressed, or suffering a return of terrible memories.

This kind of inquiry may make lawyers concerned that topics will be declared "off-limits," but, more likely, this kind of sensitive questioning will signal to a client that her experience matters to the attorney. In the author's experience, this process usually helps clients feel ready to discuss difficult memories, as their fears about becoming too distressed can be alleviated by the attorney's response. For example, reassuring the client that these disclosures are for the benefit of his case or that the lawyer will be careful and sensitive about what is discussed can alleviate anxiety.

Reflection Back

Trauma survivors often suffer intense feelings that they are damaged, different, or irrevocably altered by what has happened to them, as well as that their experiences are not tolerable or imaginable to others. One of the most powerful communication tools for speaking with trauma survivors, then, is to make them feel heard and respected, even understood. A simple tool for this is the act of reflecting back what is said, without interpretation, analysis, or disagreement. This reflection can create a powerful feeling of being a subject in one's own story, rather than being seen as an object in another's interpretation.

Reflecting back must not be rote or formulaic. Instead, in simple, genuine terms, the lawyer expresses a desire to make sure she has heard what the client is saying. Two techniques are described here.

1. *Reflecting back content.* Reflection, while simple in its idea, is complex in execution. The goal for the attorney is to state back what the client is saying, until the client verifies that the lawyer is correct. Examples include:

    ◆   "You've just said some things that are clearly very important to you. I want to make sure that I have heard you, so I would like to tell you what I hear you saying."
    ◆   "Am I right about what I am hearing you say?"

2. *Reflecting back emotion.* Reflection back can include a reflection of a client's emotion, as well as the content of what they are saying. This can be challenging terrain, as clients may feel a range of intense emotions, especially if their traumatic life experiences become part of a legal conversation. Clients may express anger, desperation, despondency, and hopelessness. Reflecting back a client's emotions must occur carefully and it is essential that the lawyer allow the client to name the feeling, if possible. Examples of reflection of emotion include:

    ◆   "I see that when you are talking about this you are looking upset. Do I have that right?" (Allow client to elaborate, if he/she/they choose to.)
    ◆   "You are talking about this with a lot of feeling. Can I make sure I understand your reaction?"

    If the client's emotion feels out of control or dangerous to the safety of the attorney (such as could happen with anger), it is important for the attorney to calmly try to contain and end the meeting if necessary. ("I see you are really upset right now. Let's take a break and try to see if we can get back to this another time.") Lawyers should never sacrifice their own sense of safety in an interaction with a client.

Reflecting back carefully to a client can create a sense of empowerment and validation. For clients who have suffered experiences of powerlessness, persecution, and erasure, this kind of communication can lay the groundwork for a positive and constructive professional relationship.

Closure

A lawyer may be able to end a meeting quickly and shift to the next task, but for a traumatized person, the conversation may have opened up intense memories and led to strong physical and emotional reactions. Ending abruptly, then, can leave a client feeling exposed and distressed, setting the stage for her to return to her cell or her family in a compromised state. Lawyers can provide closure to client meetings in ways that recognize the work the client has done, the stress she might be under, and the need for a sense of what is happening next.

Following are three examples of ways to provide closure to a conversation.

1. *Shift explicitly into closure.* Just as in anticipating what will be happening at the beginning of a meeting, signaling the end of the conversation is equally important and can help a client begin to contain what has been discussed.

   ◆ "We can wrap up in about 20 minutes. Let's make sure we have covered what you wanted today."
   ◆ "We're going to finish up soon. Is there anything else you want to discuss?"

2. *Ask for feedback on the conversation.* Lawyers can signal to clients that their opinion about how the work is going is important to the attorney. For example, as one might do with a colleague, checking in on if the client feels that the work is going well signals respect and evokes that the client has input into the working relationship.

   ◆ "As we are finishing up today, I just wanted to ask how you are feeling about our work together."
   ◆ "Is there anything you want to tell me about the way we are working together?"

The lawyer may not be able to address or fix the concerns or frustrations raised by a client but by eliciting them, the lawyer gains better understanding of how the client is perceiving the work and creates room for improving the client's experience.

3. *Help the client prepare for next steps.* If a client has had to discuss difficult memories in a meeting, she may be struggling with PTSD symptoms of arousal (feeling edgy, anxious, unfocused) or shut down (fatigue, loss of energy, feeling drained). Any of these states can make transitions back to a cell or detention area difficult, as a client may fear seeming vulnerable to others. Clients returning to their homes after a meeting may be anxious about having difficulty with family because of their distress. The attorney can assist by asking the client what they need to make the transition.

   ◆ "As we finish up, you've talked about a lot of important things. You may be feeling stressed by this. What will help you as you go back to your cell?"
   ◆ "You worked very hard today. Let's think about what you are going to do after this meeting to help yourself feel ok."

   Simple suggestions, such as that the client could do some light exercise, take a rest, or listen to music may help the client shift into a mode of self-care. Lawyers who are comfortable with talking about meditation or relaxation techniques may be able to suggest them as a resource for a client who describes difficulty with calming down. Printing out a visualization or breathing training script and offering it to a client may be appropriate.

Conclusion

Communication that follows the concepts outlined in this section—enhancing safety, giving control, reflecting back the client's words, and using closure as a way to transition the client away from traumatic material—may strengthen the professional relationship between lawyer and client by creating a trauma-informed dynamic in which the client's experiences, reactions, and opinions are paramount.[8]

Ethics and Professional Responsibility: What Lawyers Should Know and Trauma-Informed Lawyering as a Legal Competency

Kenneth Townsend[9]

Introduction

Trauma-informed lawyering aims to help lawyers spot the warning signs of trauma, both in themselves and in others, and to take the actions necessary to navigate trauma in healthy and productive ways. The stresses of law practice and the culture that stigmatizes acknowledging those stresses can undermine lawyers' effectiveness and quality of life in any number of ways. They also increase the likelihood that the lawyer will run afoul of written and unwritten rules of professional responsibility.

Trauma-Informed Lawyering and the Model Rules of Professional Conduct

Trauma-informed lawyering implicates emotional intelligence, habits of character, and other so-called soft skills in ways that are not always cognizable by a rules-oriented legal culture, including by the Model Rules of Professional Conduct. Some advocates have looked to Rule 1.1, however, as a possible avenue for re-imagining lawyer competence.[10] As a catchall provision concerning

---

[8] Attorneys who work with clients who have suffered trauma may find that they experience personal reactions to difficult or traumatic material that emerges in conversations with clients, including their own trauma history. It is strongly recommended that lawyers recognize their own reactions and find appropriate supports and resources for their own processing and well-being.

[9] Kenneth is director of Leadership and Character in the Professional Schools at Wake Forest University and Scholar-in-Residence in the Wake Forest School of Law.

[10] Nat'l Task Force on Lawyer Well-Being, *The Path to Lawyer Well-being: Practical Recommendations for Positive Change* (2017), https://www.americanbar.org/content/dam/aba/images/abanews/ThePathToLawyerWell BeingReportRevFINAL.p [https://perma.cc/UT76-Y43Y].

lawyer competence, Rule 1.1 currently states, "A lawyer shall provide competent representation to a client. Competent representation requires the legal knowledge, skill, thoroughness and preparation reasonably necessary for the representation."[11] The ABA's 2017 report *The Path to Lawyer Well-Being Report* (Report) has recommended amending Rule 1.1 to "include language . . . which defines 'competence' to include the 'mental, emotional, and physical ability reasonably necessary' for the representation."[12] Such an amendment would acknowledge that competent lawyering in the 21st century consists of more than knowing the right things and honing the necessary skills.

Alternatively, the Report suggested "amend[ing] the Comments to Rule 1.1 to clarify that professional competence requires an ability to comply with all of the Court's essential eligibility requirements,"[13] and avoiding ever-broadening conceptions of competency that risk excluding would-be lawyers with mental or physical impairments that are irrelevant for the successful practice of law.

Whether expanding definitions of competence to include emotional capacities or clarifying that definitions of competence need not exclude those experiencing trauma and related mental health issues, the Model Rules provide one pathway for helping ensure lawyers are better prepared to recognize and respond to trauma. Any amendments to the Model Rules, however, should be careful to avoid targeting, directly or indirectly, those facing mental health challenges or those who have experienced trauma in their lives or work.

Beyond the Rules

While rules are often a necessary component of cultural change, rules alone cannot fix a culture that has persistently and systematically neglected considerations of well-being in general or of trauma in particular. Changing a culture requires changing the habits, unspoken norms, and personal attitudes of those who make up the legal community. This work demands the buy-in and continued work of legal educators and of the legal profession.

Professional Responsibility and Professional Identity

Questions of professional responsibility cannot be separated from considerations of professional identity. Some lawyers view their work as something that they do but not who they are. Other lawyers identify with their work, but primarily the form of work, for example, writing briefs, preparing for trial, and so on. A relatively smaller subset of cause-based lawyers aligns their personal beliefs and causes with their professional aspirations.

---

[11] Model Rules of Pro. Conduct r. 1.1 (Am. Bar Ass'n 2020).

[12] Nat'l Task Force on Lawyer Well-Being, *supra* note 10.

[13] *Id.*

Legal education and legal practice often promote and presume a certain emotional distance between oneself and one's clients. We learn early in law school that our success is contingent upon being able to intellectually sympathize with every position and to argue every side of a case. This capacity for intellectual empathy can come at the cost, however, of a more emotive form of empathy that enables us to feel the pain of others. While important for effective lawyering, this intellectualization of empathy can prove alienating insofar as it creates a gap between our emotional and intellectual selves.

One of the greatest challenges currently facing the legal profession involves helping lawyers to think about their work and their lives in integrated, holistic ways while also preparing those lawyers for the difficulties and occasional trauma that can result when one's personal and professional identity are bound together.

Finding Agency

While much of the work required to prepare and produce trauma-informed lawyers must be undertaken by the institutions and organizations that shape legal culture, including law schools and state bar associations, it is important for individual law students and lawyers to recognize their own agency. Without overstating what any individual can do, there are a few steps that just about anyone can do to start preparing for the pressures of law practice, including for the possibility of trauma.

◆ Practice self-awareness and self-reflection.

It is all too easy to feel that law school and legal practice leave little time for the sort of self-reflection that is needed to remain tethered to one's values and commitments. For those at risk of encountering trauma, it is important to develop habits and strategies for maintaining self-awareness. Learning to spot the circumstances that trigger trauma, for example, is important in helping lawyers recognize and respond to that trauma.

◆ Seek out mentors and role models.

Mentors and role models can be invaluable to learning traditional aspects of law practice and can be just as valuable in helping new lawyers learn how to navigate unexpected pressures of law practice, including trauma. Research shows that adult learning is facilitated by having examples to follow.[14]

◆ Cultivate friendships.

Close friendships provide space to be vulnerable and to be held accountable. Cultivating intimate friendships with fellow lawyers as well as non-lawyers can be key to maintaining support and perspective when encountering difficult, or even traumatic, experiences.[15]

---

[14] Anne Colby & William Damon, Some Do Care (1992).

[15] These three strategies have been loosely adapted from Michael Lamb, Jonathan Brant & Edward Brooks, *How Is Virtue Cultivated? Seven Strategies for Postgraduate Character Development*, J. Character Educ. (2021).

Closing

The legal profession has a long way to go in preparing trauma-informed lawyers, but recent developments in legal education and legal practice suggest that this important area is beginning to receive some of the attention it deserves.

Challenges to Values and Meaning in Practice: Meaning-Making, Moral Injury, Moral Repair

Helgi Maki

Moral injury was initially defined by Jonathan Shay as the biological, psychological, and social results of the betrayal of "what's right."[16] Moral injury in the law can occur when a fundamental value or right inherent within a legal situation is violated in the name of the law.

Examples include:

◆ A legal outcome or process does more harm than good;

◆ A legal situation comes at the unacceptably high cost of violating other rights or principles; or

◆ The legal outcome is simply "technical justice" and no more than that only technically just, fair or reasonable, and justice can only be said to have been delivered in a technical manner.

Key aspects of moral injury for medical professionals are that it "occurs when we perpetrate, bear witness to, or fail to prevent an act that transgresses our deeply held moral beliefs. . . . Moral injury describes the challenge of simultaneously knowing what care patients need but being unable to provide it due to constraints that are beyond our control."[17] The legal equivalents of the doctor's oath, to first do no harm, include legal ethics upholding justice or fairness and professional responsibilities including the duty to act in the best interests of the client, and lawyers risk moral injury when some aspect of lawyering erodes justice, exacerbates unfairness, or undermines the client's best interests.

The trauma of fundamentally violating our values, even if it may be partly or wholly by our own doing, whether by our own free will or under constraint or duress is called "moral injury." Moral injury has been studied among soldiers and veterans due to its profound impact on mental and emotional well-being from shame, guilt, depression, or a sense of loss of purpose or meaning.[18] In the legal profession, moral injury is on a spectrum from minor (and likely chronic) to more

---

[16] Jonathan Shay, *Moral Injury*, 16(1) Intertexts 57–66 (2012), doi:10.1353/itx.2012.0000.

[17] W. Dean, S. Talbot & A. Dean, *Reframing Clinician Distress: Moral Injury Not Burnout*, 36(9) Fed. Practitioner 400–02 (Sept. 2019), https://www.ncbi.nlm.nih.gov/pmc/articles/PMC6752815/.

[18] W.P. Nash & Brett T. Litz, *Moral Injury: A Mechanism for War-Related Psychological Trauma in Military Family Members*, 16 Clinical Child & Fam. Psych. Rev. 365–75 (2013), https://link.springer.com/article/10.1007/s10567-013-0146-y/.

serious contraventions of our values to fundamental breach of our sense of meaning. The fundamental breach of our sense of basic fairness or morality, especially involving an organization or system that harms the people it was designed to serve or protect, has been called "institutional betrayal" by psychologist Jennifer Freyd, with its opposite, the upholding of values, referred to as "institutional courage."[19]

Our legal practices, processes, and the outcomes we pursue may inadvertently cause harm such as retraumatizing a client, or add to their experiences of trauma, such as in a sexual assault case where a victim's sexual history is scrutinized or an environmental lawyer whose practice ends up furthering harm against the environment.

Justice that hurts more than it helps isn't really justice, and if it is some form of justice then it is not sustainable. We cannot and should not expect clients to keep engaging with a legal process that involves more cost than benefit, so practicing in this way is not sustainable even from a purely economic standpoint. Morally, do lawyers want to provide legal services that clients feel hurt more than they help? And do we really want to refer our loved ones to processes or professionals practicing in this way? Perhaps this is why so many lawyers hope their children do not go to law school. No matter what profession we're in, if we would not recommend our own work (at least, as it's usually done) to our own friends and loved ones, there's a moral problem. Just as there would be a moral problem if we were doctors but would not recommend that any of our friends and loved ones have a heart operation at our own hospital.

The antidote to moral injury is moral repair, and the salve for institutional betrayal is institutional courage. Which means that, to address law-related trauma, it is necessary to find ways to engage in moral repair and institutional courage. Usually, moral repair and institutional courage require action. Lawyers may be more familiar with moral repair on an international scale than a domestic or local one. Truth and reconciliation processes, war crimes trials, and other proceedings for crimes against humanity at the International Criminal Court and in other forums are, in theory, structured to serve as acts of moral repair. (Even though sadly many of these processes may not end up benefiting from or creating moral repair as an outcome.) International peace processes may also include moral repair or institutional courage. Institutional courage involves acknowledging the harm done by the institution to those it was designed to serve or protect, as well as taking action to fulfill its intended purpose.

Collaborative family law, restorative justice, therapeutic jurisprudence, or other integrative law approaches may include moral repair by seeking to problem-solve, engage with treatment or education, or heal relationships between conflicting

---

[19] C.P. Smith & J.J. Freyd, *Institutional Betrayal*, 69(6) Am. Psych. 575 (Sept. 2014) and C.P. Smith, J.J. Gomes & J.J. Freyd, *The Psychology of Judicial Betrayal*, 19(2) Roger Williams U. L. Rev. (Spring 2014), https://docs.rwu.edu/cgi/viewcontent.cgi?referer=https://www.google.com/&httpsredir=1&article=1539&context=rwu_LR.

parties. For example, a collaborative family law practitioner (or court) using the family constellations technique (such as currently practiced in Brazil) may include words or acts of understanding or repair as part of a divorce process or custody arrangement.[20] In North America, a divorce client or collaborative family lawyer may choose to include family constellations or family trauma patterns as a support for high-conflict divorce, including cases of parental estrangement or child estrangement.[21] Internationally, the work of Vamik Volkan and the International Dialogue Initiative seek to overcome the psychological blocks to conflict resolution using Volkan's "tree model," involving collaborative community projects created through dialogue processes to reframe or gain a deeper understanding of the roots of conflict (taking analysis of underlying group psychology dynamics into account) to create a new way of co-existing after international conflict.[22]

Trauma-informed practices hold the potential to support the aims of moral repair and institutional courage by enriching legal processes for both clients and lawyers with a sense of meaning and purpose, through aligning legal or communication strategies with client needs using open, relational communication.[23] Many litigation settlements have arisen from the simple act of a client coming face to face with the question, "why are we really doing this, and what does it really mean for us?" Many lawyers have changed careers or practice areas by asking these questions, including me. Trauma irrevocably altered my sense of life's meaning. After experiencing trauma, my conventional legal practice simply no longer held the meaning it initially did for me, and often felt contrary to the practices and principles I had learned in order to heal trauma, so it seemed wiser to bear the cost of change than live with life regret. My own well-being has improved markedly by working with more sense of meaning, and engaging in my own acts of moral repair (including this book).

It's not uncommon when speaking with lawyers about trauma in the profession to hear reflections in hindsight that they "will never forget" a particular case, or that they feel "haunted" by a particular client or legal outcome. A lawyer's use of language indicating regret may suggest that moral injury has been incurred on some level, as a lawyer's own fundamental values have been contravened in a way that affects mental and emotional or even physical well-being. For example, in 2020, the language of moral injury was used in a *New York Times* OpEd written by Erica

---

[20] Sami Storch, *Constellations in the State Court*, 29 THE KNOWING FIELD: INT'L CONSTELLATIONS J. (Jan. 2017), https://www.theknowingfield.com/tkf29.

[21] For information about family trauma patterns, see MARK WOLYNN, IT DIDN'T START WITH YOU: HOW INHERITED FAMILY TRAUMA SHAPES WHO WE ARE AND HOW TO END THE CYCLE (Viking Press, 2016).

[22] Vamik Volkan, *The Tree Model: A Comprehensive Psychopolitical Approach to Unofficial Diplomacy and the Reduction of Ethnic Tension*, 10 MIND & HUMAN INTERACTION 142–206 (1999).

[23] S.E. Gold, *Trauma: What Beneath the Surface*, CLINICAL L. REV., 2018, https://papers.ssrn.com/sol3/papers.cfm?abstract_id=3035602.

Newland entitled "I'm Haunted by What I Did as a Lawyer in the Trump Justice Department."[24]

A simple way to begin including meaning-making in legal practice is to ask clients (and colleagues and ourselves): what meaning is being created with this case, personally and professionally? What will it mean in 5 years, 10 years, or 20 years and what parts of it might align with our sense of fairness, morals, and fundamental values?

No Practice Is Exempt: Some Practice Areas Affected by Trauma

No practice area is exempt from trauma but some practice areas face it on a daily basis. In this section, we review trauma and its impact in specific practice areas.

Family Law

Family Law: The Cases That Change Lives

Aida Doss Havel, Family Law Attorney[25]

In 2009, I'd been a bulldog custody litigator for 25 years. I was getting burned out, and attended the International Academy of Collaborative Professionals Forum in Minneapolis. I returned home, excited to try to sell this new model of practice to clients and colleagues. It was slow going.

Then in 2010, I tried a case that changed my life. The facts were simple: my client, the mother of a 15-year-old son and a 12-year-old daughter, wanted the judge to hear her concerns about the 15-year-old going to live with his father (which is fairly routine in North Carolina if the child desires it and the other parent is not unfit). We had a three-day trial, during which my client was shown to be a smart, devoted mother, adored by her family and friends, who had arranged her work schedule to be as available to her children as possible. She was the quintessential neighborhood mom, and she also testified about the close bond between brother and sister and how upset her daughter was that her brother wanted to go live with his father. The father was not a horrible person, just career-driven and focused on tiny grievances. When the son was with him, there were no rules or consequences.

The judge not only ruled in favor of the father (which we expected), but from the bench, in an open courtroom, she told my client what a terrible

---

[24] Erica Newland, I'm Haunted by What I Did as a Lawyer in the Trump Justice Department, N.Y. Times (Dec. 20, 2020), https://www.nytimes.com/2020/12/20/opinion/trump-justice-department-lawyer.html.

[25] Aida has been a practicing attorney in North Carolina for more than 35 years, primarily in family law (child custody, child support, alimony, property division, domestic violence, and divorce). Litigation long ago lost its appeal for her, and since 2010, she has resolved cases through mediation, collaborative law, and other peaceful dispute resolution techniques.

mother she was and how awful it was that she was trying to stand in the way of the relationship between father and son (while discounting the relationship between brother and sister). As soon as we could get out of the courtroom, I took my client into the jury room to debrief, where she promptly crawled up on top of a conference table that had been shoved into a corner, rolled herself into a ball, and began crying inconsolably. This was a woman who I'd represented for over five years, who had a master's degree, who was funny and intelligent and admired by everyone except her ex-husband. I'd never seen someone in such emotional distress, and something broke inside me that very day.

I walked out of that courtroom determined that I could no longer be a part of a system that treated families that way, and I made a conscious decision to not accept any more litigation cases. It took a year to wind up the cases I did have, during which I found a wonderful practice group of collaborative lawyers who took me in and guided my baby steps into a more healing way of practicing law. Irrelevant but interesting footnote: the 15-year-old, a year later, ended up fathering a child with a young woman the same age.

The Messiest, Worst Times to Help Clients

J. Kim Wright

If you're a lawyer, you know that there is a hierarchy in law practice. When someone introduces me as a former family lawyer, I can hear that it is code intended to diminish me or my work. Corporate lawyers with their big shiny office towers and even shinier cars make a lot more money than most family lawyers, and they measure success according to that bottom line. Many choose that area of practice because it is believed that their clients withhold their emotions and keep transactions at a safe arm's length away, always on their best behaviors. Most corporate lawyers I know discover that isn't always true. Even mergers and acquisitions can be emotional transactions.

But everyone knows that family lawyers work with messy emotions. Their clients cry, blubber even, tears and snot dripping down their faces. They have angry outbursts. Divorce is a crazy time and people are often at their worst. Family law offices are often set up with play areas, toys in a corner to occupy children while parents have conversations that destroy their worlds. Financially strapped by dividing their assets and legal bills, clients often cannot pay their bills and set up monthly payments, which sometimes they pay. Family lawyers tend to have the highest rate of accounts receivable and often write off more than half their accounts.

And yet, despite all this, family lawyers continue to practice. Is it because they lack the skills to do the high-power law in the towers?

Without trying to one-up (too much), I assert that most corporate lawyers are sorely lacking in both knowledge and skills for family law. Being a family lawyer was a surprise every day. Families are unique. The issues that arise are unique. Family lawyers have to know a little about a lot of topics, and a lot about several. As a family lawyer, I have been called to:

◆ Review and revise estate planning documents.
◆ Study and understand complex business documents for purposes of valuing the business and dividing or assigning it to one spouse (the ultimate business reorganization plan). Businesses ranged from mom-and-pop stores to national companies.
◆ Draft business documents to reflect changes, including operating agreements where the couple would continue to work together.
◆ Do bankruptcy planning and budgeting.
◆ Coordinate civil cases with related criminal cases.
◆ Become an expert on many issues relevant to the case: is schizophrenia likely to be hereditary? Which parent will best care for the anorexic teen? How do I prove over-usage of a prescription drug? What are the signs of child sexual abuse?
◆ Predict (and verify) tax consequences of asset distribution.
◆ Give an opinion about whether the marriage of a man and woman would be void when one is transgender. (This was before marriage equality.)
◆ Do numerous name changes for transgender clients who came from hundreds of miles away to hire me.
◆ Celebrate adoptions of children of all ages (including adults).
◆ Address immigration consequences of divorce.
◆ Protect my client's life from a violent spouse. On one occasion, my client was killed. It became my duty to hold the press conferences and speak for the family, all the while staying hidden, as the perpetrator was still at large. The counselor from my office became a grief counselor for the three small children and grandparents.
◆ Litigate whether we were in the proper jurisdiction.
◆ Draft conscious divorce agreements and parenting plans that reflected the couple's continued relationship as parents.
◆ Teach my client the most effective way to apologize.
◆ Talk my client out of suicidal despair.
◆ Help clients design their new futures as newly single people.
◆ Celebrate the end of a separation negotiation with ex-husband and ex-wife toasting with champagne, hugging, and sharing good wishes for the future.

Why did I do this? My undergrad degree was in business and economics. Why didn't I just take a calm job in a high-rise and choose to spend my long hours on paperwork and meetings? Why was I required to keep a box of tissue on my desk for client meetings?

I chose to work with family law because I saw that it was the place where I could make the biggest difference. I could help people transform their lives in the divorce process, create new futures, relationships that were sustainable and amicable for raising their children, building a future for all of society. I chose a practice area that demanded all my legal knowledge, not just one subject.

I chose family law because I wanted to learn about human relationship dynamics, conflict resolution, healing, and transitions.

And I wanted to help children. And create a more peaceful planet.

Immigration Law

When You Come Upon a Drowning Man: A Modest Proposal on the Immigration Crisis

Marjorie Florestal

In 1992, I was a Haitian American law student at New York University when the call came. A bloody coup in Haiti had led thousands to risk their lives on the open water in vessels not worthy of the name boat. Most were caught by the "floating Berlin Wall" the U.S. Coast Guard mounted in the Caribbean Sea; they were warehoused on Guantanamo. A relative few miraculously landed on Florida's shores. I rushed to South Florida to help process hundreds of asylum applications. There, in an old high school gymnasium that smelled of wet socks and fear, I learned of the vast divide between "classroom law" and the law as applied to Haitian asylum seekers.

These days, I am a law professor watching a new generation of law students learn a similar lesson. The arrival of the so-called immigrant caravan gives us an opportunity to teach and do differently. It is a test we are likely to fail. The efforts of some people to dismantle the scaffolding of laws meant to protect the most vulnerable threaten the end to the world as we have known it. Asylum seekers will suffer—and so will the soul of this nation.

Almost every article on this subject begins with the Voyage of the Damned—the ill-fated journey of the *MS. St. Louis* from Hitler's Germany to the Americas in 1939. When the ship arrived in Cuban waters with 937 German Jews, they were turned away. In the name of the American people, President Franklin D. Roosevelt also denied refuge (as did the Canadians). With nowhere else to go, the ship returned to Europe where 254 people perished in Nazi concentration camps.

We owe a debt to these lost souls. Their senseless slaughter pushed the international community to adopt laws, including the 1951 Refugee Convention, to ensure "never again" was more than an empty promise. To the women, men, and children of the *MS St. Louis*, and to the countless, nameless others who have perished seeking refuge, I say mournfully and with deep gratitude: I am not forgetting you. But perhaps the immigration debate would look different if our collective memories went back a bit further—526 years to be exact.

In December 1492, Christopher Columbus's ship, the Santa Maria, ran aground off the coast of northern Haiti. The Tainos—Haiti's First People, whose name means "the good people"—rushed to save Columbus's men before the ship sank, never to be seen again. The Tainos built a fort to house the New World's first migrants.

"We can't take everybody who shows up to our border." So goes the modern refrain, as if refugees hold no special status under the law. They do. But anyone with even a cursory understanding of our immigration system knows how difficult it is to be granted that status. I learned just how difficult back in 1992. Most Haitians who fled the coup were deemed "economic migrants" and shipped back to Haiti—despite the military tanks that rolled down their streets. We should not confuse "everybody who shows up to our border" with asylum seekers. We offer special protection to those who can demonstrate a well-founded fear of persecution, because we remember what the world looked like when we did not. Never again.

During his term, President Trump tried to turn a caravan of Central Americans fleeing for their lives into a national security threat. He militarized our southern border and showed the world how willing he was to flout the law—especially when it comes to those who hail from "shithole countries." But he didn't kill our immigration system—that has been decades in the making—he merely profited off its rotting corpse. He profited in the adulation of those who make no secret of their affinity to Hitler. He profited in the vitriol that makes it hard for some to acknowledge a simple truth: when you come upon a drowning man, you pull him out of the water. If you don't, the man will lose his life—and you will lose your humanity.

Classes have ended at my university. Law students are buried in their casebooks studying for exams. When they graduate, I hope the divide between the law they have learned in the classroom and the law as applied in the real world is not an unbridgeable chasm.

Repairing Fixable Trauma in Immigration

Raquel E. Aldana[26]

Migration, even when voluntary, frequently involves experiences of trauma. Some of this trauma is inevitable, such as the pain of separation or the suffering

---

[26] Raquel is Martin Luther King Jr., Professor of Law at University of California, Davis. She's a graduate of Harvard Law School and Arizona State University. She was previously a professor at the William S. Boyd School of Law, University of Nevada. Her focus is on transitional justice and criminal justice reforms in Latin America and immigrant rights in the United States.

of integration.[27] But many forms of severe trauma that accompany forced migration in particular—that is, treacherous journeys, victimization, and the brunt of immigration enforcement—could be avoided or ameliorated if nations opted to shift their practices about what it should mean to regulate borders and manage migration. This section explores a few areas of "fixable" trauma—that is, a scrutiny of immigration policies and practices that aggravate or cause trauma in migrants for reasons that are neither inevitable nor sound. It also provides recommendations for repairing this trauma through best practices that include reimagining the management and regulation of migration and embracing the science of trauma.

Fixable Trauma

Despite efforts by nations to erect physical walls,[28] shift borders though bilateral immigration enforcement agreements[29] or interdiction practices,[30] or restrict legal migration,[31] migration flows, especially forced migration, are on the rise.[32] This is hardly surprising: climate change,[33] persistent civil wars,[34] generalized violence,[35] and extreme forms of poverty[36] render these barriers permeable to the waves of people whose desperation at home thrust them often into even greater peril. Data shows a rise in migrants falling prey to human trafficking;[37]

---

[27] Raffaella Bianucci et al., *The "Ulysses Syndrome": An Eponym Identifies a Psychosomatic Disorder in Modern Migrants*, 41 European J. Internal Med. 31 (Apr. 2017).

[28] Reece Jones, *Borders and Walls: Do Barriers Deter Unauthorized Migration?*, Migration Pol'y Inst., Oct. 4, 2016, https://www.migrationpolicy.org/article/borders-and-walls-do-barriers-deter-unauthorized-migration.

[29] *See, e.g.*, Raquel Aldana et al., Global Issues in Immigration Law (St. Paul, MN: West Academic Publishing, 2013), 21–69.

[30] *See, e.g.*, Azadeh Dastyari, United States Migrant Interdiction and the Detention of Refugees in Guantánamo Bay (Cambridge: Cambridge University Press, 2015), 5.

[31] Stuart Anderson, *Trump Cuts Legal Immigrants by Half and He's Not Done Yet*, Forbes, July 21, 2020, https://www.forbes.com/sites/stuartanderson/2020/07/21/trump-cuts-legal-immigrants-by-half-and-hes-not-done-yet/?sh=1360a1dd6168.

[32] Dep't of Econ. & Social Aff., *Population Facts*, U.N. Doc. 2019/4 (Sept. 2019).

[33] Alex de Sherbinin, *Impacts of Climate Change as Drivers of Migration*, Migration Pol'y Inst., Oct. 23, 2020, https://www.migrationpolicy.org/article/impacts-climate-change-drivers-migration#:~:text=Each%20has%20a%20more%20or,likely%20to%20drive%20permanent%20migration.

[34] *See, e.g.*, Mike Giglio, *The Syrian Sisters Who Refuse to Give Up on America*, The Atlantic, Mar. 15, 2020, https://www.theatlantic.com/politics/archive/2020/03/syria-turkey-usa-refugee-crisis-trump-biden-sanders/607984/.

[35] *See, e.g.*, Forced to Flee Central America's Northern Triangle: A Neglected Humanitarian Crisis (Geneva: Medecins Sans Frontieres, 2017).

[36] *See, e.g.*, Charles T. Call, *The Imperative to Address the Root Causes of Migration from Central America*, The Brookings Institution (blog), Jan. 29, 2021, https://www.brookings.edu/blog/order-from-chaos/2021/01/29/the-imperative-to-address-the-root-causes-of-migration-from-central-america/.

[37] *See, e.g.*, Anastasia Moloney, *Venezuelan Child Migrants, Women Fall Prey to Human Traffickers in Peru*, Reuters, Mar. 12, 2019, https://www.reuters.com/article/us-peru-humantrafficking/venezuelan-child-migrants-women-fall-prey-to-human-traffickers-in-peru-idUSKBN1QT355.

deaths at sea;[38] or murder, rape, or kidnapping by drug lords,[39] all for the remote hope that if they reach their destination, life will be better for them and their families. Yet, for most, even the few who manage to reach their destination, their trauma can too easily fall outside the law's protections, as they are labeled economic or climate migrants rather than refugees.[40]

Those seeking refuge are thrust into a cruel and unfair immigration process that is uninformed by the science of trauma and often retraumatizes or perpetuates new trauma. In every immigration case, the stakes are high, but for asylum seekers, victims of human trafficking, victims of crime, abandoned children, or residents with family and ties in another nation who face community and family separation through removal, the consequences can be dire, even deadly. Despite this, most immigrants, especially the most vulnerable, such as children or the poor, are required to navigate impossibly complex legal processes on their own and without lawyers.[41] This alone is cruel and yet, rather than promote principles that would maximize access, transparency, and fairness, immigration processes are inflexible, unforgiving, opaque, and arbitrary.

One example of this is the imposition of expedited removal to asylum seekers at the border who must bear the burden of convincing asylum officers of their well-founded fear of persecution, often while in detention, without access to corroborating evidence or counsel.[42] The processes adopted to corroborate trauma and establish credibility are built on scarcity and rely too much on the migrant's repeated recounting of their trauma under conditions that retraumatize and that are scrutinized under standards of credibility that ignore how trauma affects memory and storytelling. Asylum seekers arriving at the U.S. border, in particular, exemplify these flaws. Usually, while in detention and without the safeguards of confidentiality, much less the support of mental health experts or lawyers, these applicants must tell their stories without access to corroborating evidence to help demonstrate past persecution and/or a well-founded fear of persecution to asylum officers who must assess credibility,

[38] *See, e.g.,* C.J. Chivers, *Risking Everything to Come to America on the Open Ocean,* N.Y. Times Mag., Feb. 3, 2021, https://www.nytimes.com/2021/02/03/magazine/customs-border-protection-migrants-pacific-ocean.html?auth=login-google.

[39] *See, e.g.,* Ed Vulliamy, *Kidnappers Prey with 'Total Impunity' on Migrants Waiting for Hearings in Mexico,* The Guardian, Feb. 18, 2020, https://www.theguardian.com/us-news/2020/feb/18/mexico-kidnappers-migrants-trump-immigration.

[40] *See, e.g.,* Maya Srikrishnan, *Few Central Americans Win Asylum in the United States,* New America (2018), https://www.newamerica.org/weekly/few-central-americans-win-asylum-united-states/.

[41] *See Right to Counsel for Detained Migrants in Selected Jurisdictions* (Washington, D.C.: The Law Library of Congress, May 2017), https://www.loc.gov/item/2017299989/; Ingrid Eagly & Steven Shafer, *Access to Counsel in Immigration Court* 2 (Washington, D.C.: American Immigration Council, 2016), https://www.americanimmigrationcouncil.org/sites/default/files/research/access_to_counsel_in_immigration_court.pdf.

[42] Katherine Shattuck, *Preventing Erroneous Expedited Removals: Immigration Judge Review and Requests for Reconsideration of Negative Credible Fear Determinations,* 93(1) Wash. Law Rev. 480–88 (Mar. 2018).

based on existing legislative norms,[43] which scrutinize factors such as the applicant's demeanor and the specificity and consistency in their story.[44] The applicant, when they are lucky enough to satisfy the credible fear standard,[45] must recount this story once more, this time in writing as part of a declaration in the asylum application.

And even if they manage to successfully assert their credible fear, asylum seekers, no matter their age, language abilities, or emotional well-being, must often pursue their case in immigration court without lawyers.[46]

The traumatic nature of the immigration process is paralleled by the trauma of immigration enforcement. Cloaked in the justification of deterrence, the United States has forcibly prevented asylum seekers from reaching U.S. soil,[47] placed them in makeshift refugee camps where they were vulnerable to illness and crime;[48] thrown them in prisons to await their backlogged asylum claims;[49] separated them from family, including children;[50] and even criminalized them for daring to make an "illegal entry" to assert their asylum claims.[51] As well, long-term lawful permanent residents, some of whom have lived in the United States since infancy or who have served honorably in the armed forces, face unforgiving mandatory detention or expulsion, at times for life, for the commission of crimes.[52]

Repairing Trauma

Repairing the fixable trauma of migration will require a combination of strategies and approaches.

---

[43] *The REAL ID Act of 2005: Summary and Analysis of Provisions*, American Immigration Lawyers Ass'n, Jan. 27, 2005, https://www.aila.org/infonet/the-real-id-act-of-2005-summary-and-analysis.

[44] *Id.*

[45] Dep't of Homeland Sec. v. Thuraissigiam, 140 S. Ct. 1959, 1966 (2020) ("Over the last five years, nearly 77% of screenings have resulted in a finding of credible fear."); "Human Rights First Decries Erosion of Protections for Asylum-Seekers in Supreme Court Ruling," Human Rights First, June 25, 2020, https://humanrightsfirst.org/library/human-rights-first-decries-erosion-of-protections-for-asylum-seekers-in-supreme-court-ruling/.

[46] Eagly & Shafer, *supra* note 40, at 2. Eagly and Shafer's report cites empirical evidence that, "Nationally, only 37 percent of all immigrants secured legal representation in their removal cases."

[47] Michael Garcia Bochenek, *US: 'Remain in Mexico' Program Harming Children*, Human Rights Watch, Feb. 12, 2020, https://www.hrw.org/news/2020/02/12/us-remain-mexico-program-harming-children.

[48] *Id.*

[49] *You Don't Have Any Rights Here: Illegal Pushbacks, Arbitrary Detention, and Ill-Treatment of Asylum Seekers in the United States*, Amnesty Int'l, 2018, https://www.amnesty.org/download/Documents/AMR5191012018 ENGLISH.PDF.

[50] *Id.*

[51] *Prosecuting People for Coming to the United States*, American Immigration Council, Jan. 2020, https://www .americanimmigrationcouncil.org/sites/default/files/research/prosecuting_people_for_coming_to_the _united_states.pdf.

[52] Darlene Xiomara Rodriguez & Eric Manley, *How We Fail US Foreign-Born Veterans: A Scoping Study of the Literature*, 6(3) J. Veterans Studies 1–9 (2020), http://doi.org/10.21061/jvs.v6i3.186.

Back in 2016, then Assistant Chief Judge Jack Weil shocked the nation when he said that a child age three could adequately represent himself/herself/themselves in immigration court without lawyers or adult guardians.[53] Unfortunately, the shock did not last long or impact law and policy. Despite compelling arguments advocating for a right to counsel, at least in certain immigration proceedings—that is, asylum or deportation—or types of clients—that is, children and the mentally incompetent—legal representation for the overwhelming number of immigrants remains elusive.[54] There is no question that immigration lawyers have an enormous impact on the outcome of cases, but they also embed the experience with compassion through trauma-informed lawyering. A growing contribution by immigration lawyers has been to humanize clients by making their trauma visible and documenting it with care and compassion. Lawyers have also worked hard to collaborate with forensic immigration experts to improve fairness in the adjudication of immigration cases and to understand the impact of trauma on clients and on themselves.

The editors note that lawyers in other practice areas and policy makers can learn from the practices of immigration lawyers to humanize, to make trauma visible with compassion, to collaborate, and to understand the impact of trauma in order to advocate effectively.

Sexual Assault and Sexual Harassment
Helgi Maki

Sexual assault cases reported to police, university campuses, and legal clinics spiked in North America and elsewhere after the #MeToo movement created by Tarana Burke became more widespread across the globe in 2017. Some regions of Canada saw an increase of over 70 percent in reported sexual assaults.[55] Trauma-informed practices are a particularly critical competency in sexual assault cases, whether criminal or civil litigation, due to the highly personal nature of the offense, the impact of indicia of sexual trauma in a victim or witness, and the high likelihood of trauma-impacted evidence given the inherently traumatic nature of sexual assault and the centrality of credibility in litigation.[56] Reproductive health law and reproductive rights, including abortion laws, is, of course, another critical and adjacent area meriting trauma-informed practices at all times. Sexual assault also often intersections with other areas of law such as refugee or immigration law, as people

---

[53] Maria Guerrero, *Can a 3-year-old Adequately Represent Themselves in Court? Immigration Judge: Yes*, KIRO7, Mar. 15, 2016, https://www.kiro7.com/news/can-a-3-year-old-adequately-represent-themselves-in-court -immigration-judge-yes/150047484/.

[54] Eagly & Shafer, *supra* note 40, at 2.

[55] Police-reported sexual assaults in Canada before and after #MeToo, 2016 and 2017, Statistics Canada, https://www150.statcan.gc.ca/n1/pub/85-002-x/2018001/article/54979-eng.htm.

[56] S.F. Ward, *Time's Up: Legal, Judicial Systems Slow to Adapt to Sexual Harassment and Assault Issues*, June 1, 2018, https://www.abajournal.com/magazine/article/timesup_legal_judicial_harassment_assault.

affected by war are often at high risk of sexual assault, harassment, or interpersonal violence both during and after conflict.[57] The ability to report or access legal advice for these crimes varies widely across North America and around the globe.

Traditionally, credibility assessments and related rules of evidence present challenges for complainants, witnesses, and survivors in sexual assault cases, as well as sexual harassment or interpersonal violence cases. The neurobiology of memory and narrative often doesn't match what lawyers are taught about credibility in law school. When a person perceives a threat to their lives or safety, human neurobiological and nervous system functioning prioritizes survival responses over other functions, which can mean memory is formed differently due to the brain's focus on first surviving an assault rather than merely remembering it. Memory formed in traumatic circumstances may not be linear in nature, and the resulting narrative also may not be linear, which usually does not fit well with conventional legal methods of interviewing complainants or assessing credibility.[58] In Chapter 4 on tools, we included an overview of some specialized interviewing methods that are used in sexual assault cases in some jurisdictions. The topic of trauma-informed practice in sexual assault, harassment, or interpersonal violence cases merits a book (or library) of its own, such as Elaine Craig's *Putting Trials on Trial.*[59] Some systems changes are in progress, such as judicial training in some jurisdictions on sexual assault and the social contexts in which it occurs (such as gender factors, racism, discrimination, ethnicity, sexual orientation, socio-economic factors, family violence, and systemic discrimination).[60] However such changes have not yet become widespread in most countries on a national or even regional basis, and have not been consistently connected to best practices for dealing with assault from a health and well-being perspective. Much more work remains to be done to ensure equitable access to justice and legal services as well as safe reporting conditions for people affected by sexual violence.

Stories and contributions involving sexual trauma or harassment can be found throughout this book. And, for the author of this section, listening to people affected by sexual assault describe their legal experiences since the mid-1980s has been a key driving force for creating this book. If you're reading this section with either professional or personal interest, please know the rest of this book was written with you in mind.

---

[57] Alexander Vu et al., *The Prevalence of Sexual Violence among Female Refugees in Complex Humanitarian Emergencies: a Systematic Review and Meta-analysis*, 6 PLoS Curr. (Mar. 8, 2014), https://pubmed.ncbi.nlm.nih.gov/24818066/.

[58] Lori Haskell & Melanie Randall, *Impact of Trauma on Adult Sexual Assault Victims: What the Criminal Justice System Needs to Know* (Jan. 1, 2019), https://ssrn.com/abstract=3417763 or http://dx.doi.org/10.2139/ssrn.3417763.

[59] Elaine Craig, Putting Trials on Trial: Sexual Assault and the Failure of the Legal Profession (Montreal, Toronto: McGill-Queens University Press, 2018).

[60] Department of Justice Canada, Press Release, "Amendments to the *Judges Act* and the *Criminal Code*, Sept. 9, 2021, https://www.justice.gc.ca/eng/csj-sjc/pl/jt-fj/index.html.

It is important to understand that sexual assault, harassment, and interpersonal violence cases and the people involved (including children and minors) represent a key "special population" or microcosm of all of the needs that arise in trauma-informed legal practice within the macrocosm of the legal ecosystem. Due to the personal, intimate nature of sexual assault cases, retraumatization is more likely to occur, memory and narrative are more likely to be impacted; there can be no assurance that a court or lawyer will be aware of characteristic trauma responses in complainants, victims, or witnesses; psychological safety is often at risk; credibility is more likely to be under scrutiny; and vicarious trauma is more likely for lawyers and judges.

Yet, as challenging as sexual assault cases are perceived to be in conventional terms, it is crucial for the efficacy of the legal system as a whole for the public to have faith in all aspects of the legal system, even sexual assault matters. Where there is no remedy, there can be no right, and in most of North America there is very little remedy for sexual assault, as the conviction rate in felony rape cases is less than 1 percent.[61] Although it is worth exploring whether conventional legal processes are the best approach to providing access to justice for sexual assault, surely (if conviction rates are at least some proxy for success) a less than 1 percent success rate indicates legal system failure in the same way that a less than 1 percent recovery rate for a medical procedure would be a health care system failure, fundamentally eroding faith and trust in that system.

One study of complainants in sexual assault cases in civil actions for damages and compensation claims who have been surveyed, indicated that while their therapeutic expectations of the process outweighed their financial goals, they found the negative emotional consequences (85 percent) and negative physical consequences (>50 percent) they experienced in the process alongside feelings of revictimization to be anti-therapeutic.[62] These complainants emphasized that a process where their claims were heard and listened to with empathy and compassion, and responded to, was paramount. Understandably, many potential witnesses, complainants, victims, and survivors never report what happened to them and others may be asked to sign comprehensive nondisclosure agreements that do not either address the risk of an assault happening again or the needs (or preferences) of the person who experienced the assault. One key benefit of trauma-informed lawyering is to continuously ask about and begin to meet the needs of people affected by sexual assault, and failure to address these needs is a long-standing barrier to access to justice and legal services that must be addressed in order to maintain public faith in the efficacy of the legal system. A simple place to begin is to continuously ask and reassure

---

[61] *Less than 1% of Rapes Lead to Felony Convictions*, WASH. POST, Oct. 6, 2018, https://www.washingtonpost.com /business/2018/10/06/less-than-percent-rapes-lead-felony-convictions-least-percent-victims-face-emotional -physical-consequences/.

[62] Bruce Feldthusen, Olena Hankivsky & Lorraine Greaves, *Therapeutic Consequences of Civil Actions for Damages and Compensation Claims by Victims of Sexual Abuse—An Empirical Study* 12 CAN. J. WOMEN & LAW 66 (2000) (with Olena Hankivsky and Lorraine Greaves), https://ssrn.com/abstract=2472461.

clients that lawyers both want to know and are interested in accommodating the needs of a client affected by sexual assault, especially regarding any supports that might be helpful to them in discussing their experience.

Criminal Law

The following contributions on criminal law—and related issues affecting life and liberty in connection with criminal law—illustrate key issues likely to arise in an area of law where trauma may be a factor in almost every case.

Burnout or Boundaries?

M.R.

My story is not a unique one. My work as a criminal defense lawyer and working closely with family lawyers exposed me to story upon story of our clients' traumas. I went into this work because I care deeply about improving the lives of others and hopefully, through diligent work, improving the justice system. However, I got quickly burnt out with compassion fatigue and not establishing strong emotional barriers. I left practice and took a course on feminist counseling. I now try to help clients who have experienced trauma by connecting them with the resources they need, providing legal information and addressing systemic flaws. I don't take on their stories in the same way as I did as their counsel. I have learned better coping skills and how to separate my own experiences.

I see this often from my peers—good, empathetic lawyers who either crash after taking on too much *or* who build strong, impenetrable walls around their generous hearts.

* * *

Capital Punishment and Circles of Trauma

Sarah Gerwig-Moore[63]

Five years ago, the State of Georgia executed my client and childhood friend, Joshua Bishop, right before my eyes. In a life that has included a number of heartbreaks and deaths of loved ones—including more than one lost to murder—the experience of seeing him on the gurney, strapped down, poison flowing into him, arms outstretched as on a reclining cross, stands apart. It will haunt me for the rest of my life. I see it when I close my eyes. I still dream about it.

As a law professor and in my previous career as a public defender, I have worked on many murder appeals, but only a handful of capital cases. Josh's was my first as lead counsel. I first became involved in constitutional challenges to

---

[63] Sarah Gerwig-Moore is a professor of law at Mercer Law School in Macon, Georgia, where she founded The Habeas Project and now teaches criminal law.

non-capital cases because of the difference in volume of cases; there are thousands of people in Georgia serving life or life without parole sentences for murder (hundreds of these prisoners convicted of multiple murders), and fewer than 50 men and women on Georgia's death row. It made sense to me to work on cases where there seemed—at least at the time—to be the greatest need.

In my four years working on Josh Bishop's case, however, I learned and relearned the truism penned by Supreme Court Justice Potter Stewart: death is different. The penalty, of course, is different, but so is the range of trauma in these cases, the expanding concentric circles of societal pain and harm.

In every murder case—capital or non-capital—there is a significant loss, most especially to the family and loved ones of the murder victim. But in capital cases, because of the nature of the loss to the victims' families and what is at stake for the prisoner, death truly makes these cases different. The loss is not circumscribed to those directly involved in the crime and their families: the circle is wider and expands with the years.

Over the course of my years as counsel in Josh Bishop's case, I spoke to hundreds of people who were or had been involved in his life at some point and whose opinions and experiences were relevant to his legal challenges or plea for clemency. This list is not exhaustive, of course—and still others have asked not to be included here—but it includes the people describing particular anguish because of Josh's death sentence:

Several members of the victims' families. Friends of the victims. Those first on the scene and investigating the crimes. His trial counsel. Josh's family members, particularly his brother. Members of his extended family. Former foster parents, child service's workers, and children's home personnel (this numbered in dozens). Those working in the jail while Josh awaited trial. Court personnel. Nine members of his trial and sentencing jury. Elementary school teachers. Classmates. Childhood friends.

Prison guards. Prison administrators. Fellow prisoners on death row. Medical personnel who work with prisoners. My client's friends, numerous, who wrote to and visited him over nearly 20 years. Priests and pastors who visited and ministered to Josh (and were ministered to by him). The parishioners of churches of the priests and pastors who visited and ministered to Josh.

Josh's other appellate and post-conviction attorneys. Investigators and paralegals working with his appellate and post-conviction attorneys. The loved ones and friends of his appellate and post-conviction attorneys and the paralegals, and the investigators who work with them. My law students. My law school colleagues. Colleagues of my current and former law students. My parents. My children.

I note here that I am a lawyer, not a mental health professional, so I must be careful about using those terms of art. By "trauma," I mean that the folks I talked to described combinations of worry, depression, sadness, anxiety, flashbacks, or guilt (or all of these) as a result of being caught up in the orbit of a death penalty case. There is no other word that fits the impact on our lives; we are forever changed by it. Forever affected.

Since the night Josh's death sentence was carried out, I have kept in touch with many of those listed here. We do our best to encourage one another, the pain magnified, not diminished, by his death.

These are only the people with whom I have personally discussed the case; this list does not include the many letters of condolence I received after his obituary was published and circulated, and people moved by Josh's story to whom I've never spoken. I think of the pained-looking woman in pink scrubs who started and oversaw the IV line that pumped the drugs into Josh's arm.

Perhaps as an acknowledgment of these and myriad constitutional issues, the death penalty is dying—but not soon enough to save my client and others. Even as Georgia raced to execute the last remaining souls on death row— among them, a Vietnam veteran who came home from war with PTSD; men with intellectual disabilities demonstrated by IQ scores at 70 or below; and a woman whose trigger-man co-defendant is still serving his life sentence with the possibility of parole—Georgia juries were returning fewer and fewer death sentences. Since 2014, only one person has been sentenced to death in Georgia.

And if and when those remaining sentences are carried out in the Death House of the Georgia Diagnostic and Classification Prison, the cloud of trauma will continue to grow. The anguish these prisoners caused—even assuming their legal and moral guilt is appropriately established—isn't diminished at their death. The trauma that began the night of Josh's crime didn't end the night of his execution. It spread to those of us who remain. Setting aside the financial implications (another subject entirely), we cannot afford the moral expense of capital punishment; we are buckling under its weight.

* * *

Identifying with the Convicted and Innocent[64]

Mark Godsey[65]

I am the director of the Ohio Innocence Project and have been with the organization since 2001. What we do is identify people in prison who are wrongfully convicted and innocent, and we litigate to try to get them out. Being in prison— or in the criminal justice system in general—is traumatic. But for somebody to be wrongfully convicted, just picked out of the blue and sent to prison for a crime they did not commit, is a particular kind of pain and trauma. As I got

---

[64] This contribution was originally presented at the Wake Forest Law School Trauma-Informed Lawyering Conference.

[65] Mark Godsey is a professor of law at the University of Cincinnati College of Law and is director of the Ohio Innocence Project.

more immersed in this work, I started at some level realizing I was suffering from secondary trauma. I don't think I could have fully articulated it, but I started having anger and depression and anxiety.

By 2013, it really surfaced. I was working with a client whose case I'd worked on for a decade. I came to love him and his family. I freed him from prison, and then the prosecutors were trying to retry him. I was so involved in the case, and he trusted me and not really anyone else. I was actually going to do the jury trial. I have a background as a prosecutor and I have court experience, so I could do it. In the spring of 2013, I was getting ready for a jury trial to start as soon as my classes ended. I was filing motions every week trying to stop the retrial saying it was unconstitutional. Finally, I was successful about two weeks before the trial was supposed to start. At that point it came to a head where I was just so frustrated.

The way I describe my work to people is to imagine a doctor at Ronald McDonald House who must deal with children who have cancer. Their patients are dying. Imagine the sort of trauma that would involve. I relate innocence work to that except there is an extra layer. When you're a doctor dealing with children with cancer everyone is trying to save the children. Everyone is on the same side. In our work, we have these people who have had the greatest injustices committed against them, and we have prosecutors who are putting up procedural bars and arguing dishonest things in court, and trying to stop it. It's like you're a doctor trying to save children but other people are coming in and trying to steal the medicine. So, you're seeing this intense trauma from your client, but you are also seeing, in my opinion, some of the worst of humanity. These people that are operating in their bureaucratic roles and not caring about actual justice. By the time I got to 2013 and that happened and I narrowly avoided a retrial, I was just sort of a mess. I had to step back from those cases. Fortunately, by that time I had a large staff. Other people could take on the cases while I stepped aside and focused on writing a book and fundraising. I was doing more of the high-level stuff rather than being down in the trenches because I just couldn't deal with it anymore. This has expanded into counseling my entire staff both in group meetings and individually. Then it has gone on to the students' fellows. We realized these students who worked on their cases for an entire year would be devastated and shocked at the injustice of the system. We found out they were carrying this with them two or three years later working for big firms. They were still sort of messed up over this experience.

Through this time period, 2014 to 2016, when I would start talking about this the emotions were so close and the scars so raw that I would start crying. It was hard to even talk about some of these cases. But I was fortunate to know a psychologist with a background in trauma. When she became aware of how severely my work was affecting me, she offered to start counseling with me.

She has dramatically helped me, to the point where I am able to handle it much better. I am actually doing cases again, and was I able to get out of that haze. I could focus on what the work was doing to me and what I needed to do to fix myself. For example, I did not have any self-care. I gained 60 pounds during that time. I have lost half of that, and I am on my way to losing the rest. My counselor helped me center on how I needed to take care of myself, which I was not doing because of this trauma. Meditation and other things have honestly helped to the point where I am back in the trenches again, and I am able to handle things with a better perspective.

CHAPTER 5

Tools for Lawyers and Practice Areas: Underlying Principles of Trauma-Informed Tools

Introduction

Helgi Maki

This section explores the underlying principles of several trauma-informed tools and lawyers' experiences with applying them, rather than providing a full descriptive guide to each tool. Each of these tools is subject to considerable additional research, practice, and study. Each could (and often does) have an entire area of study or book devoted to it. Trauma-informed tools used in the course of their work allow a lawyer to support a client's holistic, biopsychosocial needs that commonly arise with trauma instead of leading with an exclusively cognitive, intellectualized approach as is often taught in traditional legal settings. Often these tools also have the additional benefit of supporting a lawyer's well-being, and can be used in any part of the legal ecosystem—in a client relationship, within an organization or community, at the level of a system like schools or courts, or even individually with ourselves. Trauma-informed tools allow a client to engage in legal processes free from unnecessary constraints on capacity to respond in their own best interests. Using these tools can help clients and lawyers to move forward, step by step, in situations that may otherwise seem overwhelming, meaningless or even impossible.

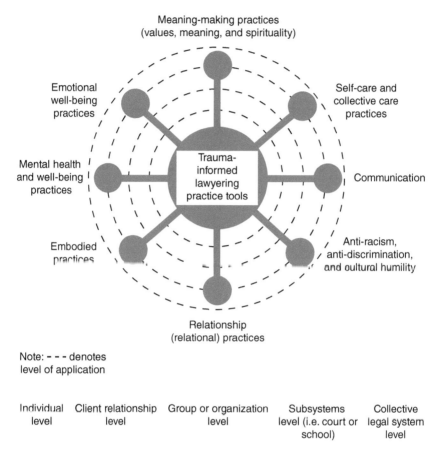

Figure 5.1 Trauma-Informed Lawyering Practice Tools
Image credit: Helgi Maki

Legal matters are already stressful and likely outside a client's comfort zone (or in trauma studies terms, their "window of tolerance"). Traumatic legal matters may fall outside a client's capacity to respond without proper resources.

With these tools, illustrated in Figure 5.1, clients are more likely to have the capacity to engage in the lawyer–client relationship in an emotionally regulated manner that allows for full engagement of the executive function in the brain's prefrontal cortex. Most simply put, when supported by trauma-informed practice, clients are less likely to feel limited by toxic stress or act as if they are in "survival mode," and are more likely to have full access to all of their capacities. They are able to make decisions or act with agency, and be in "social engagement mode."

Sometimes lawyers don't understand why tools are needed or they believe they're already too busy to learn or use these tools. However, if a matter involves factors that are not strictly intellectual, trauma-informed tools are more likely to improve outcomes than a cognitive approach alone. Stated plainly: if the case involves trauma, and therefore biopsychosocial demands, bringing only cognitive tools to the table is like bringing a knife to a gunfight. For instance, time spent communicating with care and cultivating the trust that may be slow to develop if clients perceive themselves as constantly being judged can result in more disclosure of higher quality. When an overwhelmed client can experience calmer in a legal process, that sense of calm becomes more available to the lawyer too.

In other helping professions like the medical profession, we would never question why a doctor takes steps to calm a patient before administering a vaccine, for instance. A fearful or emotional patient not only experiences distress themselves, their unaddressed distress can be transmitted to the helping professional (especially if that professional deals with patients at risk of distress all day, every day). A consistently distressed helping professional is unlikely to promote calm in their client. The function of mirror neurons, which allow us to feel empathy, also allow lawyers to sense a client's distress, which in turn can affect a lawyer, and conversely allow a client to sense and be affected by a lawyer's distress.[1] Conversely, if a lawyer is distressed and responds to a client in a judgmental or angry manner, the lawyer's distress may affect the client. A lawyer who is able to act in an emotionally self-regulated and nonreactive manner is less likely to evoke a stress response in a client, and may even support their own well-being.

Underlying Principles of Trauma-Informed Tools

Lawyers can face challenges in applying trauma-informed practice tools because these tools' underlying principles differ drastically from, and are even opposite to, the principles underlying traditional legal training. Legal training teaches us that analysis and judgment are our primary skills, the first tools to be used in any situation. Law school exams ask us to spot issues, identify problems, and present possible legal arguments about solutions. The underlying principles of each of the trauma-informed practice tools emphasize the practical utility of adopting skills and perspectives in practices of nonjudgment (as well as empathy and compassion). The value of these nonjudgment practices for lawyers is it provides them with tools for using skills that emphasize forms of knowledge other than practicing judgment. Without practice, it can be challenging for lawyers to engage with nonjudgment, which asks them to do the very opposite of what lawyers and judges are trained to do all day (judgment).

> *Legal training asks us to analyze (and/or judge) first, and trauma-informed practices ask us to provide care first and analyze (or judge) later.*

---

[1] M. Russell & Matt Brickell, *The "Double-Edge Sword" of Human Empathy: A Unifying Neurobehavioral Theory of Compassion Stress Injury*, 4(4) Social Sciences 1087–117 (2015), https://doi.org/10.3390/socsci4041087.

In order to provide both care and analysis we need to broaden our vocabulary of what judgment entails, to include discernment of when working from a place of judgment does (and does not) benefit our work, clients, and ourselves. Specifically, to provide both care and analysis lawyers must develop the skill of consciously applying their judgment (and discernment) skills, and alternating those skills with client care and service skills such as needs assessment, emotional literacy, or ethical literacy rather than using these same skills of cold analysis or judgment in every situation.

As every lawyer is called upon to act as a decision-maker, we've provided further commentary on judgment-related tools in the "Judges and Courts" section of this book. Judges may have even fewer opportunities than lawyers to use skills other than this key skill, duty and responsibility of rendering judgment for which they are named.

In this section, we give a brief overview of and provide examples and stories of how lawyers use certain representative practices to address trauma in the legal community.

Many tools relating to trauma are integrative or holistic in nature, because, both when we experience trauma and when we address it as lawyers through legal processes, we are doing it with the whole of ourselves, including our bodies, minds, emotions, ability to communicate, values and beliefs (including biases conscious and unconscious), our memories, stories and histories, and our sense of spirituality. We provide examples of tools that have a primary focus in the following areas: (1) communication and relationship formation practices, (2) anti-racism and cultural humility practices, (3) mental and emotional well-being practices, (4) embodied practices, (5) meaning-making (values, individual or collective meaning, and spirituality) practices, and (6) self-care and collective care practices.

It's important to note that, as of the time of writing, it isn't possible to include an exhaustive list of all trauma supports being used by legal professionals. It's important to know that it's not necessary or even suggested that lawyers become expert practitioners in all or any of these tools. This section simply provides a place to begin with tangible, hopeful support to help lawyers or clients navigate the discomfort, inconvenience, and distress in any practice area with more resilience, in a more sustainable manner.

Shifting Views

Nance L. Schick[2]

I frequently speak to victimology students about repeat victimization. It wasn't something I realized I had experienced—or at least not at the level I had—until

---

[2] Nance Schick is an employment lawyer, mediator, speaker, and diversity trainer in New York City.

I went to counseling at the Crime Victims Treatment Center (CVTC) in New York City after a violent assault in 2014.

I still remember vividly sitting in the waiting area, completing the checklist on the intake form. I had been to counseling before. Around age 19, I attempted suicide when my chaotic home life became too much for me to bear. I took advantage of counseling in law school, too, and again after an ex-boyfriend raped me in my current home.

In 2014, it was different. The person who attacked me this time was a stranger. He didn't have the psychological power over me the way that my abusive family member or ex-boyfriend did. Suddenly, it was clear that I was a victim like the ones I saw on TV. There wasn't so much confusion about what I did to cause the attack. At least I wasn't confused. Several people still blame me for walking home alone at night, being distracted, and even wearing clubwear that I was not wearing that night.

At the CVTC, I was not blamed. I was simply invited to heal—from every crime I had ever been the victim of. Childhood abuse? Check. Childhood sexual abuse? Check. Theft? Check. Robbery? Check. Sexual assault? Check. More than once. Violent assault? Check. F*ck. The list was longer than I expected. MY list was longer, too.

I was uncomfortable and somewhat embarrassed that I had been victimized so frequently. I didn't know if that made me weak, strong, defective, or something else. Intellectually, I knew it made me none of these. Emotionally, I wasn't sure.

I was diagnosed with PTSD after the assault. It manifested first as an inability to speak to my boyfriend about the assault. Just moments before my assailant grabbed me, I had called my boyfriend to let him know I was safely on my way home. I often called him, thinking I was safer if people could see I was talking to someone. Instead, I learned it might make me a target, and someone who loves me might have to listen helplessly to me being attacked. That's what happened to Peter.

When I first went out, even my first day of treatment, the PTSD manifested as fear of anyone wearing a hooded sweatshirt in a way that made them less identifiable. I still don't typically go out at night by myself. But that might not be a bad idea anyway.

I continued counseling at the CVTC through my assailant's sentencing, which was more than a year later. Not only did I work through the PTSD and depression from the incident itself, I struggled to accept the chronic injuries, the lack of access to medical care, the lack of a restorative justice process for my 14-year-old attacker, his disappearance (with his parents) for several months, the additional violent crimes he committed after mine, and more. I needed more sleep than I was used to. The ways I viewed issues in my law practice shifted. So did my priorities. And for some clients, my new boundaries were unacceptable.

In the long run, many of the changes have been good. I rarely work now with clients who do not appreciate the people in the process. I wrote my first book. I am fully visible as the holistic lawyer I had been somewhat quietly before. New York County has a developing restorative justice program. I am stronger mentally and spiritually, even if I still struggle with hip and back injuries. I work with other business owners, including lawyers, who have survived abuse and other crimes. I have reclaimed my power, my story, and my future.

Nevertheless, there are a few tips I consistently give to those who want to offer trauma-informed support:

1. Don't look for ways the victim could have avoided the crime. Let her come to those conclusions on her own. She has probably already rethought every single step she took before the attack and blamed herself. Yet she is not the one who committed the crime.
2. Don't take on the issue as if it is yours. The victim already feels powerless. Focus on empowering him, not fixing or controlling him—even with the best intentions.
3. Ask what the victim needs; don't assume you know better than they do. Even if you've been a victim of a similar crime, your experience will be different. Make sure you are getting the support you need, too.
4. Ask what they need frequently and listen without trying to fix anything. Again, the victim probably needs to be heard and empowered. Sometimes, they will need professional guidance for that. Be supportive of that, and trust that your relationship will be better because of that help.

* * *

Existing Trauma-Informed Legal Tools, Techniques and Practices: Interviews, Courts, Technology, Specialized Programs and Experts

Miriam Roger[3]

Interviews

The initial client interview and all subsequent information-gathering meetings are vital in establishing a trusting lawyer–client relationship. Trauma-informed techniques can be used when interviewing your client regardless of whether there is a known history of trauma. Common themes in trauma-informed

---

[3] Miriam Roger, a lawyer, advocate, and facilitator based in Toronto, is focused on improving the experiences of women and survivors of violence as they navigate the legal system.

interviews are use of empathy, preventing traumatization, rapport building, flexibility, and patience. When interviews are conducted using these competencies, clients may provide the best information possible and no additional unnecessary harm will be caused.

One established method of trauma-informed interviewing is the Forensic Experiential Trauma Interview (FETI), which was developed by Russell Strand, a retired U.S. Army CID Senior Special Agent.[4] By using empathetic, probing, open-ended questions (e.g., Where would you like to begin? What can't you forget?), including sensory questions (e.g., What are you able to remember with your six senses?), clients can provide an uninterrupted narrative with the goal of exposing corroborative information. FETI is designed to be used by various professionals and its techniques can be employed no matter the history of the client.

Motivational interviewing (MI), a client-centered counseling style used in social work, is also a strategy that can be used by legal professionals conducting interviews.[5] Developed for the treatment of substance abuse, MI was designed to explore and elicit a person's motivation to change a negative behavior.[6] For lawyers conducting interviews, the four core MI skills are transferable: open-ended questions (elicit the client's story in their own words), affirmations (acknowledge the client's strengths to build confidence for the future), reflective listening (listen carefully and repeat or rephrase to confirm your understanding), and summaries (ensure shared understanding, demonstrate interest, and address key points).

When conducting a trauma-informed interview, it is important for a lawyer to be aware of the potential for post-trauma responses during interviews. Due to the manifestation of trauma in one's brain, certain questions, environments, sounds, or other stimuli can trigger a flashback. In such a situation, the client is not merely remembering the trauma, they are reliving it. A client may also dissociate during or after an interview. It is impossible for a lawyer to predict if or when a client will experience a posttraumatic response, but a trauma-informed interviewer will be watching for such reactions and will address the needs of a client immediately.[7] Finally, a lawyer would end a trauma-informed interview by normalizing the feelings of the client, ensuring the client understands

---

[4] *The Official Forensic Experiential Trauma Interview,* Certified FETI®, Feb. 14, 2019, https://www.certifiedfeti.com/.

[5] Dalal, Payal, Rick Barinbaum & Carolyn Walther, *Motivational Interviewing: Counseling Clients in Challenging Contexts,* American Bar Association, May 1, 2017, https://www.americanbar.org/groups/public_interest/child_law/resources/child_law_practiceonline/child_law_practice/vol-36/may-june-2017/motivational-interviewing--counseling-clients-in-challenging-con/.

[6] WILLIAM R. MILLER & STEPHEN ROLLNICK, MOTIVATIONAL INTERVIEWING: HELPING PEOPLE CHANGE 29 (New York, NY: Guilford Publ., 2012).

[7] There are many resources on how to support people who are having flashbacks. Some common suggestions are to remind the client they are having a flashback, encourage the client to breathe deeply and ask them to describe the room.

the subsequent steps, and, ideally, confirming they have a support person with whom to follow up post-interview.

Courts

The physical space of a courtroom is designed to impose civility, respect, and hierarchy.[8] The movement-limiting judge's bench, the bar, and the dock as well as the many rules of a courtroom make it known this is an intimidating space with clear power dynamics. However, a judge can set the tone of their courtroom and may improve the experiences of individuals directly. Some resources suggest a judge consider the impact of an elevated seated judge's bench and how that may cause a trauma survivor to feel isolated, unworthy, or afraid. Would it be appropriate for a desk to be set up at the same level as the defendant or witness? If their testimony is going to be lengthy or intense, is it possible for the victim to sit in a separate room while they provide evidence and provide the evidence by video feed? Judges' skills can also contribute to a trauma-sensitive setting. Motivational Interviewing and FETI techniques can be employed when speaking directly to a witness or defendant.

The U.S. National Child Traumatic Stress Network has created a series of bench cards that present a trauma-informed approach to judicial decision-making relating to children.[9] These bench cards prompt judges to use tools like "emphasizing strength and resilience" and "to consider triggers" when making decisions that affect a child who has experienced trauma.

Colorado's Judge Ann Gail Meinster works with Brenidy Rice, the deputy director of court services, to implement trauma-informed practices into their jurisdiction's juvenile and child welfare court and Family Integrated Treatment court (a drug dependency court).[10] In their courtroom, it is assumed everyone has trauma and people are held to account with compassion and kindness. The physical courtroom space, language used and courtroom staff have all been considered to ensure that no unnecessary discomfort is caused to the appearing children and families.

In the United Kingdom, "special measures" are available to "help victims of serious crimes and victims and witnesses who are considered vulnerable

---

[8] Linda Mulcahy, Legal Architecture: Justice, Due Process and the Place of Law (London: Routledge, 2011).

[9] Sarah Peterson, *NCTSN Resources*, The National Child Traumatic Stress Network, Mar. 16, 2018, https://www.nctsn.org/trauma-informed-care/trauma-informed-systems/justice/nctsn-resources. *See also* NCTSN Bench Card for the Trauma-Informed Judge (Los Angeles: NCTSN, 2013), https://www.nctsn.org/resources/nctsn-bench-cards-trauma-informed-judge.

[10] Ann Gail Meinster & Brenidy Rice, *Trauma-Informed Courts: How to Create One and Why You Should*, Juvenile Justice Information Exchange, July 17, 2019, https://jjie.org/2019/07/17/trauma-informed-courts-how-to-create-one-and-why-you-should/.

and intimidated to give their best possible evidence in court."[11] These measures include various ways to provide evidence, including behind a screen, via video link, or in camera. It is also possible to provide evidence with the help of an intermediary who can assist the witness understand the question, and the court understand the witness's response.

Advocates in the courtroom can also assist in the creation of a more humane judicial system. In a recent class action lawsuit against the Royal Canadian Mounted Police for sexual harassment and discrimination, counsel for the claimants hired Primary Claims Advocates (PCAs). The PCAs had backgrounds in the social services or nursing fields and were trained in legal processes before being assigned to claimants. Counsel noticed the financial benefits of having a multidisciplinary, client-focused team as well as better client outcomes and an improved client experience.[12] In the United Kingdom and Scotland, various court support initiatives exist now and more are being considered.[13]

Specially trained therapeutic trauma-dog programs have also contributed to easing the trauma of testifying for victims. Where such programs exist, a dog is available to assist certain victim witnesses, particularly children, while they provide testimony.[14] The dog can sit with the witness and responds to the witness's cues and body language with incredible perception and kindness.

Part of having a trauma-informed courtroom is considering the secondary trauma and vicarious trauma that court and administrative staff may experience,[15] and it is essential that all court staff be included in trauma-informed training, including clerks, bailiffs, and court reporters.

Technology

Technology is another avenue that can create an accessible and trauma-informed courtroom while reducing the potential for retraumatization. Providing evidence via video one- or two-way closed-circuit television (CCTV) gives the option of not having to be in the same room as one's abuser. The United Nations has stated that in creating a child-safe environment in a courtroom, the

---

[11] *Victims & Witnesses*, The Crown Prosecution Service, accessed March 1, 2021, https://www.cps.gov.uk /victims-witnesses.

[12] Jill Taylor, *Why Does the Legal System Retraumatize Victims? Trauma-Informed Care Is Needed*, Canadian Law., Aug. 14, 2020, https://www.canadianlawyermag.com/news/opinion/why-does-the-legal-system -retraumatize-victims-trauma-informed-care-is-needed/332403.

[13] L. Ellison & V.E. Munro, "Taking trauma seriously," http://eprints.whiterose.ac.uk/100101/3/Taking%20 Trauma%20Seriously%20manuscript%20(final).pdf.

[14] Seattle's King County courtroom dog may have been one of the first courthouse dog programs in the United States. Christine Clarridge, *Courthouse Dogs Calm Victims' Fears about Testifying*, Seattle Times, Sept. 22, 2012, https://www.seattletimes.com/seattle-news/courthouse-dogs-calm-victims-fears-about-testifying/.

[15] Andrew P. Levin et al., *Secondary Traumatic Stress in Attorneys and Their Administrative Support Staff Working with Trauma-Exposed Clients*, 199(12) J. Nervous & Mental Disease 946–55 (2011), https://doi.org/10.1097 /nmd.0b013e3182392c26.

possibility for interviewing the child outside of the courtroom in child-friendly interview rooms and the avoidance of the child needing to see the abuser (i.e., use of video recordings, screens, or separate rooms) should be investigated.[16] In Scotland, research has shown "there is no compelling evidence that the use of pre-recorded evidence or live links, whether by child or adult witnesses, has a significant effect on verdicts in criminal trials."[17] Jurisdictions have different legal tests in deciding whether to allow evidence via video,[18] but it is evident that technology can improve the courtroom experience for survivors. However, the increasing prevalence of video evidence and consequent avalanche of digital evidence in litigation discovery from cell phone videos to bodycams to surveillance camera videos may increase the risk of secondary trauma.[19]

Integrative or Specialized Programs, Supports, or Training

Innovative, specialized programs have also been developed to address the needs of certain groups. For example, in response to the specific needs of veterans, more than 300 veteran's treatment courts have been established in the United States.[20] Exposure to the realities of combat as well as the loss of military structure can result in serious mental health concerns and can land veterans in conflict with the law.[21] Using a collaborative, multidisciplinary approach, veterans' courts offer wraparound support and camaraderie to veterans accused. Veterans involved in the specialized treatment court report significant improvements, including their mental health stability, emotional well-being, and family functioning.[22]

Some restorative justice or therapeutic jurisprudence initiatives for court innovation or support may also be considered trauma-informed, including mental health court and drug or substance abuse courts.

---

[16] United Nations Committee on the Rights of the Child *UNICEF Every Child's Right to Be Heard* (London: United Nations, 2011), https://www.unicef.org/files/Every_Childs_Right_to_be_Heard.pdf.

[17] Vanessa Munro, *The Impact of Pre-Recorded Evidence on Juror Decision-Making: An Evidence Review* (Scottish Government - Crime and Justice, 2018), https://www.gov.scot/binaries/content/documents/govscot/publications/research-and-analysis/2018/03/impact-use-pre-recorded-evidence-juror-decision-making-evidence-review/documents/00532556-pdf/00532556-pdf/govscot%3Adocument/00532556.pdf.

[18] In the United States, one test courts apply in deciding whether to allow one-way CCTV is that of Maryland v. Craig 497 U.S. 836 (1990), which balances the defendant's right to confront their accuser and the public policy interest of protecting those who are too mentally vulnerable to testify in the courtroom.

[19] Amy F. Kimpel, *Violent Videos: Criminal Defense in a Digital Age*, 37 GA. ST. L. REV. 305 (Jan. 28, 2021), https://ssrn.com/abstract=3671638.

[20] Treatment Courts Are Justice Reform, Justice for Vets, Feb. 26, 2021, https://justiceforvets.org/.

[21] It is estimated that as many as 43 percent of current veterans suffer from some sort of significant mental health issues, including PTSD, major depression, or alcohol misuse. *See* Eric Elbogen et al., *Are Iraq and Afghanistan Veterans Using Mental Health Services? New Data From a National Random-Sample Survey*, 64(2) PSYCHIATRIC SERVS. 134–41 (Feb. 1, 2013), https://doi.org/10.1176/appi.ps.004792011.

[22] Kraig J. Knudsen & Scott Wingenfeld, *A Specialized Treatment Court for Veterans with Trauma Exposure: Implications for the Field*, 52(2) COMMUNITY MENTAL HEALTH J. 127–35 (2015), https://doi.org/10.1007/s10597-015-9845-9.

Use of Experts

Since PTSD's introduction into the DSM-III in 1980, experts have been increasingly called upon to discuss trauma's impacts in all types of courts, including international and domestic criminal courts and civil courts.[23] The purpose of calling an expert on trauma is to provide triers of fact the appropriate context through which to process a victim's, witness's, or accused person's testimony or actions. A trauma expert's testimony may be relied upon when a victim's behavior is connected to a trauma syndrome (broad testimony) or when an individual has been diagnosed with a mental health condition related to their trauma (applied testimony or fact witness).

When it comes to syndrome testimony (e.g., battered women syndrome and rape trauma syndrome), a DSM diagnosis is not required for an expert to be called. When deciding whether an expert should be called to provide broad testimony, a lawyer should consider whether the victim's mental and physical reactions lie outside the common understanding of an average juror or judge. This can include behavior during the traumatic event (e.g., not fighting back, sustaining only minor injuries) or behavior after the event (e.g., continued contact with the accused, waiting to report to authorities). However, every jurisdiction has different standards, requirements, tests, and/or laws regarding the admissibility of broad evidence.

In 2007, the American National District Attorneys Association released a monograph for prosecutors which contains "Recommended Practices for Introducing Expert Testimony to Explain Victim Behavior."[24] This helpful document recommends a three-step strategy when introducing expert evidence in sexual or domestic-violence prosecution: identify the victim behavior that jurors will perceive as counterintuitive, determine the admissibility of expert testimony on victim behavior, and explain the victim's behavior. It also contains many sample questions for qualifying experts and eliciting evidence.

When considering whether to call an expert to testify to your specific client's trauma and their psychiatric diagnosis, a lawyer must ensure the situation calls for expert opinion. For example, in a case of PTSD, it is unlikely that an expert will testify unless the person in question meets the diagnostic criterion listed in the DSM-V. A clinician may also be called as a fact witness or participant expert, and will be asked to provide information based on their firsthand knowledge or observations, rather than providing expert testimony on a particular subject. In this circumstance, the fact a witness can only testify regarding

[23] Ralph Slovenko, *Legal Aspects of Post-Traumatic Stress Disorder*, 17(2) PSYCHIATRIC CLINICS OF N. AM. 439–46 (1994), https://doi.org/10.1016/s0193-953x(18)30124-2.

[24] JENNIFER G. LON, INTRODUCING EXPERT TESTIMONY TO EXPLAIN VICTIM BEHAVIOR IN SEXUAL AND DOMESTIC VIOLENCE PROSECUTIONS (National District Attorneys Association, Aug. 2007), https://www.ojp.gov/library/abstracts/introducing-expert-testimony-explain-victim-behavior-sexual-and-domestic-violence.

the specific client in question, and cannot provide their opinion regarding people or circumstances that they have not directly encountered.

The National Child Traumatic Stress Network has created two Fact Sheets for clinicians who are called as expert witnesses.[25] These Fact Sheets are wonderful resources to share with an expert before their testimony to assist in their preparation.

Communication and Relationship Formation Practices

The following four contributions consider emotional competence, strengths-based communication, and communication with the support of embodied practices as tools. In addition to the following, the ABA has guidance about creating a trauma-informed client relationship, aimed at child law practitioners and with some generally applicable tips.[26]

Soft Skills as a Vital Component of Trauma-Informed Practice

Dr. Emma Jones[27]

In recent years, the topic of "soft skills" has become increasingly discussed within the legal profession.[28] Such discussion often revolves around the argument that skills involving the affective domain (emotions and feelings) are important for client care, enabling lawyers to attract and retain clients successfully. Examples often refer to the concepts of emotional intelligence[29] and empathy.[30]

This increase in awareness is a positive development, demonstrating that soft skills are an integral and vital part of legal practice.[31] It is certainly the case that they are necessary for a trauma-informed approach to client care. For example, when working with a client who has experienced trauma, it is important to be able to gauge their emotional responses, understand potential triggers, and demonstrate sensitivity and empathy while also maintaining appropriate

---

[25] *Testifying in Court about Trauma: How to Prepare*, The National Child Traumatic Stress Network, Mar. 24, 2018, https://www.nctsn.org/resources/testifying-court-about-trauma-how-prepare.

[26] Establishing a Trauma-Informed Lawyer-Client Relationship, American Bar Association, Oct. 1, 2014, https://www.americanbar.org/groups/public_interest/child_law/resources/child_law_practiceonline/child_law_practice/vol-33/october-2014/establishing-a-trauma-informed-lawyer-client-relationship/.

[27] Dr. Emma Jones is a former lawyer (solicitor in the UK) and a legal educator. She writes about emotion in legal practice and the importance of "emotional competence."

[28] *See, e.g.*, Randall Kiser, Soft Skills for the Effective Lawyer (Cambridge, Cambridge University Press, 2017).

[29] Peter Salovey & John D. Mayer, *Emotional Intelligence*, 9(3) Imagination, Cognition & Personality 185–211 (1990); Daniel Goleman, Emotional Intelligence (London, Bloomsbury 1996).

[30] Lynne N. Henderson, *Legality and Empathy*, 85(7) Mich. L. Rev. 1574–653 (1987).

[31] Marjorie A. Silver, The Affective Assistance of Counsel: Practicing Law as a Healing Profession (Durham, Carolina Academic Press, 2007).

professional boundaries. Even for those clients in matters not overtly related to traumatic events there is a need to read emotional cues and build rapport—no client comes to a lawyer as an emotion-free zone.

However, such soft skills are also vital to the well-being of lawyers themselves. Understanding your own responses and reactions to clients and reading the emotional early warning signs about your own state of well-being are crucial in developing a sustainable trauma-informed practice.[32] The risks of experiencing vicarious or secondary trauma, even forms of posttraumatic stress disorder, means that lawyers must prioritize understanding and responding to their own well-being.[33]

A problem arises because such soft skills have traditionally been disregarded or undervalued by the legal profession. As such, they are not always taught within vocational training and they often do not form an explicit part of competency frameworks and codes of conduct.[34] This means that often there is no clear guidance and support in developing such skills. Rather than seeing these skills as an adjunct to so-called hard skills such as legal research, analysis, and advocacy, it is important to acknowledge soft skills as an integral part of trauma-informed legal practice. Not so much soft skills as vital lawyering skills.

It is important to appreciate that these vital skills can be taught to and developed by trauma-informed lawyers. They are not something you either have or you don't. Spending time evaluating your existing skills and seeking out training and support to develop key soft skills is an important part of continued professional development and a sign of emotionally aware and astute lawyering, which will benefit both you and your clients.

Strengths-Based Communication

Iain Smith[35]

Brendon's father left the family home shortly after he was born and his mother had a number of relationships with angry, drug-addicted, and violent partners. As an infant he was taken into local authority care, in various children's homes

---

[32] Sarah Katz & Deeya Halder, *The Pedagogy of Trauma-Informed Lawyering*, 22 CLINICAL L. REV. 359–93 (2016).

[33] Colin James, *Towards trauma-informed legal practice: a review*, 27(2) PSYCHIATRY PSYCHOLOGY & LAW. 275–99 (2020).

[34] *See, e.g.*, Emma Jones, *Affective or defective? The LETR's Characterization of Affect and Its Implementation into Practice*, 52(4) THE LAW TEACHER 478–89 (2018).

[35] Iain Smith is the winner of Scottish Lawyer of the Year Legal Award 2020. Iain specializes in criminal law and has been involved in a number of high-profile High Court trials. He fights hard to protect people's rights and passionately defends his clients. His career as a solicitor started in 1993 and five years later he formed Keegan Smith with Jim Keegan QC. Iain is actively involved in creating a fairer criminal justice system and is the leading trauma informed lawyer in Scotland. He is a core group member of West Lothian Adverse Childhood Experiences Hub and a Trustee of the charity Aid & Abet, who try to assist people get out of the cycle of offending. Iain is also boldly asking all judges in Scotland to treat those appearing before the court with respect and dignity.

and foster care, and was separated from siblings. This chaos, violence, neglect, and feeling of being unloved left this child in a constant state of fear and stress. By the age of ten he was consuming alcohol. By 11 he was smoking cannabis, and by 13 his first shot of heroin was administered by his mother herself.

His self-soothing on opiates continued into adulthood. There followed an abandonment of hope, absence of love, and inevitable entry to the criminal justice system at 17.

Brendon began to steal to fund his drug habit. The court decided to punish him in the community by what is known as a community payback order. This is a direct alternative to custody. It sets unpaid work and social work control to create obedience. Yet traumatized people cannot be punished out of their addiction and often the timetables set people up to fail.

Brendon's sad life continued to deteriorate and he remained unemployed and to an extent with his lack of skills, criminal record and trauma—unemployable. He became homeless. Sold his phone. Impecunious. Inevitably his court order failed and the social workers brought it back to the judge for a breach of the order.

During the gap before he was arrested for the breach, Brendon met a "Good Samaritan," a charity worker who decided to help Brendon. He was provided with a home, assistance to obtain state benefits, prescriptive medications, mentoring, and friendship. With this positive turnaround in his life, he was arrested and appeared in Edinburgh Sheriff Court.

As his defense lawyer, I explained to the judge the nature of his horrific childhood, the biological effect that stress would have had on his development and the long-lasting impact of trauma. I explained how he self-soothed on drugs and with the help of several charities he was working with managed to turn his life around.

She paused then sneered "Mr. Smith, What are you asking me to do with him?"

In a packed court I quietly implored her to "praise him."

"I'm sorry," she replied, stunned.

Thinking she hasn't heard me due to the ambient noise of a busy court, I raised my voice and boomed "PRAISE HIM!" Everyone, including the judge, fell silent.

Genuinely shocked, the judge said she was considering jailing him (and probably me) for what she viewed as a contemptible suggestion.

Bail was allowed and four weeks later, armed with reports from the various charities, his mentor, his doctor, and housing, I was ready for battle. Even the social work report had catalogued his blighted upbringing and used the words "childhood trauma" to explain (not to excuse) his actions.

Then, like some form of miracle, the judge spent ten minutes praising Brendon for his good efforts and his attempts to improve his life. She allowed the order to continue and wished him well. Her anger was gone, her empathy engaged, compassion flowed, and she gifted him hope.

I could feel tears fill my eyes. At last, a judge found the formula to stop the revolving door. It is counterintuitive for judges in Scotland to look beyond punishment and retribution. And yet repair and rehabilitation are the only long-term solutions to reduce crime. Compassion. Hope. And when that fails, Perseverance.

Brendon left the court with me and beamed. "No one in authority has ever spoken to me like that before. I feel good about myself."

My one regret. Not telling the judge the effect of her smart application of justice. Maybe she will read this book one day. Let's hope all the judges do. The following story provides one example of a lawyer and social worker's perspective on why trauma-informed principles (including for communication) are needed in the legal system.

What I Want Judges to Know and Do

M. Frances (pseudonym)[36]

This is my dream essay: to write to judges from the triple perspectives of having been a child abuse and domestic violence survivor in my family of origin, and being both an actively practicing lawyer and clinical social worker.

I have spent a considerable amount of time pondering the question about how, when I was growing up, so many people had sufficient information or awareness that I was in peril and did nothing about it. I even returned to my high school and asked my guidance counselor if he'd had thoughts about why I had run away from home. "I was being abused," I told him, and he didn't skip a breath. "I thought so."

"Why didn't you report? I asked him, my heart beating wildly at the thought that someone could have saved me. His response was, "I was scared your father would have my job."

It wasn't until January 6, 2021, when I witnessed myself and a significant portion of our nation and world, huddled in an emotional corner, wondering what the U.S. president might do next, that I clearly understood. It wasn't until I witnessed the paralysis of congressional leaders, outspoken psychiatrists with specialization in human violence, who'd spent years warning of just this

---

[36] M. Frances JD, LICSW is an active lawyer, clinical social worker, part-time exhibiting artist, and published essayist. Her career has primarily been in the adoption field and she is very proud of having helped place 200 children in happy, safe, and loving homes. This essay is published under a pseudonym with the kind understanding of the editors.

Frances credits her survival to the generosity, courage, and grace of administrators at Mount Holyoke College, excellent therapists, a solid practice of Vipassana meditation, and the love of her long-time partner and co-parent. She is proudest of their having raised their daughter in a climate of encouragement, safety, and love.

danger, that I understood why I'd been so victimized despite what was in plain sight: people were terrified of my father, who suffered from a harmful mixture of psychological difficulties.

I will share my story because the reader may pull questions or insights from this. I no longer have the question: "How could 20 adults have known I was in constant risk and not taken steps to rescue me?" My question, now, is, "When an ordinarily well-meaning teacher, psychotherapist, doctor, lawyer, or judge runs up against a situation in which they feel scared, for their own well-being and safety, when a parent with personality disorders, aggression and perhaps human evil are involved, how do we, as a society, create sufficient structures, "a sufficiently protective professional deliberating community" and resources so that that professional does not feel too scared to prioritize the safety of the child (and the safety of the child's other caretaker(s))?

My mother's first husband, on the face of him, would have been deemed a "good guy." A graduate of an Ivy League law school, reasonably attractive with his pearly white teeth and thick black hair. For my mother and those looking over her shoulder, this man, soon to serve in the Anti-Trust division of the Justice Department, was a "catch." However, he was actually evil. I mean evil in the way clinician/psychiatrist M. Scott Peck described in his brilliant book, *People of the Lie*. Peck said that hallmarks of evil were lying, scapegoating, and lacking empathy.

As a small child, I was neglected in ways that openly endangered my life. My parents' fighting was awful and frequently bottomed out with the presence of police cars at the house. These were the days when women were not believed and police did not remove offenders nor arrest them. There were no such things as restraining orders. Years later, I learned that their separation was hastened by an occasion where my mother's first husband tried to murder her by strangulation. She managed to break free and go to the hospital where she explained her presence there with a story, as many women did then and still do now, because she knew that the truth would not be believed, nor would she (or I as a grade school child) be helped to greater safety.

These were the days before "no fault" divorce and my mother only was able to divorce by agreeing to the threat that she not tell anyone what he'd done, or else. . . .

Over the course of my childhood, I was beaten, raped, and terrorized by the man I came to call "my mother's first husband." Prior to the rapes, I had been a straight A student, a member of my state student government, and a serious piano student—after the rapes, I became a runaway. I was in college before I learned that diarrhea was not the natural state of bowels.

After he showed up, uninvited, at my college graduation, I changed my name so he couldn't find me. Despite my efforts to hide, after I graduated law school with my new name, he showed up at a Federal Court hearing where I was expected to argue. I contacted many law firms after that, seeking representation for a civil suit. What was then called the Women's Legal Defense Fund agreed to take my case. But, then, I, too, understandably, became scared.

I asked him to meet me in the office of a psychiatrist. This was the same doctor who'd refused my mother's earlier request to protect me; she asked him to recommend cessation of visitation with him to the court. The psychiatrist had clung to the worn-out trope that children need both their parents, denying the harm of his abuse. This doctor now bore witness as my father closed the shades to the doctor's office, looked at me with the eyes of a man imbued with human evil, and hissed, "If you sue me, you'll be a leaf in the wind." The psychiatrist didn't have the presence to apologize for his earlier underestimate of his maliciousness or the harm to me and only stated, "He did not speak as an innocent man."

There were a number of points when a trauma-informed probate court judge could have made a difference. My mother's first husband, a highly trained attorney, openly weaponized the legal system against my artist mother. She had to beg lawyers to represent her, pay as much as she could while also supporting me. And he just looked like a "good" lawyer—there wasn't anyone with a capacity to see the sadism between the well-written lines or the courage to use their power to end it.

How might judges have had the strength of training, insight, and courage to refuse to be bullied by my mother's first husband? How might they have served the bench far better than being accurate, according to a very narrow view, in their rulings and steps taken from the bench?

There is a skill that probate and family court judges need to have. The skill involves seeing between the lines, around the corners of sharp edges presented by others as your limits. The skill involves listening to your gut, even if the motion or document before you fit the rules and canon, and knowing when something is terribly wrong and that, without your involvement, the life and well-being of the other caretaker and child are threatened.

I used to think perhaps it was that professionals didn't recognize the signs that there were serious difficulties. Now I think that people let that awareness in—it's not that ongoing education in recognizing sadistic parents with complex personality disorders and, at times, human evil, isn't still needed. Instead, I think the real issue is creating sufficient professional and personal safety so that the "reporter" or good Samaritan actor or judge, entrusted with carrying out true justice on behalf of the child, doesn't fear they're committing professional suicide by stepping forward or, perhaps worse, putting themselves and their family in danger of violent revenge.

The skill is one that I have taught many mandated child abuse and neglect reporters. So many ask, "When do you know that you need to report?" I answer: "The time to ask for guidance from a reporting office, even if anonymously at first, is when you are beginning to ask yourself the question, 'Is this a case I might need to report?' That is when you should be contacting your support team." The support team (or "sufficiently protective professional community") referenced earlier in this essay, should have been formed just before the beginning of your job, not in a crisis. It can be comprised of individuals from separate offices who don't know each other so long as confidentiality is maintained and they have expertise in supporting you.

Likewise, judges who are trained to ascend to the bench based on individual work and to hold so much, alone, should not attempt to discern, identify, grapple with, or make decisions in cases involving human evil without a support team. This is not a straight-line approach—you have to let evil pass through you—the way to do this is to share both what you know from a factual perspective and the thoughts that cross your mind, the thoughts that more resemble animals from the wild crossing a highway where they are perceived to not belong, with a team of individuals who you trust to listen deeply and hold a protective space for you. Assume that any evil you see is just the "tip of the iceberg." That was certainly true for my mother and for me. The judges either chose not to see or were blinded by their solitary roles and fears for their own professional and personal well-being. There needs to be line items in state judicial budgets to cover the extra expertise needed to acknowledge and respond to human evil in family court cases. Not allocating funds perpetuates denial.

When you have random thoughts that go through your mind—is this child ok?—this is when you should talk with clinical social workers, retired judges with a greater experience in the emotional realm, and your own therapist. You can maintain confidentiality and also engage in therapy so that the worries don't tangle like pasta and seem unsortable. Don't hold the worries alone. Create a larger circle of care for yourself. Evil is too hot to handle in your own bare hands.

You don't want to hold the worries alone because denial is a genuine stage for judges, too, and without the help of a supportive ally team, you are likely to rationalize your way out of awareness of the child's peril. You will make a decision limited to the four corners of the document before you and tell yourself that more has not been asked of you; that's not part of your job. That's for the therapists to figure out and for the counselors to heal.

There are two bright moments in my personal history that I want to also share. This is not to minimize my suffering, but to point out what was needed to fight back.

Though I had run away from home, I had not been able to tell anyone what happened. That requires another essay about shame and our society's utter lack of support for child abuse survivors. Although my mother's first husband had initially agreed to cover the costs of my college education, toward the end of my first semester, he said that, for tax purposes, I had to have lived at his home for at least two weeks in the calendar year. He would only continue to pay for college, if I would return on the holidays.

This is what I mean, judges. It may have been an accurate reading of the tax code. He could have said this in a reasonable tone. But he also stated he wished I had stayed at his home, lived in the upstairs apartment, so we could "continue our relationship," when there was no such thing. There was only a terrified child uncertain about whether I could run away or whether he would lock me up in a juvenile prison—something he threatened to do if I told anyone.

I went to my college's counseling center and explained everything. My therapist asked if he could have my permission to talk with the dean of students on my behalf. The next thing I knew, I was in the dean's office and she said to me, "I spoke with your father. He said you were a very bad girl; he would no longer support you in college and that we should send you home. I told your father that, at Mount Holyoke College, we don't send girls home simply because they can't pay their bills. And then, frankly, I told your father exactly what I thought of him and hung up on him."

No lawyer. No trial court judge. No appellate judge. No therapist. No rabbi. No parent. No teacher. No grandparent. No piano teacher. No extended family. No person who had reason to know he was delusional and vindictive, evil and imperious, gaslighting and totally vacuous where empathy should have been, protected me. But the dean did. And the financial aid director sat me down and laid out the financial aid plan that would ensure that I could complete my college education. They did so because they had an institution behind them, one dedicated to the safety, well-being, and education of girls and women.

All forward-thinking judges should take the time to understand psychological concepts of complex personality disorders and human evil and the dangers posed for children. Truly capable judges, making decisions in the family law arena, should have a solid interdisciplinary team to support them when evil shows up between the lines and openly. It would be naïve to think that clinical skills held by social workers and psychologists only involve empathic listening and hand-holding—you need to coordinate with those who have those expert skills.

I survived, but, at great cost. If the ACEs scale is true to form, the abuse I suffered may have cost years of my life, the cut-off as yet unmeasured. But, judges, his evil should not have been unleashed, unfettered, ignored, and allowed, in the name of gaslit statements of the law. I want you to do better at reading situations with a wider, trauma-informed, and, indeed, psychiatrically informed lens. And don't do this alone. It is bigger than you. A truly wise judge knows when something is bigger than their skillsets and asks for help.

It is up to probate and family court judges to learn much, much more than solely about the law. Ongoing judicial training will give you the opportunity to feel more confident in this area where children need your judicial eye. And to hear much, much more than just legal arguments. And to know how to develop the space within you and with a strong established support team of allied professionals to entertain the worst and not flee from it out of parallel fear for your own safety or well-being.

The children, who are the often invisible clients in your court, are counting on you. I was failed. I speak now for so many children who didn't survive those mistakes, for those who can't find the words, and for those who were not as fortunate as I to have this opportunity to share these thoughts. Thank you for listening.

* * *

The following contribution focuses on working with communication and language, as well as teamwork and collaboration, to help clients with the difficult topic of death and dying.

A Multidisciplinary Approach to Death and Dying

Rhiannon Thomas[37]

How comfortable are you discussing dying and death, especially with someone who knows that they will die soon? Do you feel you can manage this conversation? What will you do if they start crying? How will you deal with your own experience or relationship with dying and death? Will you feel so overwhelmed that you forget to ask an important question, one which you might not get the opportunity to ask again?

These are just some of the questions I've asked myself over the years while consulting with clients seeking a will.

In 2013, I approached two mental health professionals—Victoria Mayer, a clinical psychologist and family mediator (and ex-lawyer) and Di Burger, a family counselor whose expertise lies in adult and pediatric palliative care and bereavement support. Together, we developed Milkwood,[38] a new breed of legal practice based within the new paradigm of integrative law. Our legal services would be expansive, including the heart and soul in the consultation and the resulting legal document. We wanted to provide a values-driven service, which would result in values-based wills and other documents.

We designed Milkwood to be meaningful for our clients—the name has a special meaning to us, the logo and the website were thoughtfully created, our relationship as colleagues, our own personal development and emotional

---

[37] Rhiannon Thomas is an integrative lawyer with a vision: to offer the best, most meaningful encounter that a person can have with the law; to work collaboratively with other professionals; to inspire other lawyers to reassess the way in which they practice law and serve their clients; and to take her firm, Milkwood's, methods into mainstream law firms by providing training and workshops on using this approach.

[38] You can learn more about Milkwood at www.milkwoodlaw.co.za.

well-being, our client's individual circumstances and the contracts we create collaboratively with them. We even offered an ongoing relationship with Victoria or Di for those clients who needed further assistance with the non-legal issues that arose during their initial consultations—from how to have constructive conversations about each other's unique values, their relationship to money, conflict resolution styles or how they felt about the prospect of a certain death (the "when" rather than the "if"), or their "non-legal" plans for the future.

Instead of asking clients just the usual questions to draft a valid legal will, we ask additional questions, which allowed us to get to know the client in a more personal way, resulting in a fuller, holistic, and more meaningful conversation about their mortality. The questions are simple, but ones which generally go unasked, especially when consulting with a legal professional: What is important for me to know about you? What is most important to you? What is worrying you most? How can I best support you? These additional questions and the support of a trained multidisciplinary team leads to a better outcome for the clients and has relieved my stress and feelings of being in over my head. Knowing my clients can follow up with trusted colleagues who will meet non-legal needs gives me a sense of comfort as well.

* * *

Nonviolent Communication (NVC)
J. Kim Wright

Nonviolent communication was developed by Marshall Rosenberg who wrote several books on the topic. We recommend a more thorough study of the topic.

In brief, NVC recognizes that humans are trying to meet their own needs and values, that we all share the same basic human needs, and that our differences are often the result of different strategies for meeting those needs. The NVC model is multipart: Identifying feelings, giving and receiving empathy, recognizing how those feelings reflect met and unmet needs, and making requests.

One aspect of NVC worth noting here is that of Other Conversational Responses. Often, we think we are giving empathy but we choose strategies that are not helpful and could even be harmful.

Other Conversational Responses

The following is excerpted from a web post on www.cnvc.org. It has been adapted by Rachel Monde and reprinted with permission of the Center for Nonviolent Communication.

Each of us has learned a number of different conversational styles or responses that we may tend to use habitually. Some of these are mentioned here.

Sometimes the following responses can lead to misunderstanding, hurt feelings, anger, disconnection, loneliness, and depression, which is why in his book *Nonviolent Communication: A Language of the Heart*, Marshall Rosenberg suggests using NVC empathy, suggesting that it is possible to have a conversational response that leads to understanding, acceptance, connection, and caring.

The following responses are *not* being implied as always "wrong" or "bad." Only that being aware of our habitual conversational responses and using them as "bells of awareness" can remind us that we have choice in how we want to interact with, and the type of responses we can hope, therefore, to receive in return from others.

As a society, we have been trained that the following conversational responses are efforts to connect, which may be why these responses are used so frequently. Knowing this, when you encounter others responding to you using one of these styles, have compassion; they may be trying to give you empathy!

Note: some of these responses, such as educating or strategies, might serve the other person, if they are used after NVC empathy, and upon asking whether the person would like to hear them.

1. Advising/strategies: "What you should do is. . ."
2. Analyzing/diagnosing: "You're acting schizophrenic. . ."
3. Blame: "You made me. . ." or "You hurt me when you. . ."
4. Championing: "You can do it. . ."
5. Consoling: "It wasn't your fault; you did the best you could. . ." Or touching the other person, "there, there."
6. Correcting: "That is not how it happened. I did not do that. . . ."
7. Devil's Advocate: "But they work hard and they really try. . . ."
8. Educating: "You know, x happened because people. . . ."
9. Explaining/Justifying: "I would have . . . (e.g., called). . . but. . ."
10. Guilting or Shaming: "How could you do such a thing. . ." or "You are so selfish. . ."
11. Honesty (Judging or Criticizing): "The trouble with you is. . ."
12. Being "NICE": "No, I am not upset. I'm FINE."
13. One-Upmanship: "That is nothing. What happened to me was. . ."
14. Questioning: "When did that actually happen?"
15. Realistic: "That will never work because. . ."
16. Relating: "Oh I know how you feel because x happened to me. . ."
17. Shutting Down: "Cheer up now, you'll get over it."
18. Sympathizing: "Oh you poor thing" or using sympathetic eyes, tone of voice, or body posture.
19. Sarcastic humor.

Each of those conversational styles may have its proper purpose, but a better alternative is to learn to listen empathetically.

Powerful NonDefensive Communication

Another communication model that is helpful is that of Powerful NonDefensive Communication (PNDC). Based on the book by Sharon Ellison, *Taking the War Out of Our Words*, PNDC focuses on how we can protect ourselves without getting defensive and achieve our goals without resorting to a power struggle. With the PNDC model, it is possible to be direct and honest as well as open and transparent, thereby increasing our integrity without losing spontaneity. We recommend the audio version of the book because a lot of the communication depends on tone of voice.

* * *

Anti-Racism and Cultural Humility Practices

Myrna McCallum

Cultural humility is a framework which was created by Dr. Melanie Tervalon and Dr. Jann Murray-Garcia, which focuses on the life-long commitment to self-reflection, self-critique, openness, respect, and the genuine commitment to engage with those who come from different backgrounds than ourselves. Dr. Tervalon and Dr. Murray-Garcia, who are both Black physicians from the LA-area, were inspired to create this framework after witnessing the beating of Rodney King by members of the LAPD.

The cultural humility framework is intended to build bridges between people and groups for the ultimate purpose of moving us toward fairness and justice for all and to help correct the racial and inequitable imbalances which exist within the organizations and systems within which we work—like the legal profession. This framework is the preferred approach, especially when working with those who are not representative of the mainstream, cis-gendered, able-bodied, White, middle-class, heteronormative backgrounds.

> The lawyer, as a listener, will begin to grasp the systemic inequalities many complainants from these communities have lived with as a result of inherent injustices within the policing, corrections and court systems. When you actively listen, you practice cultural humility. Cultural humility will encourage you to critically examine common unconscious biases which feed myths and stereotypes, question your knowledge sources and open your mind to new perspectives; all of which are the same components underpinning trauma-informed approaches to practice.
>
> – Nisha Sikka & Myrna McCallum

The guiding principles of cultural humility according to Tervalon and Murray-Garcia include recognizing and changing power imbalances and institutional accountability, alongside lifelong learning, self-reflection, and self-critique.[39] While conventional legal education still teaches future lawyers not to ask a question they don't already know the answer to, the focus on self-reflection, self-critique which cultural humility promotes asks lawyers to adjust some of their own core practices to improve the lawyer–client relationship and advocacy experience. Humility, for example, is a critical component which has the potential to dramatically improve the client experience by centering and prioritizing the client's lived experience.

As we assist clients in their journey through the many stresses of a legal process, it's important to be aware that justice work tainted with racism of any kind including White supremacy is highly unlikely to be experienced as helpful legal services by a client. Since the death of George Floyd in 2020 and collective increased focus on improving civil rights in response to systemic racism, many law schools and bar associations (including the ABA) have bolstered and updated their resources for anti-racism education and practices, and the calls for further resources and system change continue.

Anti-racism studies as they're taught by Ibram X. Kendi, equal justice as taught and practiced by Bryan Stevenson, racialized trauma training and cultural somatics as taught by Resmaa Menakem, ABA resources such as the ABA Men of Color Project, Black Lawyers in America Toolkit, ABA Task Force Report on Reversing the School-to-Prison Pipeline and other resources on cross-cultural communication like the cultural detective work of Dr. Eun Kim are among the resources that lawyers will want to refer to and reflect in ensuring that their trauma-informed legal services embody anti-racism practices.

In addition, the Transgender Law Center maintains a resource center for legal services and has observed that transgender people are frequently compelled to interact with legal systems that are not designed for transgender persons, describing even fundamental legal services like identity document correction as potentially overwhelming, confusing or isolating.

Embodied Practices: Awareness, Nonjudgment and Movement

Helgi Maki

"Exercise is the key not only to physical health but to peace of mind."[40]

– Nelson Mandela

---

[39] M. Tervalon & J. Murray-Garcia, *Cultural Humility Versus Cultural Competence: A Critical Distinction in Defining Physician Training Outcomes in Multicultural Education*, 0(2) J. Health Care for the Poor & Underserved 117–25 (May 1998), https://muse.jhu.edu/article/268076/summary.

[40] Nelson Mandela, Long Walk to Freedom (London, England: Abacus, 1995).

"I do a variety of weight-lifting, elliptical glider, stretching exercises, push-ups...and I do the Canadian Air Force exercises almost every day."[41]

– Ruth Bader Ginsburg

In addition to respecting the body's needs for nutrition, sleep, time not working, and exercise, each being health supports that have been shown to help improve well-being in response to or even to prevent toxic stress, embodied practices to support nervous system regulation and their benefits in dealing with trauma are sufficient for these practices to be considered essential by trauma experts.[42] Instead of defaulting to our primary tools of analyzing, judging, discerning, or deciding, we become aware (with nonjudgment) of what clients, colleagues, and ourselves are experiencing physically and respond to physical needs.

Movement practices were used as a support by the editors in preparing this book to reduce stress, tension and chronic pain and promote healthy stress response cycles, which you'll read about next. Even simple movements and exercises that can be done in five minutes or less, while sitting in an office, can assist lawyers and clients with experiencing healthy stress response cycles instead of getting stuck in distressed bodily states. A "body scan" exercise is an example of a body-based mindfulness exercise of being present with body sensations that can be learned easily in minutes, even by the busiest lawyers by internally sensing the state of the body from head to toe at some point in the day instead of forgetting the body. A simple way to begin an embodied approach to legal practice is to notice how clients, colleagues and ourselves may convey signs regarding their state of being with body signals such as breathing or posture. For instance, we can begin to notice whether a person's breathing appears to be calm or labored such as rapid, shallow or even non-existent breath. Or whether a person's bodily posture appears grounded and upright, collapsed or hyperalert.

We recommend that readers read further about and explore movement and body-based practices including Somatic Experiencing, polyvagal theory training, embodied forms of mindfulness meditation such as Mindfulness-Based Stress Reduction (MBSR), and the other approaches described in this chapter. It's important to engage the expertise of trained practitioners and of course appropriate to seek the advice of your doctor before you begin a new practice.

---

[41] Ruth Bader Ginsburg as quoted by Andrew Prokop, *Ruth Bader Ginsburg works out like a Canadian Air Force Pilot*, Vox.com, Sept. 30, 2014, https://www.vox.com/xpress/2014/9/30/6871539/ruth-bader-ginsburg-healthy.

[42] N. Burke Harris, The Deepest Well: Healing the Long-Term Effects of Childhood Adversity (New York: HMH Books, 2018).

Embodied Trauma and How to Respond to It

Rebecca M. Stahl, JD, LLM, SEP[43]

Responding to Trauma in the Moment

When we consider trauma from an embodied perspective, we can think about how to respond to its manifestations in the moment. These are simple techniques that you can use to help yourself and those around you, including clients, down regulate enough that the prefrontal cortex can come back online, and you can all respond rather than react automatically from a trauma response. Each of these techniques work differently for different people, so try them all and discover which ones work best for you.[44]

Try the following exercises as you read and notice your breath before, during, and after. Notice if any of them work better for you than others. This list goes in order from easiest to do in the courtroom to techniques that require you to leave the room.

1. Noticing the breath. This is as simple as it sounds. There is no need to try to change the breath for this exercise. Notice the inhale. Notice the exhale. Notice where it moves freely. Notice where it gets more stuck. Just notice. And as you notice, see if anything changes. Do this for five to ten breaths.

2. Grounding. Feel whether there is a space within your body where you feel connected to what is beneath you. This could be anywhere, but many people feel this in their feet on the floor, their legs and buttocks on the chair, their arms on the arm rests, or their backs on the chair. And for most of us, where we feel grounded will change. Take a few moments to notice where in yourself, right now, you feel the most grounded, and pay attention to that area for 30 to 60 seconds.

3. Somatic hug. This is great during virtual meetings where no one can see your arms! Place your right hand in the middle of your ribcage about six inches below your armpit. Place your left arm over your right arm and your left hand on your right rib cage. Do this for at least 60 seconds, but there is no limit to how long you can rest like this.

---

[43] Rebecca Stahl is deputy director of the Sayra and Neil Meyerhoff Center for Families, Children and the Courts at the University of Baltimore School of Law. Rebecca previously represented children and as a Fulbright Scholar in New Zealand. Rebecca earned a master of law degree from the University of Otago. Rebecca co-authored, *Representing Children in Dependency and Family Law: Beyond the Law*. Rebecca is chair of the board of directors of Somatic Experiencing International, an international organization dedicated to healing trauma.

[44] One note: if the trauma manifestations are taking over your life and your practice, seeking professional help from someone trained in an embodied trauma therapy (somatic experiencing, Eye Movement Desensitization and Reprocessing [EMDR], sensorimotor psychotherapy, or Internal Family Systems [IFS] therapy) is suggested.

4. Pushing hands together. This is great if you are angry from an email or something someone says to you. Place your hands together in front of your chest. Using approximately 15 percent of your strength, push your hands together for three to five seconds. Do this three times, resting between each one for three to five seconds. After the third time, rest for 30 to 60 seconds.
5. Orienting. This tells your nervous system there is no external threat, so it can down regulate. Slowly move your neck and allow your eyes to follow. Pay attention to what you see, even if you have seen the room for years. Slowly move your head from one side to the other as your eyes follow the neck's movements.
6. Placing your forehead in your palms. Rest your elbows on the table in front of you and place the heel of your hand on your eyebrows and place your fingers on your scalp. Allow the shoulders to soften down the back and your head to relax into your hands. Rest here for 30 to 60 seconds.
7. Push-ups. Push-ups are one of the best ways to move energy, particularly fight energy. You do not have to be able to do "perfect" push-ups. They work just as well if you are on your knees, or standing by pushing against a wall or a desk.
8. Take a walk. Just move! You can walk around the office or better yet go outside and walk around the building, even for five minutes or less. Just move!

You can also use these techniques with clients and sometimes even with other professionals. One counterintuitive way to help clients is to interrupt them. We have all experienced times when clients get extremely activated by the story they are telling. Interrupting someone so you can speak instead is very rude, but interrupting to help a client down regulate their nervous system (come out of sympathetic activation toward "rest and digest") can be helpful for everyone involved, as long as you do it respectfully and with purpose.

The best way to interrupt someone who is speaking very quickly, not breathing, and not able to tell a coherent story is to make sure that you are paying close attention to where they are in the story. You can kindly stop them, ask them if it feels overwhelming to tell the story, and then ask if it would be okay to take a short break while you discuss something else and you will remind them where they were in the story to come back to it later. Remember to ask if they are okay with the break and then talk about anything at all that is likely not to be overwhelming for them. I often use favorite or recent good movies as a talking point. When you notice that their breathing deepens, their speech patterns get slower, and they look a bit more relaxed, you can ask if they are ready to go back to the story. You can even ask them to try one of the techniques above, such as orienting, while you take your break.

References and Resources

Representing Children in Family and Dependency Court: Beyond the Law, Rebecca M. Stahl and Dr. Philip M. Stahl

My Grandmother's Hands: Racialized Trauma and the Pathway to Mending Our Hearts and Bodies, Resmaa Menakham

In an Unspoken Voice: How the Body Releases Trauma and Restores Goodness, Dr. Peter Levine

The Deepest Well: Healing the Long-term Effects of Childhood Adversity, Dr. Nadine Burke Harris

The Boy Who Was Raised as a Dog: And Other Stories from a Child Psychiatrist's Notebook—What Traumatized Children Can Teach Us About Loss, Love, and Healing, Dr. Bruce Perry and Maia Szalavitz

Rebecca M. Stahl, *Responding Effectively to Trauma Manifestations in Child Welfare Cases*, 58 Family Ct. Rev. 920 (2020).

The Score Isn't Final: Mind-Body Practices to Release Trauma

Stephanie M. Shorter, PhD[45]

The Body Keeps the Score

These words distill the essence of the work and clinical practice of psychiatrist Dr. Bessel van der Kolk, a leading researcher who has studied how people process and adapt to traumatic life experiences since the 1970s. He is absolutely correct—trauma leaves its mark in our tissues and chemistry, so the body *does* keep a cumulative scorecard of the past. However, that scorecard does not have to be the final one.

Beyond talk therapy, residual changes following trauma can get dislodged from tissues through the body-based practices. That is, the body can release trauma and reprogram itself. The goal of this chapter is to introduce you to some simple physical practices that can alleviate trauma and anxiety, all of which are supported by rigorous empirical standards in fields like behavioral neuroscience and psychoneuroimmunology.

The autonomic nervous system is comprised of the peripheral nerves that run throughout the body. The two divisions of this system work as counterparts: the sympathetic division is the "fight or flight" system that revs up when danger is impending, while the parasympathetic division involves "rest and digest" processes that help the body maintain and repair itself. Within the autonomic nervous system, the vagus nerves are a major player in stress

---

[45] Stephanie M. Shorter, PhD, has an eclectic professional background that ranges from serving as a neuroscience professor at Vanderbilt University to editing several journals and books related to behavior change, design thinking, social transformation, and yoga therapy. Now based in Silicon Valley, she works in venture capital and is honored to serve as the neuroscience advisor for Cutting Edge Law.

management and the (subjective) perception of safety. Vagal activity regulates heart rate, blood pressure, metabolism, cellular repair, inflammation, detoxification, digestive peristalsis, immune function, and sexual arousal.

A common misconception is that a person is either in parasympathetic mode or sympathetic mode, as if it is possible to flip a toggle switch and be solely in one mode or the other. In fact, both systems are active at all times. There is always a balancing act, occurring at a very fast time scale. Optimal health is not the absence of fight or flight activity; it is reflected in the *balance within the autonomic nervous system.*

This balance of the autonomic nervous system has a quantified signature, something that you can measure in your daily life. If you can measure something, you can improve it, and that is the rationale for some mind-body practices that are suggested later. You can train your nervous system to become more adaptive. Respiratory rate and the cadence of the heartbeat are the telltale signs of whether all of this dynamic autonomic activity sums to a net healthy balance.

When the breath is short, jagged, irregular or suspended (holding one's breath), the fight or flight sympathetic nervous system is exerting control to an unhealthy degree. As a result, the cognitive and behavioral skills to best cope with the stressor are not available at that moment. Conversely, when the breath is slow and controlled, there is greater autonomic balance. Breathing is the only autonomic process able to be brought under our control. We can slow the breath at will, leading to a calmer mood and correlated physiology.

Having a regular breathing practice is one of the most effective treatments to ameliorate the effects of acute trauma and chronic daily stressors. Breathing at a rate of six cycles per minute, with each inhalation + exhalation cycle lasting about ten seconds, is optimal. This slow rate of breathing coordinates the activity of the heart and lungs and increases arterial baroreflex sensitivity (important for blood pressure homeostasis). A wide range of studies, even some that compared the respiratory systems of yoga practitioners and Himalayan mountain climbers,[46] have shown that a breath rate of 6 cycles per minute induces a state of cardiopulmonary synergy that is beneficial down to the cellular level, including antioxidant protection and decreased acidity (tissues heal best when they are more alkaline than acidic). The most effective way to breathe at a rate of 6 cycles per minute involves elongating the exhalation. Inhaling for 4 seconds and exhaling for 6 seconds has been shown to have a very soothing effect while also inducing the cardiopulmonary waves to be in sync, shifting the CO_2 composition and acidity of the blood, and promoting antioxidant processes. A

---

[46] Bernardi, L., Passino, C., Spadacini, G., et al. (2007). *Reduced Hypoxic Ventilator Response with Preserved Blood Oxygenation in Yoga Trainees and Himalayan Buddhist Monks at Altitude: Evidence of a Different Adaptive Strategy?*, 99 EUROPEAN J. APPLIED PHYSIOLOGY, 511–18.

breath cycle of 10 seconds can feel really slow at first. Start where you are, be patient, and keep the exhale longer than the inhale.

You can learn more about many different controlled breath techniques by Googling the term *pranayama*. *Prana* is from the Sanskrit referring to *life force* and *yama* is an *observance or in service of*. The breath serves the maintenance of life in the body – it does this by bolstering the balance of the autonomic nervous system. Importantly, for a trauma-sensitive breath practice, one should always opt for a slow, deep, "cooling" pranayama practice. Simple is best. Elevated, forceful, invigorating, or "heating" pranayama techniques can have negative effects that can range from agitating to fully triggering PTSD symptoms.

If breathing doesn't seem like much of an intervention to you (as in *don't just do something, sit there!*), realize that you can get the same benefits out of singing. Depending on the song, the vocal control of singing can simulate breathwork and generate the same physiological benefits. Consider that Buddhist monks chanting are not just reciting words but are also engaging in breathwork by drawing in oxygen and then chanting (exhaling) a long series of syllables. One study compared the effects of monks chanting and other research participants singing "Ave Maria" in Latin.[47] Tempo dictates the pace of breath control. The tempo of a pop song is too fast to induce this kind of restorative breathing, but you can look to slower tempo songs with sustained notes and find something that pleases you and also naturally makes you breathe about six times per minute. That's now your go-to mind-body song.

Other mind-body practices that are stretching- or movement-based, such as yoga and tai chi/qi gong, also increase vagal tone, especially when the movements are executed so that breath and movement are coordinated. Stretching and movement of the torso can provide mechanical stimulation of the vagus nerves. Whether a nerve is stimulated "organically" by electrochemical processes internal to the body or from some kind of external force (e.g., light, heat, movement, stroking, pressure, electrical stimulation), the effect is the same. Now, imagining how the vagus nerves intertwine with the organs of the torso, it is easy to see that changing the shape of the body will exert pressure at different points along the nerves. Any movement, twisting, or inversion that alters the organs' position relative to each other will also exert pressure upon (stimulate) the vagus nerves.

One of the most effective movements for elevating mood and increasing vagal tone is a backbend. Interestingly, the yoga postures that Westerners call backbends are actually described in the opposite way in Sanskrit, the language

---

[47] Bernardi, L., Sleight, P., Bandinelli, G., et al. (2001). *Effect of Rosary Prayer and Yoga Mantra on Autonomic Cardiovascular Rhythms: Comparative Study*, 323 BRITISH MEDICAL J., 1446–49.

of the original teachings of yoga. Instead of bending the back, the Sanskrit terms instruct to expand the front. The true goal of these postures is to open the front torso rather than compress the spine. Therefore, the most effective and safe form of doing a "backbend" is to stretch and expand the tissues around the collarbones, sternum, thoracic chest, and abdomen, like a majestic and proud Sphinx statue. Chest-opening postures increase lung capacity to enable deeper breathing and increased blood flow, thereby enhancing the body's rest-and-digest capacity. These postures also alleviate anxiety and significantly improve mood. Even seated at your desk, you can take a minute or two to shift your posture in a way that opens your chest. Adding several cycles of the 4:6 inhale:exhale breathing, you can improve your physiology and sense of calmness in a very short timeframe.

Trauma is a part of human society. When traumatic events happen, the body keeps score. But being able to train your nervous system and increase your HRV opens the possibility of rewriting the scorecard. These mind-body practices can often release what years of talk therapy could not.

Considerable research has been done for decades on trauma and its effects, posttraumatic stress disorder. Only recently, just since the mid-1990s, have scientists studied posttraumatic growth. When posttraumatic growth occurs, the individual has actively revised the scorecard. Mind-body practices offer the real possibility to move beyond any long-term cognitive, emotional, or behavioral damage of trauma, to move into nonjudgmental awareness, and ultimately to move into the realm of posttraumatic growth. The ability to reflect without emotional valence or judgment is at the heart of posttraumatic growth: to transmute the pain of something that was once traumatic and evolve into a more sophisticated version of oneself.

Mental and Emotional Well-Being Practices

Helgi Maki

The legal profession has a complicated relationship with mental and emotional health, and especially with emotions. Beginning in law school we are taught that judges will analyze every case according to the standard of a so-called reasonable person. We're given the mixed message to care for our mental and emotional health yet always remain "reasonable" or "rational." Lawyers usually don't receive training in the skills underlying the ability of a supreme court justice to avoid applying feelings to facts, prevent ourselves or others from being consumed by emotions or to recognize the humanity of our clients and colleagues.

Trauma-informed tools for mental and emotional well-being include (among others) mindfulness, mental health support from a qualified practitioner or group, emotional literacy, emotional intelligence and the ability to self-regulate and maintain appropriate emotional boundaries in our work. Mindfulness allows us to remain free from judgment, with awareness of the present moment and unconstrained by thoughts of the past or future. Mental health practitioners help us support healthy cognition, mood, and behavior. Both of these tools are frequently incorporated into law firm or law school wellness programs and legal clinic wellness resources. With well documented benefits, there seems to be less resistance to including mindfulness in lawyer well-being suggestions (since it tends to address other common complaints such as anxiety or attention space) than tools directly dealing with emotions.[48] While mindfulness has also been shown to reduce negative emotions, many lawyer well-being programs have yet to embrace practices that turn toward or deal directly with emotions.

The practice of law emphasizes the importance of facts and objectivity over subjective experiences including feelings and emotions. It's understandable to assume that a lawyer's (or client's) state of mind and mental or emotional health are mere inconveniences to be ignored unless legally relevant such as determining *mens rea* or capacity. However, powerful emotional experiences such as grief are likely to arise in traumatic legal matters.

The underlying principles of mental and emotional well-being practices for lawyers and clients affected by trauma focus on nonjudgment, empathy, compassion, and awareness. The views on which practices are the most useful to support trauma are diverse, and evidence-based options include mindfulness, developing emotional self-regulation (through co-regulation with a helping professional) and self-compassion. Emotional intelligence practices also support well-being, and lawyers working with trauma often need to attend to issues like emotional boundaries, refraining from taking on clients' issues on a personal level outside of work. A deep dive into nonjudgment, empathy, and compassion is helpful for lawyers but beyond the scope of this book. As a starting point, it is useful to ask where in your practice and in your life, you are spending time practicing nonjudgment? In trauma-informed practice, lawyers practice nonjudgment with clients, themselves, and colleagues, which does not mean that actions of any of these parties are without consequence. Rather, lawyers and clients who are not acting, thinking, or feeling reactively from a state of fear can consciously choose from a larger opportunity set of options in the legal process.

Since lawyers rely on their minds all day, every day, in their work it should not be surprising that care is merited for the parts of ourselves most often relied upon for productivity. Some representative tools for putting mental and emotional

---

[48] S.J. GEORGE, WHY LAW SCHOOLS SHOULD TEACH MINDFULNESS, http://sites.law.duq.edu/lawreview/wp-content/uploads/2017/09/53.1_George_Article.pdf. *See also* https://www.natlawreview.com/article/attorney-wellness-and-mindfulness-part-2-what-does-mindfulness-practice-look.

well-being tools into action are described later. It's important to select tools that feel the most relevant to your practice, your clients and your own needs.

A simple way to begin working with emotional intelligence is to notice the emotions and facial expressions of clients, colleagues and ourselves, which we might start to do by asking ourselves what emotion we observe that the person we're working with may be experiencing. This practice can be supported by learning more about emotional intelligence from experts such as Daniel Goleman.[49] Or by reading about emotional regulation (and co-regulation) for lawyers.[50]

Lawyer Well-Being and Self-Examination Tools

Alyssa Johnson[51]

Practicing law took a toll on my physical, emotional, and mental health. I was constantly stressed, exhausted, and anxious. In the end, I quit practicing as an act of self-love because I was so depleted. It has taken a lot of inner work for me to find my way back to myself and re-engage with the legal field in a much healthier way.

As part of my reclamation, I've learned a number of tools that help me regulate my feelings, bring me back to my center, and create spaciousness within my being so that I can hear my inner voice more clearly.

The most important tool that I have is heart listening. One of the many beautiful things about being a lawyer is how we develop our brains. It's a highly cerebral profession. We're able to take very challenging, abstract ideas and put them into form in a way that helps our clients. The shadow side of this, however, is that we can become almost solely reliant on our minds rather than incorporating our hearts into our decisions. This can leave us feeling unbalanced and unintegrated. Heart listening is a key piece in rebalancing and reintegrating ourselves.

If you're new to listening to your heart, it may be challenging to move around your mind enough to listen deeper. But with practice it gets easier. To use this tool, take a few deep breaths and settle more deeply into your chair. As you lean into your breath, become aware of your heart. Notice how it feels. If brain chatter comes up, that's totally fine. Keep breathing and thank your brilliant mind for its thoughts. Go back to your heart. Ask your heart for guidance.

---

[49] Goleman, *supra* note 29.

[50] Debra S. Austin, & Rob Durr, *Emotion Regulation for Lawyers: A Mind Is a Challenging Thing to Tame* (December 4, 2015). 16 Wyo. L. Rev. 387 (2016), U Denver Legal Studies Research Paper No. 15-60, https://ssrn.com/abstract=2699330.

[51] Alyssa Johnson is a former lawyer who now helps attorneys find more joy in their work. Specializing in mind-body-spirit integration, Alyssa teaches lawyers how to incorporate their heart's wisdom into their work and their lives. Utilizing embodiment tools, spiritual and well-being practices, and trauma-informed body exercises, Alyssa helps lawyers live heart-centered, nourishing, and rewarding lives. You can learn more about Alyssa at www.AlyssaJohnson.love.

You can ask for guidance on a specific question or you can just open and allow your heart to provide whatever it wants. Let the answer come however it may. It could be a color, a picture, a feeling. You may feel really good or you may feel rage, grief or some other feeling that causes discomfort. Let it be whatever it is. Your heart is communicating with you in its own extraordinary way.

Another tool I use that works beautifully with heart listening is setting Sacred Space. This is a prayer or invocation that you say before beginning your day, your work, or a task with which you want to be intentional. When you set Sacred Space, you're creating a focused container for your task. Your mind, body and heart become clear as to what you desire to feel, accomplish or experience and it allows your energy to flow in a directed way. Setting Sacred Space also has an element of trust in it. Trusting that you're asking for the right things, trusting that your requests will be delivered to you in the perfect way. The practice of law can be very distrustful depending upon our experiences. Implicitly trusting that we're setting Sacred Space in the way that it needs to be set can be a really healing antidote for the distrust many of us carry.

Since setting Sacred Space is about asking for what you desire, you can't do it wrong. Include whatever feels right to you. Trust that you're asking for exactly the right thing and that it will be delivered to you in its exact right form.

Breathwork is another tool I use as it's extremely effective at regulating my nervous system. A side effect of trauma is that our breathing can become too shallow or too rapid. Our bodies then become stressed because they're fighting for oxygen. A helpful tool to come back to center and check in with your body is to do conscious breathwork. There are many types of breathwork, but a very simple one is a circular breath. Imagine inhaling and the breath moving all the way down to your belly. On the exhale, imagine the breath moving back up and out through your nose or mouth. Repeat this circular breath and track it through your body. What do you notice? How do you feel? Do any areas of your body feel loose, tight, relaxed, constricted? There is no right or wrong here. Only curiosity and nonjudgment. The more you become conscious of your breath, the more you can slow your breathing down and become inwardly quiet. This opens up space for you to respond to life rather than react. It also gives you space to deeply listen to your inner being.

The last tool I want to share addresses our innate need for connection. An aspect of law that can be really harmful to our nervous systems is the isolation that we may experience. Humans are built for connection and it's traumatizing to our nervous systems to be isolated for long periods of time. And yet many lawyers spend much of their time working alone on their projects. To combat isolation try co-working with colleagues or friends. Hop on Zoom together, share how you're feeling and what you intend to work on, set a timer for however long you want to work, and then check-in when the timer goes off. Sharing how you're feeling helps you feel connected, seen, and heard. Sharing what you're working on helps you stay focused and on task.

Practicing law is tough regardless of an attorney's experiences with trauma. But it can be extraordinarily hard for those who are exposed to painful client stories or those who have a history of trauma and are trying to do their best work while their trauma responses are running in the background. The tools I've shared can help you become more aware of your own body and what you need at any moment in time. Self-awareness is power because we can make more thoughtful, informed choices when we have a greater understanding of what's going on.

If we focus on seeing the world and ourselves exclusively through the lens of our legal training we may diminish awareness of emotions, whether our own or within others. Emotional literacy or intelligence along with continuously learning to self-regulate can keep us connected to emotional responses that can be key signs of impact from "vicarious trauma" or "secondary trauma" described in the following section. Vicarious and secondary trauma can arise from situations where a lawyer witnesses the suffering of others, rather than experiencing their own direct situation of adversity in their own lives. The editors note that some leading trauma experts believe that there is no such thing as vicarious or secondary trauma, that it is all trauma. However, the terms are in common use and we will include references here.

Common Signs and Symptoms of Vicarious Trauma

Nazanin Moghadami[52]

A lawyer should consider checking in with themselves about vicarious trauma if they notice a change in their mannerisms or thinking styles that cannot be explained by other factors. Following is a list of changes in mannerism and attitude that might point to vicarious trauma:

- Irritability
- Fatigue
- Sleep disturbance
- Substance use
- Relationship breakdown
- Nightmares
- Rapid weight change
- Change in eating habits
- Social isolation

---

[52] Nazanin Moghadami is a Registered Clinical Counselor with an MCP from Adler University. She lives in Vancouver, British Columbia.

 ◆ Fear of being alone
 ◆ Distorted sense of safety
 ◆ Losing flexibility
 ◆ Withdrawal
 ◆ Overworking
 ◆ Being easy to upset and cry
 ◆ Anger outburst
 ◆ Rage
 ◆ Persistent feeling of shame or guilt
 ◆ Hopelessness
 ◆ Impatience
 ◆ Hypervigilance and paranoia
 ◆ Loss of faith in own work or legal system[53]

In the following section, Eileen Barker discusses the role of emotional literacy and boundaries for lawyers and mediators.

Emotional Literacy and Boundaries

Eileen Barker[54]

1. Begin thinking about the emotional climate of a case early on. Sometimes it will be apparent. If not, inquire of the parties and/or attorneys.
2. When dealing with emotionally charged situations, safety and trust are critical. Give thought (in advance if possible) to what the parties and lawyers may need to establish a sense of safety and trust.
3. When appropriate, encourage direct emotional expression. ("Talking about the feelings underlying the conflict can be very helpful.") This requires discernment. One situation in which this is not appropriate is when the client is already emotionally flooded.
4. When emotions surface in mediation, normalize them. ("It's normal to feel anger/sadness/grief in this situation.")
5. Learn to recognize emotional blocks when they arise in mediation, and how to facilitate constructive emotional expression. The parties

---

[53] Excerpted with permission from N. Moghadami, *Chapter 7: Vicarious Trauma & You*, in Trauma-Informed Legal Practice Toolkit (Golden Eagle Rising Society, 2020), https://www.goldeneaglerising.org/initiatives-and-actions/trauma-informed-toolkit-for-legal-professionals/. For more details on identifying and addressing vicarious trauma (including thinking styles), please refer to the Self-Assessment Tool in the full version of the Toolkit at https://www.goldeneaglerising.org.

[54] Eileen Barker has been writing and speaking on forgiveness, and guiding people who need to either forgive themselves or someone else, for many years. A practicing litigation lawyer who rejected the traditional adversarial role, Eileen has focused her practice on mediation, helping thousands of people resolve disputes outside of court.

will usually flag emotional issues for you, but they will often do so indirectly.

6. Distinguish between feelings and behavior. Inappropriate behavior can be addressed through ground rules, and should not be confused with responsible expression of strong emotion.

7. Stay with the heat. Allow each person to have his feelings straight out, without stifling or interfering with them. When an opening presents itself, put your active listening and empathy skills in gear. Reflect back the emotional content and intensity.

8. Promote emotional literacy amongst parties and attorneys. Explain that acknowledging feelings can be a very important step in conflict resolution (and no, it is not therapy).

9. Give the parties options. "Are you comfortable discussing this in the joint session? Would you prefer to talk privately?"

10. Give the attorneys options. "It would be helpful for me to talk with your client about her underlying feelings. Would you prefer to take a break while I speak with her?"

11. Be aware of your own internal response to strong emotions. Are you contracting or resisting? Are you judging? If so, can you set that aside and support the party?

12. Learn to embrace healthy emotional expression. Recognize that emotions tend to connect people in a very human way, and often hold the key to unlocking conflict at a profound level.

Boundaries

For many people, boundaries are a foreign concept. Most people weren't taught about boundaries, and don't know what they are or how to establish them. Most of us didn't have good role models for setting healthy boundaries. Instead, we learned to accommodate other people and put the other person's needs above our own. That's fine up to a point. But, when someone is being treated poorly, it may indicate their boundaries are weak or nonexistent. Our clients need to learn to establish and maintain healthy boundaries, and so do we all.

The essence of a boundary is "here is what is ok with me, and here is what isn't ok with me." You have a right to set boundaries. In fact, it's your job to set clear boundaries—to let others know what is ok with you and what is not ok—and stick to them.

So, what do healthy boundaries look like? Here are some examples:

◆   It is not my job to fix others.
◆   It is okay if others feel angry, but it's not okay for anyone to lash out at me.
◆   It is okay for me to say no.

◆ I'm not responsible for how others feel.
◆ I don't have to anticipate the needs of others.
◆ My needs matter.
◆ Nobody has to agree with me.
◆ I have a right to my own feelings.

If your boundaries are breached, you need to enforce the boundaries in a manner appropriate to the circumstances. Once again, this requires discernment.

At a minimum, you need to reassert the boundary. You need to restate what is not ok and why. If, after doing so, you feel the other person understands what you need and why it is important to you, then you may feel safe and confident continuing in the relationship.

However, if you lack trust that the other person can or is willing to honor your boundaries, you have a harder decision to make. You might choose to take a break from the relationship. Although hard to do sometimes, it is usually best to let the other person know the reasons for this. Set a time period for the break, or tell the other person you will let them know when and how you are ready to resume contact. This approach can reduce stress, because both of you will then know what to expect, and it allows you to take small steps (when you're ready) to see if you can establish trust.[55]

The Four States of Distress: How to Comfort Someone When Something Bad Happens to Them

Spencer Greenberg and Kat Woods[56]

When a friend or loved one has something bad happen to them, what should you do to help them feel better? This question can be difficult to answer because people want different things at different times: empathy, problem-solving, optimism, distraction, and so on. We propose that there are four general states that a person may be in when something bad happens, and that knowing which of these states they are in can help you figure out how you can best comfort them.

Note that we are only considering non-emergency situations for this model, since emergencies require immediate action. Furthermore, note that while people do not always pass through all of these different states when something bad happens (so they are not really "stages" per se), when they do all occur, they tend to happen in a predictable order.

---

[55] Reprinted with the author's permission.

[56] Spencer Greenberg is an entrepreneur and mathematician with a focus on improving human well-being. He founded ClearerThinking.org, which makes free, digital tools for improving lives. Kat Woods is the president of The Nonlinear Fund, which searches for high impact strategies to reduce existential risks.

The Four States of Distress Model
State 1: Shocked or confused

When something negative and unexpected occurs, we may need time to understand what actually happened and how we feel about it. A friend can help facilitate that process. If you know someone in this state, you can help them understand what happened and how they feel about it.

Most common potential emotions: shock, confusion, surprise, fear, dread, denial

- Example situation 1: your friend comes home from vacation and finds that their apartment is wrecked.
- Example situation 2: your friend who thought their relationship was going great is suddenly dumped by their partner.

Strategies more likely to be helpful:

- Active listening
- Helping to resolve confusion
- Expression of concern
- Validating their confusion
- Reflecting back to them your understanding of what they have said

State 2: Feeling bad and not ready to feel better

When we're feeling strong negative emotions, we may actually want to be feeling them. For instance, if someone we love dies, we likely will want to be sad about it for some period of time. Or if we are betrayed, we may well want to stay angry at the person for a while because we feel that anger is deserved. If you know someone in this state, you can help them express their feelings and feel validated.

Most common potential emotions: intense forms of sadness, depression, anxiety, anger, contempt, guilt, jealousy

- Example situation 1: your friend whose home was wrecked is feeling highly anxious about the expensive damages and furiously angry at the person whom they let stay there while they were gone.
- Example situation 2: your friend who was broken up with yesterday is feeling very sad about the loss of the relationship.

Strategies more likely to be helpful:

- Active listening
- Empathy
- Validating their emotions
- Reflecting back to them your understanding of what they have said
- Help them get into a mindset where they are ready to feel better

State 3: Feeling bad but wants to feel better

After feeling bad for a while, at some point we are likely to get sick of those negative feelings and wish that we could feel better again. At this point, a friend can help alleviate those negative feelings. If you know someone in this state, you can help them feel better.

Most common potential emotions: intense to moderate forms of sadness, depression, anxiety, anger, contempt, guilt, jealousy [same list as State 2]

- ◆ Example situation 1: your friend whose home was wrecked is still feeling anxious about the cost of replacing their possessions and angry at the person who caused the damage, but they are sick of thinking about it all the time and want to move past it.
- ◆ Example situation 2: your friend who was broken up with still feels very sad about it, but wants to feel better, move on, and focus on the future

Strategies more likely to be helpful (note that this section is especially person dependent, with different people having different Comfort Languages[57]):

- ◆ Optimism and reframing (e.g., seeing it in a less negative light or finding a silver lining)
- ◆ Physical comforting (e.g., a hug)
- ◆ Validating their emotions
- ◆ Distraction (e.g., doing a fun activity)
- ◆ Helping them explore and understand their feelings
- ◆ Problem-solving (especially if there is a way to quickly fix much of the problem)

Since people really do differ in their preferred ways to be comforted (e.g., some people love optimism while some hate it, some people love hugs and others don't like to be touched), it's really important at this stage to use your knowledge of the person to figure out how to best comfort them. If you don't know, you can simply ask them how you can help them feel better, and then suggest options that they can choose from.

State 4: Feeling better and wants solutions

When we're feeling intensely bad, it's often both difficult and unappealing to problem-solve. After we start to feel better, however, we may start to feel motivated to find a way to improve our situation. If you know someone in this state, you can help them move forward past the problem.

Most common potential emotions: more manageable or minor forms of sadness, depression, anxiety, anger, contempt, guilt, or jealousy

---

[57] https://www.youtube.com/watch?v=mswQdZed51M.

◆ Example situation 1: your friend whose home was wrecked is feeling somewhat less bad about it, but now they want help figuring out how they are going to get their stuff replaced and whether they can get the guest who caused the damage to pay.

◆ Example situation 2: your friend who was broken up with is feeling somewhat less bad about it and wants your help meeting someone new.

Strategies more likely to be helpful (though your choice will depend on the person and your relationship to them):

◆ Brainstorming solutions
◆ Problem solving
◆ Advice
◆ Volunteering your time to actually help on the solution
◆ Providing resources to help solve the problem

A lawyer's values, beliefs, and culture (including cultural knowledge) are also integral to meaning-making. The following contributions examine how the sense of meaning can be enriched by these deep forms of knowledge, or by defining traumatic conflict as including an opportunity for transformative growth or forgiveness.

Conflict as an Opportunity for Growth

Brittany Bisson[58]

"Rather than being dangerous, conflict holds within it vital messages, regarding unmet needs and areas of necessary change. Given this understanding, safety is increased not by avoiding conflict, but by moving toward it with the intention of hearing the messages within."

– Dominic Barter

I spent the majority of my life actively and intentionally avoiding all conflict. I had a preconceived idea that conflict was violent, destructive, and unproductive. Naturally, this stems from childhood trauma. I wanted to be the opposite of what I was exposed to . . . which I conflated with the absence of conflict. It was not until *very* recently that my perspective shifted. In processing my divorce, I realized that by avoiding *all* conflict I absolutely missed opportunities for growth and understanding. Similarly, when I encountered conflict at work, I would avoid it. This was a very disempowering place to stand. I missed out on opportunities for more money, better hours, etc. because I was so concerned with walking into conflict.

---

[58] Brittany Bisson is a 2022 graduate of Quinnipiac University School of Law.

Also, conflict doesn't just exist and dissipate organically. Instead of directly confronting conflict, I suppressed conflict. For me, suppressed conflict was toxic. It manifested as frustration, internalized blame, resentment . . . I could go on. Eventually, I grew tired of my own avoidant behavior. I think it has been a slow creep towards engaging in conflict in a meaningful, healthy, restorative way. I have to actively choose conflict. It is not my default.

Warrior of Law, Warrior of Dream, Warrior with Beatitude, Warrior TIL, Me!
Warriors of Law, Warriors of Dream, Warriors with Beatitudes, Warriors TIL, We!

Joseph Thomas Flies-Away, JD, MPA[59]

The most impressive question asked of me as a judge for my people is: "What do you think about when you sentence me, Joey?" In the Hualapai Tribal Court, my home court where I am related to many, minors called me by my first name. I was entering a final disposition in a delinquency matter. This delinquency engaged, though intelligent, young man forced me to consider all of those thoughts. What do I think about when determining penalties, especially when taking one's freedom away? At the hearing I explained the influence of the scale and brevity of his offenses and conduct, the victims' harm and hurt, and the associated damage. I also described how I review his record, his family history, what is going on currently, and what might happen in the future to deter future visits with me. I did not stop thinking about the youth's question after the hearing, however. I eventually expanded the question placing crime or delinquency into the context of Conflict and how It is best addressed. I previously developed a planning tool or paradigm while a Planner for my Tribe that identifies a number of key considerations that facilitate Cooperation. By connecting the Conflict considerations to Cooperation, the flat tool became a Sphere, the foci for the Spirituality of Law Analysis. The question of a curious and courageous young Hualapai inspired the Warrior of Law Approach. The Spherical Analysis and Approach are practices that I believe champion trauma informed law.

The Warrior of Law Approach and Spirituality of Law Analysis derive from applying the considerations of the Sphere.[60] The Sphere in its most practi-

---

[59] Joseph Flies-Away formerly served as Chief Justice and Chief Judge of the Hualapai Tribal Court, and he has served as a pro tem judge for several tribal courts in the Southwest. In addition, he works as a Community Nation Building Consultant in Phoenix, Arizona. He has also been a lecturer at Stanford University School of Law and adjunct faculty at Arizona Summit Law School. In addition to his JD from the Sandra Day O'Connor College of Law, he has a master's degree in public administration from Harvard's Kennedy School of Government.

[60] For a fuller description of the Sphere, see Joseph Thomas Flies-Away & Carrie Garrow, *Healing to Wellness Courts, Therapeutic Jurisprudence +*, 2013(2) Mich. St. L. Rev. 425–39.

cal sense is a tool, in its most defensive sense a shield, and in its most aggressive sense, a weapon. It serves the needs of many including a jurist and justice system, an advocate, a community and nation builder, a family, and a nation. When used to solve problems, disagreement or disputes, the Sphere guides the Spirituality of Law Analysis. When used as a development or planning device it directs the Warrior of Law Approach. Both processes confront conflict, a crime or delinquent act, and coordinate cooperation, ways to remediate harm. They help push parties and people forward in a positive direction. Because the Spherical Analysis and Approach focus on key aspects or components of life, they support comprehensive determinations of penalties and rehabilitation plans, and embrace holistic and sound sentencing and disposition.

Most, if not all, of those I listened to in court experienced trauma throughout their life. Alcohol caused a great deal of pain, hurt, and worry for them, their family and friends. Alcoholism and alcohol abuse still remain a source of pain and frustration. Drunk people yelling and fighting around town severs our collective sense of peace. In preparing for arraignment, I read many complaints full of trauma-laden allegations. The conduct and actions described scenes where the offenders seemed totally disconnected to those they were allegedly hurting.

Emeritus Chief Justice Robert Yazzie of the Navajo Nation Supreme Court describes a criminal as "one who acts like he has no relatives." The complaints I read described exactly this. The defendant's or minor's conduct showed complete disengagement from those they presumably loved and shared family. I witnessed these very same people out in the community interacting in a safe and happy space, so I knew they shared and depended on family ties. The alcohol and other substances negatively influenced their inherent feelings and thoughts of togetherness and belonging. Drinking affected their spirituality and became disconnected. The disconnection led to formidable physical, emotional, and intellectual harm to their relatives and others. The alleged conduct or action, including what was said, resulted in trauma to its receivers.

The harmed persons, the victims, were many times overwhelmed and deeply affected. When I had the perpetrator and victims before me at the end of it all, I talked with them, encouraged apologies, and reviewed any orders given to promote reconnection and healing, including counseling to address a number of issues for the defendant and the trauma experienced by the victims.

Up until 2004 Hualapai Tribal judges served as coroners. As the Chief Judge I was the Chief Coroner. In talks or conversations about being a judge I often said, "I see dead people," humor being a very important weapon against trauma.

Seriously and sadly however I knew almost every one of the persons whose body I had to enter an order for removal and release to county officials. It was the worst part of judging for me.

One order that strained my spirit the most was regarding a young lady who took her own life by hanging. It is one of those experiences that really cannot be unremembered.

The majority of deaths and attending conduct that became Court cases were caused by drinking and drugging. Our tribe and many others lose many family and tribal members far before their time due to substance abuse, especially alcohol.

Our community response was to plan the Hualapai Wellness Court, a tribal institution that is empowered by the formula TJ +, Therapeutic Jurisprudence Plus.[61] We first operated an adult wellness court and worked with the juveniles. The Hualapai Wellness Court became one of the first tribal mentor courts for a short time. Tribal court staff from Tribal Nations visited us and observed how we operated our Court. In one session one young lady did not want to cooperate and ran out the door, an incident that the observers probably experienced at some point later.

The hope for each Wellness Court defendant, each minor and family, with the help of the Team and counselor(s), was that they create a Wellness Plan that directed a more positive path and journey. Wellness Plans incorporated a number of what was at that time called wellness activities like counseling and exercise. We hoped that counseling would lead to the root of the abusive behavior, recognize the source of the disconnection—whatever it was that affected the participant's sense of peace.

Other activities like exercise were included as Wellness Plan elements in order to promote health and wellness. Wellness Plans sought reconnection for the Participant, new and better connections, and stronger internal and external relationships that support a healing journey.

Our Wellness Court participants, as did the enquiring minor, experienced a history of disconnecting events and situations. They experienced a lot of trauma. Part of the healing required that they talk trauma out somehow, let it go, learn what lessons are available, then move on. While the counseling ordered was intended to allow both individual and group communication for Wellness Court participants, the Wellness Court Team looked for other ways to promote connectivity and positive relationships.

My experience shows me that without confronting the source of trauma fully, the individual is less able to cope with all sorts of stimuli and can end up drinking again, perhaps causing more stress and trauma to others and themselves.

The goal, however, of having sustained sources of positive connection, activity, support, was and is difficult to obtain in a community where many are disconnected and disengaged. It remains tremendously challenging to maintain visions of health, wellness and peace for one's community and relatives

---

[61] *Id.* at 424–36, for further description about therapeutic jurisprudence and Tribal Healing to Wellness Courts.

when there are so many obstacles and struggles. In my talking with those who appeared before me I attempted to extend a tether, particular to the minors, a link to some significant fact or observation that might stimulate sight. For instance, I would say, "you descend from a chief and start acting like it," a connection that most of the time the juvenile was not aware of.

Possibility, fortunately, is one of the Sphere's primary considerations. Positive visions for the future, seeing something far ahead that's good, is one of the ways to maintain a forward motion. Seeking visions is a primary ceremony for Indigenous people throughout the world.

The sense of working towards both personal and collective goals provides a much-needed motivation to maintain pace and stamina.

Identifying and securing useful connections and relationships that further momentum are central to the Spirituality of Law Analysis and Warrior of Law Approach. In the Analysis and Approach Confrontation is compelled, Communication is engaged, and Compromise is negotiated in order to move towards Concord, Accord, or Peace. All Spherical considerations are applied and studied as thoroughly as possible to gain the most insight. The situation is looked at from both a conflict and cooperation perspective. Individual or citizen and collective or community aspects are explored, and understandings and perceptions of right and wrong are acknowledged. After all the aspects and considerations of the Sphere are contemplated a complete record of information is assembled and available to help make comprehensive decisions and plans.

The U.S. Substance Abuse and Mental Health Services Administration (SAMSHA) references the following terms in describing a trauma informed approach: realizes, recognizes, responds, and retraumatizes. These terms generally reflect the importance of acknowledging trauma exists, that it may be a factor, that the response is informative and appropriate, and that actions and conduct do not cause the person to be retraumatized. I think I SAMSHA-fy this trauma-informed characterization. I also think that my personality and nature, and my life experiences lay a solid informational base and foundation that helped prepare me for serving as a judge for my people.

My efforts to assist in the development of the Hualapai Wellness Court were encouraged and guided by my understanding of how alcohol abuse restrains my Peoples' ability to Gather, Ground, and Grow. Serving as both a planner and judge allowed me to help plan and build or rebuild our Nation as well as address all sorts of disconnection, that is, crime and conflict.

The spiritual nature of law helps tie society and people together. Law prescribes the parameters of human relationships and interaction. The lack of a legal framework or a general code of conduct creates chaos for a society. A body of rules and guidelines encourages and prescribes acceptable behavior, in hopes of discouraging conflict and disconnection. Trauma is a source of significant disconnection.

A Warrior of Law

1. Considers, appreciates and calculates the spiritual nature of law;
2. Is conscious of the need to maintain connection;
3. Identifies disconnection and works to secure reconnections or new and better connections.

I understand, describe and address law in a particular way. I believe law as a very spiritual construct, that is, law is about relationships, between the government and the citizen, between individuals, between nations. Law provides the framework with which a People Gather Ground and Grow. The building of the Sphere places Law and Spirituality/Spirit together on the same axis. In other words, in the Sphere, Law and Spirituality are synonymous.

Spherical Approach and Analysis facilitate the formulation of personal and collective visions and provide structure from which to produce roadmaps and guides for strategic responses. Warriors of Law are trauma informed

Self-Care and Collective Care Practices

Self-care is often seen by trauma experts as being integral to working with trauma, as part of what Laura van Dernoot Lipsky[62] calls "trauma stewardship" which is the connection in working with trauma between our responsibilities to both provide care and to support our own capacity to help. In writing this book, self-care and connecting with care from helping professionals was seen as part of the process as was collective-care through regular group processing and debriefing. Below we reflect on the importance of not only self-care but collective care, as trauma arises not just in individuals but in a collective manner, from both collective trauma and the trauma people experience uniquely as individuals.

Self-Care and Collective Care

Self-care and collective care both involve mindful awareness and presence with our own needs for support, and the needs of others, usually in both cases involving the vulnerable step of asking for help. Law is imbued with a "do it yourself" mentality. However, we lawyers are also human beings who, just like all other humans, are social beings who cannot self-regulate solely in isolation. Well-being requires having the awareness and capacity to have a nonjudgmental relationship with ourselves, and our communities, and the needs that arise in each. Collective care practices can include providing a positive culture to support needs that may differ from our own, or the practice of some of the tools described in this chapter alongside or

---

[62] Laura van Dernoot Lipsky & Connie Burk, Trauma stewardship: an everyday guide to caring for self while caring for others (San Francisco: Berrett-Koehler Publishers, 2009).

in dialogue with others. In the next section on judges and courts you'll find a discussion of self-care and collective care from Myrna McCallum.

Some Trauma-Informed Practices for Self or Collective Care: Self-Awareness, Support, and Referrals

Increasing Self-Awareness and the Ability to Be Present

Helgi Maki

After a traumatic loss, I experienced decades of insomnia plus chronic back pain and body tension sometimes called "body armoring." It was distracting and interfered with my ability to be present with clients or even myself. Despite experiencing discomfort for a long time, once I began learning to practice movement and mindfulness regularly (meaning daily or weekly, depending on the practice) the sleeplessness and pain dramatically improved. After only a few months of dedicated practice with professional instructors, my experience with pain shifted. Some clients commented that I seemed more calm or positive and a few remarked on feeling "safe" with me. My practices include strengthening exercises, restorative movement and a variety of meditation practices including mindful walking (written about by Thich Nhat Hanh) and yoga nidra (a mindful body-scan technique). In addition, I have received support and education through psychotherapy for many years. During times of loss or grief I've found that insomnia or chronic pain can return somewhat, so I am reminded that the journey of trauma and grief is a continuous learning process at all levels and I need to learn new trauma-informed skills on an ongoing basis.

Finding Support

J. Kim Wright

In my first book, *Lawyers as Peacemakers*, I shared the story about being traumatized by a case. The basic facts were horrible enough: three small children, a house fire, a meth-addicted mother was convicted of intentionally setting the fire. The father, grandfather, and aunt of the children sat with me for seven hours as they told all the grisly details. He shared photos of the children and newspaper articles and told me about the evidence that was presented in court. The fire chief and police chief who investigated the case died of suicide and a heart attack not long after the fire. At trial, the judge apologized to the jury and offered counseling to them all.

At the end of our meeting, they told me that no one else had ever listened to them the way I had. They had never been able to share all of their pain and memories. Their church family was polite but avoided them. Neighbors nodded and rushed inside. They'd been left to handle their pain on their own. Not everyone had done well with that. The distraught father was on a disability pension and living in his parents' basement. The parents held their own grief and watched their son deteriorate from his grief.

On the way to the train after the long day of listening, the grandfather took me aside and told me that they felt transformed; that they felt like they had a new beginning and could now heal from their losses. A few months later, an email came that let me know that they had indeed moved on with their lives. The father was working again and dating someone he hoped to marry. It was the best possible outcome for them, even though the mother later asked to pull out of the restorative justice documentary and we didn't finish that process.

But that day, I was completely depleted. I am good at my job and I listened to them like emptying a vessel of their pain. I gave everything I had and then some.

But the tiredness didn't just go away. It stayed with me. I felt numb for months.

Three months later, my next restorative justice case was a famous murder case with a lot of previous media attention. I was hired by a producer who was pushing to get it done and filmed. The military officer husband (who I will call Gary) had killed his wife, dumped her body on a deserted road, and then walked around free for years before the wife's family hired a private investigator to uncover the facts. [That story isn't quite accurate but you really don't want to know the rest.]

A male colleague and I were sent to interview Gary in prison. As anyone who has visited a prison knows, we had to go through a search, produce identification, and were under careful watch during the visit. Gary spent the entire interview talking to me, ignoring my male colleague. To me, it was obvious that he was trying to manipulate me. He really wanted to be on television and to look like he was rehabilitated and it was all just a mistake (evidence and conviction notwithstanding). There was no genuine remorse. I was uncomfortable and told my colleague that I would not be taking the case. I said that I believed we'd just spoken with a sociopath. My colleague was oblivious and thought I was making it all up.

Two weeks later, my opinion was further validated when a letter from the prison arrived at my home address. Gary had obtained my address from the ID which I used to enter the prison and was still trying to persuade me. Knowing he would someday be released was a factor in moving out of my house later that year.

These two cases represented all my nightmares come true. I was not equipped or supported in how to deal with such matters. It might expand the picture if you know that I am one of those mothers who not only raised my birth children but several step-children and foster children. The idea of a mother killing her own children goes against everything I am. I also experienced years of domestic violence and death threats in my first marriage. There were many times when I feared for my life. I was the director of a domestic violence shelter and worked closely with victims and one of my clients was killed by her husband. The two cases were way too close to home.

I decided to quit restorative justice, although I was exceptionally skilled and did a lot of good work there. I thought I just wasn't good at compartmentalizing.

Years later, in a conversation with international restorative justice leader, Dominic Barter, he told me that he never led a workshop or worked with clients without having a full team on stand-by. This team was not for client emergencies, rather it was for his own support, a container for the emotions that arise in him.

We lawyers are taught that we can't discuss our cases with anyone due to confidentiality concerns. We are cautioned to keep it all to ourselves, to be rational and distant from our feelings. Therapists, on the other hand, also hold their clients' confidences but create outlets for themselves. Supervision is a long-valued tradition among therapists. It is sometimes seen as advanced training but often includes mentorship, counseling, and support. It is thought that therapists can be better at their jobs if they can discuss their cases, look at their own triggers, and develop action plans with another trained therapist.

How can we lawyers get the support we need? The collaborative practice model offers possibilities for lawyers to consider. In collaborative practice, a team works together to support divorcing couples. The team generally includes at least one mental health practitioner. (Depending on the model, there may be two mental health practitioners, each working with one of the parties.) The participation agreement and engagement with the client set out this relationship which are generally intended to benefit the clients. They make it clear that information is going to be shared and the therapists provide emotional and psychological support to the clients to help them in the divorce process.

Sometimes the mental health practitioners come in handy for the lawyers, too.

I was representing a medical professional in his divorce. His wife had initiated the divorce. They had two children. He worked all the time and was a distant dad. The case went like most cases do until one day my client came into my office. He explained that he wanted to transfer all the property to the wife, that he'd set up accounts for the children, and that he planned to kill himself in a few weeks when I'd completed the appropriate transfers.

They really didn't train us for this in law school but what is there to do when the client is sitting in front of me? I was nonjudgmental. I listened, asked curious questions, including asking him if he'd thought about the impact on the children. He assured me that it would look like a terrible accident and they wouldn't have to live with the fact of their father's suicide. I asked him if he was under a doctor's care and he explained that he couldn't be straight with his own doctor and wouldn't ask for counseling or medication, out of fear of losing his own professional license. We talked about PTSD and whether that might be playing a role in his decision. He'd never heard of it but proceeded to tell me stories about what he'd seen in the emergency room, horrible stories that I don't want to remember even as I write this. I let him tell them, relieving himself of the pain and the secrecy.

And when he left the office, I called the mental health practitioner on the collaborative team, as much for me as for the client. He listened as I told him the story, what I said, what might happen next. He helped me devise a plan of action.

And, the plan apparently worked. The client decided that maybe he wasn't going to work in the emergency room anymore and opened a different kind of practice . [As I wrote this, I decided to check to see how he was and searched Google. I'm happy to report that he is still working in a small-town practice in a less traumatic specialty, many years later.]

The feelings around the third story and the first two are very different for me. The latter is a memory that I can recall but has very little charge. The first two are often cause for reflection. I notice that I still hold that lawyer attitude that I should have been better, should have been able to compartmentalize my feelings and carry on.

The work of Evan Seamone on Veterans Treatment Courts is a rich repository of information worthy of a book of its own, including the below contribution on effective referral strategies for special populations like veterans.

The Art of Referral[63]

Evan Seamone[64]

Key elements of effective referral apply regardless of whether the "other professional" is a doctor, psychiatrist, priest, shaman, spiritual guide, or even a veterans' peer group leader. Within the area of clergy-clinician collaboration, researchers note that referrals can be done competently or ineffectively.[65] Along these lines, legal scholars observe that "[t]he lawyer's advice [regarding referral] should be substantive and not end with a general recommendation to get

---

[63] Excerpted with the author's permission from EVAN R. SEAMONE, THE COUNTERINSURGENCY IN LEGAL COUNSELING: PREPARING ATTORNEYS TO DEFEND COMBAT VETERANS AGAINST THEMSELVES IN CRIMINAL CASES IN THE ATTORNEY'S GUIDE TO DEFENDING VETERANS IN CRIMINAL COURT 299–336, 309 (Brockton D. Hunter & Ryan C. Else, Editors, 2014).

[64] Evan R. Seamone is a health care law attorney at Loxley Services, specializing in veterans' health care issues.

[65] See generally Mark R. McMinn et al., Basic and Advanced Competence in Collaborating with Clergy, 34 PROF. PSYCHOLOGY: RES. & PRAC. 197 (2002).

help," since "vague advice . . . may be viewed as unhelpful to a client."[66] Building on this important lesson, the defense attorney should consider the following measures as means to ensure the effective representation of the combat veteran client.

Key Attributes of Effective Referral

♦ Make personal contact with prospective referral sources before recommending them to clients.

♦ Interview professionals to determine their experience treating clients with PTSD or service-connected disorders.

♦ Obtain their views on continued relationships with attorneys, sharing information, and collaborating in furtherance of the client's well-being.

♦ Identify potential conflicting aims, such as differing views on sin, repentance, confessions, and other matters that could interfere with the objectives of the legal representation.

♦ Consider measures to avoid triggering professional reporting requirements of domestic violence or other matters that would harm the client's legal interests.

♦ Explore the other professional's treatment objectives and whether the professional is willing to address litigation-related stressors.

Many of the above concerns are based on "mutual knowledge problems" in which the two professionals operate on "different information and contextual understandings," including "different vocabularies, value assumptions, and helping milieus."[67] Attorneys easily miss these distinctions because referral normally marks the termination of a relationship for persons other than lawyers.[68] However, this is not an option for the defense counsel given the ongoing nature of the legal relationship. When attorneys are unmindful of these referral considerations, opportunities abound for inconsistent and conflicting advice from counselors. The client's dilemma becomes prioritizing which counselor's concerns are valid and which are not. Placing a traumatized veteran client in the

---

[66] For more on the value of attorney referral to clergy members, see generally Evan R. Seamone, *Divine Intervention: The Ethics of Religion, Spirituality, and Clergy Collaboration in Legal Counseling*, 29 QUINNIPIAC L. REV. 289 (2011).

[67] Carol M. Suzuki, *When Something Is Not Quite Right: Considerations for Advising a Client to Seek Mental Health Treatment*, 6 HASTINGS RACE & POVERTY L.J. 244 (2009) ("Some lawyers are resistant to considering psychological needs of a client when providing legal counseling, believing that mental health referral is 'social work' that is not appropriate for lawyers.").

[68] McMinn et al., *supra* note 65, at 201. *See also* GARY B. MELTON ET AL., PSYCHOLOGICAL EVALUATIONS FOR THE COURTS: A HANDBOOK FOR MENTAL HEALTH PROFESSIONALS AND LAWYERS 5–15 (3d ed. 2007) (describing "some of the perceived 'clashes' between law and mental health professions [that] reflect fundamental conceptual differences").

position where he is forced to prefer one professional over the other cannot help the legal representation. The resulting distress may very well aggravate the client's symptoms and erode established trust in the attorney–client relationship. It can equally distance the attorney from the other professional.

PART II

Systems, Groups (or Organizations), and Legal Culture

Trauma can impact or even overwhelm systems, groups, or organizations, and systems recognizing this have already begun trauma-informed systems changes.[1] Numerous trauma experts, including Nadine Burke Harris, Gabor Maté, and Bessel van der Kolk, have observed that trauma is a silent epidemic in North America and in many countries around the world. Significant law and policy responses have also begun to emerge. Federal U.S. legislation has been introduced as well, and "bench cards" have been created for judges working in juvenile justice to better deal with trauma. Many states, including Massachusetts, California, and Oregon, have begun including lawyers and legal clinics in their trauma-informed care initiatives.[2] Trauma-informed courts exist in Arizona, Colorado, Idaho, and Tennessee, and restorative (or wellness) courts such as addiction courts, mental health courts, and veterans' courts exist in many other jurisdictions in North America and around the world.[3] Canada has begun offering or requiring training about trauma for judges in some jurisdictions. Globally, trauma-informed justice work is being done at community and government levels in numerous regions and countries, including the Caribbean, the Democratic Republic of Congo, India, Kenya, Nigeria, Rwanda, Scotland, and Vietnam.

Legal Systems and the Impact of Trauma

In the following chapters, our focus shifts from addressing trauma in individuals and practices to addressing it (including as a leverage point for systems change) in

[1] Judith Herman discusses the capacity of trauma to overwhelm systems of care. JUDITH HERMAN, TRAUMA AND RECOVERY: THE AFTERMATH OF VIOLENCE—FROM DOMESTIC ABUSE TO POLITICAL TERROR (New York: Basic Books, 1992).

[2] Mallika Kaur, *Negotiating Trauma & Teaching Law*, 35 J. LAW & SOCIAL POL'Y, 113–19 (2021), https://digital commons.osgoode.yorku.ca/jlsp/vol35/iss1/6.

[3] Other "training for change" initiatives have been educating professionals to effect systems change, for instance the "Smart Justice" and trauma-informed care training approach in Scotland and the "training for change" approach developed by Dr. Alisha Moreland-Capuia, which began in Oregon and has since moved to the Harvard Law School and Harvard Medical Network through McLean Hospital. For further information, see https://home.mcleanhospital.org/ce-itisc.

the legal system as a whole, including its key parts—the courts that are our forums, the legal education we all continuously engage in, and the systemic legal culture as a whole as illustrated in the figure below. Of course, the people who work in these systems, including judges, law professors, and other legal professionals, are individuals whose experiences are worthy of considering through the lens of the principles discussed in Part I.

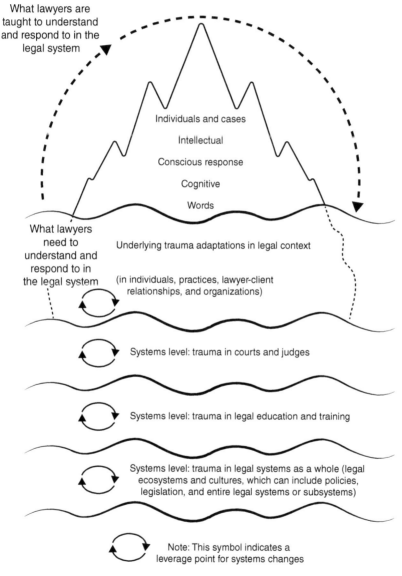

Understanding and Responding to Trauma in the Legal System
Image credit: Helgi Maki

We emphasize in this section that systems include collectives of humanity—human collectives and the collective trauma they carry. Attorney and activist Sherri Mitchell from the Penobscot Nation writes about the collective trauma and "soul wound" that Native Americans have suffered. Myrna McCallum has observed that there's a parallel to be found between the group trauma and patterns of historical pain Mitchell is acknowledging and what we experience individually and collectively in the legal profession. Mitchell describes group trauma as follows:

> Group trauma is passed along in ways that impact the entire group. Group trauma can lead to distorted thinking, which often manifests as internalized oppression, as people try to maintain some sense of misplaced control over the circumstances of their oppression. In addition, trauma from longstanding oppression can leave the group huddled together in a form of stagnated solidarity. When anyone tries to move beyond the place of suffering that the group has occupied, they are attacked by the group and brought back down. Some within the group may feel a sense of loyalty to the suffering that the group has endured, and they hold onto it as an act of allegiance. Others attach their identity to the suffering and no longer know who they are beyond its boundaries. In instances like this, the group has become a place holder for the pain, a living memorial to the trauma that the group has experienced. When the trauma becomes a badge of identity or a living shrine, it's very difficult for the people to consider a new path forward.[4]

Mitchell encourages the acknowledgment of the pain carried individually and collectively, instead of allowing it to persist silently within people and groups:

> When we don't allow ourselves to acknowledge the pain—the deep, agonizing soul pain that results from historical trauma—we aren't able to recognize that we are all carrying some measure of that pain within us. Instead, we allow it to isolate us and keep us cut off from one another. We also fail to recognize that the cause of that pain is not only a violation against us, it is a violation against life itself, and its mournful cries echo through our DNA, and become lodged in our genetic memory.[5]

The importance of understanding the impact of trauma on legal systems, including large groups within the system, cannot be overstated, as political unrest, crimes against humanity, war, and trauma are inseparable. Trauma expert Vamik Volkan[6]

---

[4] SHERRI MITCHELL, SACRED INSTRUCTIONS: INDIGENOUS WISDOM FOR LIVING SPIRIT-BASED CHANGE (Berkeley, CA: North Atlantic Books, 2018).

[5] Id.

[6] VAMIK VOLKAN, KILLING IN THE NAME OF IDENTITY: A STUDY OF BLOODY CONFLICTS (Charlottesville, VA: Pitchstone Publishers, 2006). Vamik D. Volkan, *Trauma, Prejudice, Large-Group Identity and Psychoanalysis*, 81(2) AM. J. PSYCHOANALYSIS 137–54 (2021), doi:10.1057/s11231-021-09285-z, https://www.ncbi.nlm.nih.gov/pmc/articles/PMC8097112/; VAMIK VOLKAN, PSYCHOANALYSIS, INTERNATIONAL RELATIONS AND DIPLOMACY (London: Routledge, 2019), https://www.taylorfrancis.com/books/mono/10.4324/9780429478871/psychoanalysis-international-relations-diplomacy-vamik-volkan?refId=f2d66c23-6b91-4514-8971-f2605959ab1d&context=ubx.

has observed from his work facilitating international peace negotiations, including in the Middle East and former Soviet Union, that political ideology (including fascism and other extremisms) and trauma transmission are intertwined, as a population's prior historical experience of trauma may create underlying psychological dynamics that can motivate aggression.

David Bedrick[7] observed (on Facebook):

Did you know that trauma makes it more likely folks will turn to fundamentalisms and forms of spiritual bypass? Here's how.

Firstly, a traumatic event is often more powerful than anything we have experienced before; it is too big for us to cope with or to hold. In this way, it appears to be all powerful—omnipotent.

Secondly, the unyielding grip it has on our lives demands relief. As such, we are desperate for a kind of redemption—to be rescued, "saved" from its torment.

Thirdly, wrestling with trauma leads us on a confused search for understanding, for meaning. Its impact transcends the mundane and all logic. It seems mysterious, numinous. In this way, our relationship with its impact may be interpreted as spiritual.

When we don't deal with our trauma directly, we abandon not only the terrifying and painful crisis, we also abandon ourselves. In this abandonment and trauma's seemingly spiritual dimension, we may reach out to a belief system that affords us some hope.

We grasp onto this belief with a religious zeal and are threatened by anything that calls that belief into question. We protect it with our lives, knowing somewhere inside of us that if the belief weren't there, we would fall back into trauma's abyss.

We become fundamentalists, proselytizing and "selling" the insights, "truths," and path that has saved us from our horror. However, in our blindness to our own pain, we also become blind to others. This is what I believe are the underlying dynamics of what is now called spiritual bypass.

---

[7] David Bedrick, "Did You Know that Trauma Makes It More Likely Folks Will Turn to Fundamentalisms and Forms of Spiritual Bypass?" Apr. 6, 2022, https://www.facebook.com/DBedrick/. Reprinted with permission of the author. David is a speaker, teacher, and attorney and author of the acclaimed *Talking Back to Dr. Phil: Alternatives to Mainstream Psychology* and his new book *Revisioning Activism: Bringing Depth, Dialogue, and Diversity to Individual and Social Change.* David spent eight years on the faculty of the University of Phoenix and has taught for the U.S. Navy, 3M, psychological associations, and small groups. He has received notable awards for teaching, employee development, and legal service to the community. David completed graduate work in psychology at the University of Minnesota and clinical training at the Process Work Institute, where he is a diplomate and adjunct faculty member as well as a member of the ethics committee and the advisory board for the master of arts program in conflict facilitation. As a practitioner of process-oriented psychology—a branch of Jungian psychology—he has worked with groups, couples, and individuals for more than 20 years.

CHAPTER 6

Trauma and Healing in Legal Systems: Courts and Judges

We Need Judges to Embrace a Trauma-Informed Judicial Practice

Myrna McCallum

You need not be a trauma expert to take on a trauma-informed judicial practice or to embrace trauma-informed lawyering. Do you meet trauma in the courtroom? Do you sometimes feel the traumas of others following you home? If your answer is yes to either question, then this approach to practice is for you.

I am often quick to admit that I am no expert in trauma, but I am not convinced that is an entirely correct statement. I was born into a violent environment, so trauma has lived with me for a long time. I have also worked as a defense lawyer and a prosecutor, so I can rightly state that I have worked in an environment that routinely displayed violence, communicated violence, felt like violence, and called on me to participate in perpetuating violence.

I believe my personal and professional exposure and responses to traumas makes me sufficiently qualified to engage you in this conversation. After all, who better to contemplate trauma-informed courts and judges than a former litigator and adjudicator who not only knows trauma but participated in causing trauma for others? What does this admission mean? It means that our legal processes are inherently traumatizing, we must acknowledge this fact. Once we do, we can begin to explore ways in which we can minimize the traumatic impact our courts have on everyone who enters.

This chapter explains why we need trauma-informed judges and identifies key focus areas that can turn even the most "thick-skinned" and resistant jurists into practitioners of compassionate inquiry (as per Gabor Maté's practice). In this chapter, I also explore how trial judges can cause trauma for themselves and others by unknowingly or recklessly permitting trauma to enter the courtroom with little to no regard for their gatekeeping responsibility; and by not giving a second thought to how the presentation of traumatic evidence is admitted in proceedings where the evidence is not being challenged by the litigants without regard for how the exposure may adversely impact court staff, litigants, and lawyers. I also introduce the subject of vicarious trauma as I have come to recognize it in myself, some colleagues, and some judges so we can all learn to identify when we are slipping before we find ourselves on our knees unable to get up. One quick note, I recently spoke with Gabor Maté and he said that vicarious trauma is not what we experience, in fact, it is personal trauma triggered. Something to consider.

This chapter concludes with recommendations that every justice participant and especially system leaders who value the mental health and wellness of their judges can act upon to identify, prevent, and possibly eliminate harm and trauma experienced in the workplace.

Reliving Trauma

We are, as a collective, a traumatized society. If we had not already experienced direct or intergenerational trauma prior to the Covid-19 pandemic, we are certainly experiencing mass pandemic trauma, here and now. Yes, it is a thing, look it up. I am often shocked at how many participants in my various training sessions tell me that they have never experienced any trauma. However, when I ask participants to think of "trauma" as "loss," more people are quick to acknowledge their losses and feelings of instability, disconnection, and vulnerability following a loss. From loss, most folks can directly link the loss to an event, usually a traumatic or distressing event. I think every traumatic event creates loss.

Once participants have accepted that they have experienced trauma, I invite them to engage in a self-awareness exercise. How have your traumas created triggers? What are your triggers? You know, those swift and irrational emotional reactions that erupt without warning, especially in the face of shame, anger, rage, grief, sorrow, or silence, which may take you by surprise and are rarely considered reasonable in the circumstances. Lawyers, I am sure you have seen triggers in judges. Judges, I am certain you have seen triggers present in counsel, accused persons, victims, and witnesses. Triggers present when you do not feel safe or, more pointedly, when you feel under threat—even when no threat is present.

You may be wondering what triggers have to do with trauma in the courtroom and why your triggers matter. The easiest explanation is this: you bring your entire self to the workplace, to your professional relationships, to the dais from whereupon you judge matters, day in and day out. If you have not engaged in a self-awareness practice, your traumas and triggers will ultimately drive your engagement in the courtroom. You may become explosive, avoidant, withdrawn or detached, and desensitized. There is no judgment in this statement, this is simply how the brain responds when it is either reliving trauma or experiencing triggers. It is in this reactive state that we often do so much harm to ourselves and to others. This chapter has been written to help you reflect on how we can all do less harm by embracing a trauma-informed practice.

Practice Self-Reflection

We cannot change what we refuse to see. Self-reflection can serve as your best friend to help you determine what you can and cannot change about the way you and others experience the courtroom. Are there decisions that you make each day that may adversely impact your mental health and the well-being of those who work in or visit your courtroom? When you are about to sit for a trial involving significant acts of violence, especially sexual violence perpetuated on the vulnerable, which may include images and sounds, how do you prepare yourself and your court staff for the trauma that will inevitably enter the courtroom and their consciousness? What, if any, conversations do you engage in with counsel to determine whether any uncontested evidence can be submitted by way of a written agreed statement of facts? What about after the fact? What conversations do you have then? And with whom?

It is critical to understand that although you may have grown "a thick-skin" or believe yourself to be impervious to the effects of human suffering experienced by others, the same may not be true for those who are sitting in the courtroom with you. When trauma is invited in unchecked and allowed to take up space so those present have no choice but to look at it and listen to it, in all its damaging forms, do you ask yourself: What harm am I causing? What harm am I perpetuating against myself and those who work around me?

Everyone needs a safe and healthy workplace, but not everyone experiences the workplace in this way. Oftentimes safety and health in the legal workplace is eroded due to the continuous decisions of judges throughout a proceeding (which are not restricted to evidentiary issues and the conduct of direct and cross examination of witnesses). These decisions include how they respond to counsel or witnesses, including the hostile or impatient messaging presenting in their demeanor (especially when frustrated with counsel), and extending to how they open and close the courtroom, which communicate expressly and implicitly their role and relationship to the participants in the courtroom. Sometimes, simply opening court with a pleasant "good morning" can go a long way to easing folks into what everyone knows could be a challenging workday.

Even though some employee groups have unions representing their interests, not all employees will speak up when they experience harm for a variety of reasons. Trauma, sometimes, is a silencer. So, I invite you to ask yourself: What is your responsibility for creating a safe and healthy workplace for yourself, litigants, lawyers, and court staff? Are you open and sufficiently welcoming so others can approach you with their traumatizing experiences? Your increased awareness on this issue coupled with these self-reflection questions are foundational to becoming a trauma-informed judge.

What Is a Trauma-Informed Judge?

A trauma-informed judge has been trained to recognize trauma when it presents and has learned how trauma impacts the brain, especially communication, memory, and attention. A trauma-informed judge has learned critical skills, such as empathy, patience, and compassionate inquiry, and can recognize when these skills require application. A trauma-informed judge can respond to trauma when it presents in others by creating space for emotional expression or inquiring about whether litigants have had access to available support. A trauma-informed judge is sufficiently skilled to recognize when warnings are required for court staff who may be emotionally unprepared or ill-equipped psychologically to confront the harm they may experience as a result of exposure to graphic and traumatic evidence. A trauma-informed judge will be able to apply their knowledge and skills to create a safe space where participants in the system, including witnesses, are better able to provide the evidence necessary for the judge to make a fair decision.

Undoubtedly, some judges will read this and infer that by demonstrating a responsive, empathetic, and compassionate demeanor in the courtroom in particular may make them vulnerable to claims of bias or a loss of objectivity. That argument is flawed, because practicing compassion is no different from practicing respect, especially if a compassionate approach applies to all persons in the courtroom and not just a single litigant. It is also critical to point out that our legal systems and justice processes have gained an unfavorable reputation, largely due to judges withholding compassion, patience, and empathy in the courtroom, opting instead to display arrogance, intolerance, and indignation. Choosing to display a trauma-informed practice could only serve to improve a feared, flawed, and fraught environment.

Why Do We Need Trauma-Informed Judges?

If you are not feeling psychologically safe, centered, and well when you come into the courtroom, no one else will feel psychologically safe, centered, and well either, because we cannot offer what we do not have. In addition to ensuring that court staff enjoy a safe and healthy workplace, which respects their mental health, litigants are entitled to be free from excessively traumatizing practices when they come into the courtroom. I state "excessively" because I am fully aware that our court processes and justice system is fundamentally traumatizing for many litigants, especially victims of violence.

There are steps, however, that judges can take to ensure that no single person is excessively subjected to dehumanizing, degrading, and disrespectful experiences in the courtroom that add to their traumas. Judges are aware of their duty to act as gatekeepers and to ensure that any line of questioning by lawyers is reasonable in the circumstances. When judges fail to act on their duties and responsibilities then a traumatic experience is a likely outcome for the litigant—and others who witness the verbal or psychological attack on the litigant.

A trauma-informed judge will not only recognize and uphold their gatekeeping duties but also proactively inquire with counsel about any possibilities to admit graphic evidence in a manner that does not expose everyone in the courtroom to the risk of traumatization. Where mitigation or prevention of displaying traumatic evidence is not possible, a trauma-informed judge will inquire about the needs of court staff to either take several breaks throughout the proceeding and/or switch out with other colleagues.

Finally, a trauma-informed trial judge will check-in with court staff and others to remind every person present that self-care and collective-care practices, including peer support, may be necessary to address and debrief their exposure to traumatic material. This same check-in applies to judges, too. You should be asking: What did I see? What did I hear? How did it impact me? Do I need to talk it out or otherwise let it go, or am I going to take it home?

Self-Care and Collective Care

Now, I am certain you are wondering what "care" has to do with the courtroom experience? The simple answer is everything. Furthermore, I am fully aware that the concept of "self-care" may be foreign to some, especially those who have lived lives of survival, which demanded that they care for others, at the cost of neglecting their own needs; this can especially be the case for Black, brown, and Indigenous people. However, I need to communicate that regardless of how you perceive the practice of self-care and collective care, it is imperative that you, as a leader in the courtroom with all your power and privilege, engage others in this conversation while also making this practice a priority.

What you need to understand is that without taking on a routine practice that prioritizes checking in with yourself (self-care) to see how you are coping while also checking in with those around you (collective care) to ask how they are coping, there will never be honest conversations about how mental health can be adversely impacted in the courtroom. Empathetic judges will leave the judiciary devastated and forever damaged. Committed court staff will leave their jobs to engage in intensive and extensive therapy. Driven lawyers will find themselves drowning in addiction, debt, or depression, resulting from their futile attempts to suppress their adverse and traumatic experiences so they can continue to do the job. We have seen far too many times how the legal profession has destroyed the mental health and wellness of lawyers, not only in leading them to experience depression and addiction but also disbarment and, sometimes, death by suicide.

We need to hear judges openly engage in conversations about mental health and the effect of trauma on the judiciary and the legal profession, if we are ever going to make space for understanding the extent to which trauma impacts judges, lawyers, and court staff. Judges have a critical role to play in modeling a practice of openness and creating psychological safety so that it becomes permissible to discuss how trauma in the courts has adversely impacted ourselves and others.

Contrary to what you may tell yourself about being able to separate your heart from your mind, compartmentalizing or suppressing your fears and traumas is not always an accessible or reliable strategy. I can also tell you that when a judge or lawyer is not prioritizing their mental health and wellness, they usually display explosive, disorganized, distracted, or disassociated characteristics, which everyone can see and feel. These are the judges no one wants to appear in front of, and these are the judges who cause lawyers to experience a sinking, dreadful feeling when they know they will have to enter their courtroom. Are you one of those judges? If so, to borrow from Gabor Maté's compassionate inquiry approach, what happened to you?

Trauma is a traveler and if you are experiencing the impacts of trauma but not doing anything to address those impacts, you will intentionally, or unintentionally, cause trauma for others who work around you. Judges can unknowingly cause others trauma in many ways. As individuals who enjoy tremendous privilege, I ask that you critically reflect on the ways in which you have seen yourself (and others) invite trauma in or allow individuals to experience emotional distress in the courtroom with no regard for the long-term implications of such a traumatizing and reckless practice.

How Can We Recognize Vicarious Trauma?

In the context of the legal system, vicarious trauma is the phenomenon experienced by lawyers and judges who hear, see, or read about trauma on a regular basis, then begin to experience adverse mental health impacts similar to those who were directly victimized or traumatized. In effect, by being a witness to a traumatic event, we can experience the same or similar traumatic effects such as those described by Bessel van der Kolk.

In addition to experiencing irrational fears, intrusive thoughts, nightmares, migraines, insomnia, anxiety, depression, hopelessness, helplessness, or an inability to concentrate (just to name a few experiences), which are usually followed by unhealthy coping mechanisms, our views about the world change significantly or become damaged. For example, long-time lawyers and judges who have had repeated exposure to child pornography may be unable to walk by a playground and upon seeing a father play with his child look for signs of abuse or begin to believe that the world is an unsafe place for children. We may even become uncomfortable with showing our own children and grandchildren physical affection.

Once you commit to learning about trauma, including vicarious trauma, judges and lawyers can start to recognize to what extent they have been adversely affected by their repeated exposure to the traumas of others. They may even begin to recognize their own personal, unhealed traumas and how their own trauma experiences have collided with the traumas of others. Once awareness has been achieved, a resilience or, better yet, a recovery strategy can be put in place to begin to address, release, and overcome the debilitating, immobilizing, and traumatizing effects you have carried and attempted to hide from the view of others.

Resilience strategies are essential to addressing mental health and wellness in the judiciary. Every person needs a healthy coping strategy that will allow us to get through adversity and hard times. "Hard times" should not be interpreted solely as court matters involving graphic subject matter but should also contemplate the cumulative adverse impact that sometimes shows up weeks, months, and even years after exposure to graphic and traumatic content. Oftentimes, these effects are exacerbated by heavy workloads, exhaustion, isolation, and psychological stress in the workplace.

I cannot provide you with a "get-it-together quick" resilience recipe because it is not a one-size-fits-all sort of practice. What I can say is that it is imperative that you create a trusted support system that will hold you up when you are falling and will keep you accountable when you slip into negative coping practices. Engaging your colleagues in peer-support strategies such as a debriefing practice, which addresses how what you heard or saw impacted or triggered you and what you can do to address and release that as it comes up (and not later, because later hardly ever arrives for busy people) helps to curb the isolation many judges experience. It is important to understand that debriefing requires consent and is not an opportunity to share details about what you saw that triggered you or to engage in dark humor with a colleague; that practice does nothing but pass the trauma around.

Collective-care and self-care practices are critical, as is utilizing mindfulness methods to create an environment that is calm and focused. Identifying boundaries is equally important, because without healthy boundaries that allow you to feel safe and respected in the workplace, a terrible practice of martyrdom, inequity, and workaholism will emerge. In case you are not clear on how boundaries apply to your role on the court, consider this: boundaries mean that you are clear in your mind about what your role is and what you are there to do and what you cannot do. Litigants may come into court with unrealistic expectations of what can be achieved through a trial. When they arrive, they bring all their hurts, and often, a lifetime of injustices, seeking redress. You need to be transparent in what the court can and cannot do (in case their counsel has not taken the time to do so) and explain these limitations using plain language.

Finally, we all benefit from a daily ritual of releasing the traumas people bring into our work environments, so the stories, images, and experiences do not follow you home. For some, this means taking a walk to clear your head, and for others, it means getting some cardio going or taking up a yoga practice. For others, it is a mindfulness practice focused on releasing and restoring (see other sections of this book, which provide tools and resources on healing modalities and mindfulness practices). Whichever ritual you decide upon, you will experience benefits almost immediately. And, incidentally, so will everyone else who comes into contact with you.

Trauma-Informed Transformation in the Courts Requires Action

Becoming a trauma-informed judge is a significant step in the right direction; however, an individual approach to trauma-informed judicial practice cannot achieve lasting transformation. A trauma-informed approach to judicial practice requires rule changes, policy amendments, and action from leadership, including lawmakers, to achieve acceptance and sustainability.

It is also imperative that those who appoint judges reevaluate the qualities and competencies we value in judicial candidates. These competencies must include a proven practice of empathy, compassion, resilience, and a meaningful understanding and application of trauma-informed practice, including emotional intelligence. Maybe at the very least, judicial candidates must be forever teachable and possess an open mind, which will allow them to learn more about the lived experiences of those who will appear before them.

Lawmakers and those who are responsible for disciplining judges will also have to rethink how they provide support for judges who are adversely impacted by the exposure to graphic evidence in the execution of their judicial responsibilities. This includes creating a workplace culture that supports judges coming forward to disclose and requesting a leave to address and maintain their wellness. When a judge begins to demonstrate behaviors that suggest that their mental health is deteriorating, courts should have active support systems to hold that judge up. Upon their return to work, a collective-care practice must be operationalized to ensure that the reintegration experience is not overwhelming, alienating, or otherwise unsupported. This is a practice that must be modeled and prioritized in order to create and maintain a healthy workplace.

I cannot underscore enough how responses to judges who request support should be about rehabilitation and recovery, rather than ousting judges who display and communicate that they need help. Proactive steps taken by leaders, judicial council members, and lawmakers that center the mental health and well-being of judges will only positively influence the reputation of the judiciary as whole. A judge who experiences safety, support, and protection from their superiors will bring safety, support, and protection into the courtroom, which will benefit everyone. This is where real transformation begins, and this is how true trauma-informed justice happens.

Some Trauma-Informed Practice Frameworks for Judges and Courts: Judicial Distress, Trauma-Informed Courtrooms, and Sentencing

Australia's First Research Measuring Judicial Stress: What Does It Mean for Judicial Officers and the Courts?

Carly Schrever[1]

While recent decades had seen a seismic shift in awareness and understanding of mental ill-health within the legal profession, propelled by empirical research from around the world that consistently revealed alarmingly high rates of stress and depression among law students and practicing lawyers,[2] there remained no empirical research in Australia concerning work-related stress and vicarious trauma among the judiciary. To respond to this identified gap, a psychologically grounded, mixed-methods research project was undertaken through the University of Melbourne, in which 152 judicial officers from five Australian courts participated. The findings of the research are published, or are scheduled to be published, across three reports. The first report was published in 2019,[3] and it looked at *whether* judicial officers are stressed, compared to lawyers and the general population. The second, published in early 2021,[4] looked at *which* judicial officers are most stressed, and *why*. The third, to be published soon, explores the perceived sources and impacts of judicial stress, and ideas for court responses. The following is a summary of the key findings of the first and second reports. The key findings of the first report are as follows:

- On a standardized measure of "non-specific psychological distress," 52.9 percent scored in the moderate to very high ranges (compared with 32.8 percent of the general population: Schrever, Hulbert, and Sourdin 2019, 155).

[1] Carly Schrever is a lawyer, psychologist, and award-winning empirical researcher. She undertook Australia's first empirical study measuring stress and well-being among judges and magistrates.

[2] *See, e.g.,* Norm Kelk et al., *Courting the Blues: Attitudes towards Depression in Australian Law Students and Legal Practitioners*, Monograph, 2009-1, Brain & Mind Rsch. Inst. (Jan. 2009); Jared Chamberlain & James T. Richardson, *Judicial Stress: A Topic in Need of Research, in* STRESS, TRAUMA, AND WELLBEING IN THE LEGAL SYSTEM 269 (Monica K. Miller & Brian H. Bornstein eds., Oxford University Press, 2013).

[3] The first report: Carly Schrever, Carol Hulbert & Tania Sourdin, *The Psychological Impact of Judicial Work: Australia's First Research Measuring Judicial Stress and Wellbeing*, 28(3) J. JUD. ADMIN. 141–68 (2019).

[4] The second report: Carly Schrever, Carol Hulbert & Tania Sourdin, *Where Stress Presides: Predictors and Correlates of Stress among Australian Judges and Magistrates*, 29(2) PSYCHIATRY, PSYCH. & L., 290–322 (2022).

- On the World Health Organization's "Alcohol Use Disorders Identification Test" (AUDIT: Saunders et al. 1993), 30.6 percent of judicial officers scored in the medium to high-risk ranges (sometimes referred to as the ranges indicating "problematic" alcohol use)—a rate similar to the Australian legal profession (32 percent) but considerably higher than the general population (18.8 percent): Schrever, Hulbert, and Sourdin 2019, 162).

- Three-quarters (75.2 percent) of judicial officers had scores on at least one of the three burnout factors (exhaustion, cynicism, and reduced professional efficacy) that indicated some level of burnout risk—only one-quarter (24.8 percent) scored in the low-risk range all on three burnout factors (Schrever, Hulbert, and Sourdin 2019, 162).

- The overwhelming majority (83.6 percent) of judicial officers reported experiencing at least one symptom of secondary traumatic stress in the one week prior to completing the survey, and almost one-third (30.4 percent) scored in the moderate to severe ranges—the level at which formal assessment for PTSD may be warranted (Schrever, Hulbert, and Sourdin 2019, 159–161).

- Despite this, judicial officers' reported levels of mental health concerns were comparatively low—their rates of "moderate to severe" depressive and anxious symptoms were dramatically lower (approximately one third) than those of lawyers, and slightly lower also than those suggested for the general population (Schrever, Hulbert, and Sourdin 2019, 156–157).

- In addition, 62 percent reported finding judicial office a little or much less stressful than their previous careers (Schrever, Hulbert, and Sourdin 2019, 154), and 76 percent reported experiencing personal wellbeing and satisfaction related to their work most or almost all of the time (Schrever, Hulbert, and Sourdin 2019, 153–154).

The key findings of the second report were:

- Judicial stress across the jurisdictions was predicted by the extent to which judicial officers' "basic psychological needs" of autonomy, competence and relatedness were satisfied within their working environments. Relatedness satisfaction (i.e., the number and quality of authentic and trusting collegial relationships a judicial officer experiences) was the best predictor of judicial wellbeing (Schrever, Hulbert, and Sourdin 2022, 307–8).

- The *only* demographic factor that was robustly associated with levels of judicial stress was *jurisdiction*: judicial officers in the high-volume, lower courts were significantly more stressed across a range of measures than those in the higher and appellate courts. The greatest disparity was in levels of burnout exhaustion. There were no differences in judicial stress levels according to age, gender, seniority, geographical location, or area of legal practice (Schrever, Hulbert, and Sourdin 2022, 307–12).

◆ The higher stress experienced by lower-court judicial officers was almost entirely explained by their lower levels of basic psychological needs satisfaction—especially autonomy and relatedness (Schrever, Hulbert, and Sourdin 2022, 312).

The first report of Australia's first research measuring judicial stress and well-being has revealed a judiciary not yet in a mental health crisis but under considerable stress. The second report showed unequivocally that it is judicial officers in the high-volume, lower courts that experience the most stress, and that this appears to be due to fewer opportunities for autonomy and relatedness in those courts. This research provides the basis for beginning an *evidence-based* conversation on judicial well-being in Australia—which would be one that acknowledges the inevitability of some distress in judicial work, recognizes that judicial distress is not necessarily incompatible with high-level judicial performance, promotes open dialogue among judicial officers about the personal challenges of the work, encourages judges and magistrates to engage proactively with professional and peer support, and fosters a deepening of the sense of meaning and satisfaction that judicial officers derive from their work. In many Australian jurisdictions, this kind of conversation is already well underway, and underpinning structural and systemic changes to support judicial well-being.

Building a Trauma-Informed Court in Memphis, Tennessee[5]

Claire Chiamulera[6]

In downtown Memphis, three blocks from the Mississippi River, the Memphis and Shelby County Juvenile Court welcomes children and families who enter

---

[5] Claire Chiamulera, *Building a Trauma-Informed Court in Memphis, TN*, ABA, Apr. 1, 2021, https://www.americanbar.org/groups/public_interest/child_law/resources/child_law_practiceonline/january---december-2021/building-a-trauma-informed-court/. Reprinted with permission. This article highlights the innovative work of one of the National Council of Juvenile and Family Court Judges' Implementation Courts. It is reprinted from the recent publication, *Redefining Judicial Leadership: Stories of Transformative Practice*, a collection of articles showcasing several Implementation Courts and their work to improve court practice for children and families. Note that some time passed between when the articles were originally written and publication of the book so new developments at the court are not reflected. We are also aware that many of the innovations had to be discontinued when courts went on line during the pandemic.

[6] Claire Chiamulera is a legal editor for the ABA Center on Children and the Law, Washington, DC. She provides research, writing, editing, and design support for center projects focused on improving access to justice for children and families in the child welfare legal system.

its doors with a warm embrace. Classical music plays on the piano in the lobby. Doors are painted the colors of the rainbow, and a Dr. Seuss mural consumes a wall on the way to the child abuse department. Staff smile and show families where to wait. Signs indicate when and where cases will be heard. Attorneys quietly escort clients to assigned courtrooms when cases are called.

It wasn't always that way. When Judge Dan Michael became judge of the court in 2014, he walked into a courthouse with dark, paneled courtrooms, staid corridors lined with headshots of past judges, and closed windows with shades drawn. Families waited in an overcrowded, chaotic main hall, craning to hear each time the bailiff appeared and shouted the case name at the top of his lungs.

A trauma assessment conducted in 2015 by the National Council of Juvenile and Family Court Judges (NCJFCJ) outlined actions the court needed to take to become more trauma informed, and Judge Michael wasted no time in following through on those recommendations. He and his staff dramatically transformed the court culture and physical environment and adopted practices that were sensitive to child and family trauma. In the following pages, Judge Michael shares practices that he and his staff have adopted. For a more detailed picture of this court's efforts to become trauma-informed, see *Redefining Judicial Leadership: Stories of Transformative Practice.*

Assisting Children and Families Who Come to Court

Court staff greet children and families when they arrive, tell them where to sit, and ask them to watch whiteboards and an electronic case board for case information and court assignments. When a case is called, attorneys meet their clients in the waiting area and escort them to the courtroom. These efforts replace an age-old practice of having the courtroom bailiff yell case names as they are called, a practice that created chaos and confusion and left the safety of the courtroom unattended.

The court is also leveraging technology to inform clients about their cases. A software program allows the court to enter cell phone numbers of case parties. The program will then automatically send a text message reminder to parties the day before their case hearing with the hearing date, court address, and assigned courtroom number. On the day of the case, the parties, witnesses, and attorneys will receive a text informing them when their case is ready and the courtroom number.

Respecting Clients and Helping Them Understand Court Processes

Court staff are trained on how to talk to and engage children and families who come to court. Following guidance in the NCJFCJ Enhanced Resource Guidelines, judges control the courtroom in a way that is respectful and nonthreatening and engages the parties. For example, Judge Michael says he'll ask a child's name, then ask if the child prefers to be called Sam or Mr. Smith. He also asks the child a direct question, such as how the child is doing in school, if the child got a good night's sleep, and so on. Similarly, he will put the child's family at ease by asking the parents' names and engaging them directly and respectfully.

Judge Michael explains the proceedings to parties and encourages questions. "I tell litigants all the time: Consider yourself in a foreign country. We speak a foreign language called legalese so if I say anything you don't understand, raise your hand and I will explain it to you." Parties also receive a copy of the court order before they leave the courtroom, so they know specifically what is required of them.

Providing Therapy Dogs

A collaboration with Western Tennessee Therapy Dog Services brings therapy dogs into the court to sit with children during trials and hearings. For many children, a dog at the child's feet or side is calming and helps the child feel safe and protected. "We know the benefits of having animals around children," said Judge Michael. "It relaxes them."

Offering Parent Orientation and Education Programs

Judge Michael's staff provide parent orientation programs in the community to help parents understand the legal process and expectations. Parent education programs were first started to teach parents whose children were detained by law enforcement about the legal process and requirements around attending probation meetings. The program had a positive impact by reducing the number of warrants the judge had to issue and giving parents a roadmap of how the system worked. Parent education programs were then broadened to all legal matters the court handles—child abuse and neglect, custody and visitation, delinquency, and child support. Increasing understanding of how the system works decreases the stress and anxiety of participating in the legal system, and in many cases prevents court involvement.

Assessing and Responding to Family Trauma

Assessing Clients' Trauma

Court staff are trained on trauma-responsive approaches and validated tools to assess family trauma. Voluntary trauma assessments are conducted on each family that comes to court. Judge Michael and the court magistrates only see the assessment findings after adjudication and use the findings to make informed decisions about how to treat children and families and provide rehabilitative services. The court has relationships with community service providers who provide trauma-informed services (e.g., psychologists, group homes, religious institutions), so if a family or child presents with serious trauma in their background, the court will refer them to one of those providers.

Introducing Trauma-Responsive Programs

Several court-based programs reduce trauma by diverting children and families from the court system. A juvenile detention diversion program reduces the number of children who come to court by working with law enforcement to develop a detention assessment tool. Youth who do not need to be detained are sent home, given a summons, and asked to participate in a 45-minute educational program. They don't get juvenile court records. Judge Michael says this program has reduced the numbers of youth who come to court by more than 85 percent. Similar programs designed to divert youth who carry guns and juvenile sex offenders from the juvenile system are also shielding youth from the legal system.

Applying a Trauma-Informed Practice Framework to Sentencing

Katherine J. McLachlan[7]

In some ways, trauma-informed sentencing is an oxymoron. If a sanction intends to punish through incarceration, its very purpose is to traumatize the defendant with an experience so unpleasant as to promote both specific and general deterrence. However, prison sentences are criminogenic and traumagenic. Trauma-informed practices aim to reduce or minimize harms experienced by everyone involved, while also reducing crime.

To be trauma informed "is to understand and recognize trauma and its impacts, and to respond in a manner that is person centered, strengths based and seeks to further empower the individual and actively prevent retraumatization."[8] Trauma-informed practice is not designed to resolve the impacts of trauma; that is the purpose of "trauma-focused" practice. A trauma-informed service works to "recognize, understand and minimize" the long-term impact of trauma.[9] This has been articulated as four key assumptions—to realize, recognize, and respond to trauma, and resist retraumatization—by the Substance Abuse and Mental Health Services Administration (SAMHSA).[10]

[7] Katherine McLachlan, BA (Hons), LLB (Hons), LLM, GDLP, completed a PhD in criminology/law focusing on trauma-informed practice in the criminal justice system in 2022. She has more than 20 years working in criminal and social justice roles, with South Australia Police, Attorney-General's Department (SA), the Australian Institute of Criminology, Victim Support Service and currently Flinders University. She established the online bachelor of criminal justice at the University of South Australia. She has been the victim representative on the Parole Board of South Australia since 2015. https://orcid.org/0000-0001-7171-2089.

[8] Parkerville Children and Youth Care. *Taking a Trauma Informed Approach: A practice framework* (Perth: Parkerville, 2018), 1.

[9] Sheryl P. Kubiak, Stephanie S. Covington & Carmen Hillier, *Trauma-Informed Corrections*, in Social Work in Juvenile and Criminal Justice Systems 92–104, 92 (D. Springer & A. Robert eds., Springfield: Charles Thomas, 2017).

[10] Substance Abuse and Mental Health Services Administration. *SAMHSA's Concept of Trauma and Guidance for a Trauma-Informed Approach* (Rockville: SAMHSA, 2014), 9–10.

Sentencing judges may be trauma informed if they realize that trauma is often present in defendants' lives and recognize the impacts of an individual defendant's trauma experiences on their offending behavior. Trauma-informed sentencing also requires that judges resist retraumatizing the defendant both in the sentencing process and the sanction/outcome.[11] A trauma-informed response is based on five key principles: safety, trustworthiness, choice, collaboration, and empowerment.[12]

1. **Safety** entails the provision of effective physical and emotional safety to service users when they access services. Service users feel welcome, included, and heard by the service provider. Users and workers understand client rights, feedback processes, and protective policies and practices. When applied to sentencing, safety, for example, is present when judges ensure that defendants feel included, able to participate, and heard.

2. **Trustworthiness and transparency** refers to the establishment of mutually understood, clear, and consistent expectations and boundaries, such that trust is built between the service provider and the service user. In sentencing, trustworthiness is demonstrated when judges ensure defendants understand both the court process and the implications of the sentencing decision.

3. **Choice** maximizes service users' sense of control regarding their service preferences, through the provision of information, options, and an awareness of their rights and responsibilities. Choice in sentencing may be demonstrated when judges discuss with defendants the implications of the sentencing decision.

4. **Collaboration** involves service users' participation in the planning and shared decision making around activities and settings related to service provision. Collaboration in sentencing is difficult to demonstrate, as shared decision making is rarely possible. However, judges may ensure defense counsel present individual factors that the defendant

---

[11] Gene Griffin & Sarah Sallen, *Considering Child Trauma Issues in Juvenile Court Sentencing*, 34(1) CHILDREN'S LEGAL RIGHTS J., 1–22, 17 (2013); SAMHSA, *Concept of Trauma*.

[12] STEPHANIE S. COVINGTON, BECOMING TRAUMA INFORMED: TOOL KIT FOR WOMEN'S COMMUNITY SERVICE PROVIDERS (London: One Small Thing, 2016); ROGER D. FALLOT & MAXINE HARRIS, CREATING CULTURES OF TRAUMA-INFORMED CARE (CCTIC): A SELF-ASSESSMENT AND PLANNING PROTOCOL, VERSION 2.3 (Washington: Community Connections, 2011); Maxine Harris & Roger D. Fallot, *Envisioning a Trauma-Informed Service System: A Vital Paradigm Shift*, NEW DIRECTIONS FOR MENTAL HEALTH SERVICES, Spring, no. 89 (2001): 3–22; C. HENDERSON, M. EVERETT & S. ISOBEL. TRAUMA-INFORMED CARE AND PRACTICE ORGANIZATIONAL TOOL-KIT (TICPOT): AN ORGANIZATIONAL CHANGE PROCESS RESOURCE, STAGE 1 - PLANNING AND AUDIT (Sydney: Mental Health Coordinating Council, 2018); CATHY KEZELMAN & PAM STAVROLPOULOS, PRACTICE GUIDELINES FOR CLINICAL TREATMENT OF COMPLEX TRAUMA (Sydney: Blue Knot Foundation, 2019); SAMHSA, *Concept of Trauma*; Katherine J. McLachlan, *Same, Same or Different? Is Trauma-Informed Sentencing a Form of Therapeutic Jurisprudence?*, 25(1) EUR. J. CURRENT LEGAL ISSUES 1–18 (2021).

believes are relevant to sentencing and the defendant's preferred outcome.

5. **Empowerment** promotes skills development of service users through a strengths-based approach, recognizing the importance of individual characteristics such as culture, history, and gender. Empowerment in sentencing is best demonstrated when rehabilitation is prioritized, as well as through statements that recognize individual strengths.

References

Australian Institute of Judicial Administration. *Guide to Judicial Conduct*, 3rd ed., (Melbourne: AIJA, 2017).

Cooper, A. *Indigenous Disadvantage a Focus in Sentence Appeal for Aiia's Killer*, The Age, (Dec. 17, 2020), https://www.theage.com.au/national/victoria /indigenous-disadvantage-a-focus-in-sentence-appeal-for-aiia-s-killer -20201217-p56ock.html.

McLachlan, Katherine J. *Using a Trauma-Informed Practice Framework to Examine How South Australian Judges Respond to Trauma in the Lives of Aboriginal Defendants* 11(2) J. Qualitative Crim. Just. & Criminology (Jan. 20, 2022).

Sapouna, Maria, Catherine Bisset & Anne-Marie Conlong. *What Works to Reduce Reoffending: A Summary of the Evidence* (Edinburgh: Scottish Government, 2011).

CHAPTER 7

Legal Education and Trauma

Law School as Trauma

Marjorie Florestal

On the night John Wilkes Booth murdered President Lincoln, he was said to look wild and haggard with hair standing on end and eyes "bolting from his head."[1] His breath might have caught in his throat. His heart must have raced in his chest. The amygdala would have taken over, partially shutting down the higher brain to focus on the primitive survival instincts of fight or flight. Booth wasn't about to flee. He was a man on a mission to do what he could for "a poor, oppressed, downtrodden people"—southern whites who had suffered the humiliation of defeat on the battlefield. These once proud Aryans were now forced to recognize their black chattel as human beings.

Booth lurked in the shadows of the Ford Theater with his derringer at the ready, waiting for a chance to right that fundamental wrong. A roar of laughter filled the theater. "Freedom!" Booth shouted before pulling the trigger. The bullet pierced Lincoln's skull, pulverizing flesh and bone. It lodged at the back of the president's head where it remained until the attending physician cracked Lincoln's skull open to perform an autopsy.

What if, in that moment of dismemberment, Lincoln was forced to evidence his capacity for critical thinking by arguing "both sides" of a hypothetical about the rights of southern slaveholders? The murdered president would need to give equal weight to the longing for freedom in the slaves, and the longing for freedom

---

[1] T. Alford, Fortune's Fool: The Life of John Wilkes Booth 268 (New York, NY: Oxford University Press, 2015).

171

to *enslave* in southern whites. While this might seem a far-fetched scenario to some, it is the felt experience of many students in the law school classroom.

Black students grapple with legal doctrines like "stand your ground," which was used to justify the murder of Trayvon Martin, a Black teenager walking around his father's gated community dressed in a hoodie with a bag of Skittles in his pocket. Indigenous students regurgitate principles of property law that reduce their eons-old connection to the land to a mere possessory interest that can be terminated at will in favor of the rights of "discoverers." Survivors of rape confront graphic cases and hypotheticals, forcing them to relive the trauma of their experience without so much as a trigger warning to prepare them. All students are trained to "think like a lawyer," an epistemological approach that some argue rejects "the intuitive, the emotive, and the personal" and contributes to an epidemic of depression among law students.[2]

The law school classroom can be a trauma-filled environment for students, and it is an experience that stays with them long after law school. In this chapter, we move beyond definitions to focus on how trauma shows up in the law school classroom. We further explore how law professors and law students might create trauma-informed spaces that encourage more effective teaching and learning.

Trauma in the Law School Classroom

For lawyers of a certain age, the name Professor Kingsfield evokes a visceral reaction. Kingsfield is the iconic law professor in *The Paper Chase*, a movie based on the novel by John Jay Osbourn. Aggressive to the point of rudeness, Professor Kingsfield defines his teaching objective as follows: "You teach yourselves the law, but I train your minds. You come in here with a skull full of mush; you leave thinking like a lawyer."[3] In a classroom encounter with Mr. Hart, a student, Professor Kingsfield unleashes a Socratic dialogue that ends with Hart running to the bathroom to lose his breakfast.

Kingsfield would undoubtedly reject the notion of a trauma-informed law school classroom. For him, the study of law is a rigorous, trial-by-fire ritual. In the Kingsfieldian worldview, the objective is to train students to "grow a thicker skin" in order to withstand the rigors of legal study. Those deemed incapable of the task should be "encouraged" to leave the study of law behind. (Kingsfield famously offered Mr. Hart a dime to call his mother and tell her he was unlikely to become a lawyer.) While most modern law professors would not adopt this view, in the absence of a trauma-informed pedagogy, Kingsfield's ghost still lurks in the law school classroom. He can be found in the resistance to adopting best practices like trigger warnings before requiring students to engage with graphic or emotionally charged material. He looms large in the legal canon where "classic" cases erase the

---

[2] M. Meltsner, *Feeling Like a Lawyer*, 33 J. Legal Educ. 624, 633 (1983).

[3] The Paper Chase (James Bridges dir., 1973).

presence of racialized and marginalized communities—except in select criminal and constitutional law cases. He exists when professors normalize the abnormal by adopting a business-as-usual approach in the classroom even as the world shuts down in the face of a pandemic or rioters storm the U.S. Capitol under the banner of the Confederate flag.

The Trauma-Informed Classroom: What Professors Can Do

A trauma-informed law school classroom is one in which professors and students have a basic understanding of how trauma impacts the body, emotions, and cognition. Beginning from this shared knowledge base enables both parties to create a space in which difficult material and difficult conversations can be tolerated without resorting to emotional shut-down, silence, or maladaptive coping mechanisms. This book provides a wealth of information on that score, as well as practical tools for self-regulation and self-care. Beyond basic knowledge, professors seeking to create a trauma-informed law school classroom could benefit from the following suggestions:

1. *Begin with the presumption that students want to learn and are not seeking "an easy way out."*

When students appear unprepared, checked-out, or are frequently absent, it can be easy to assume a lack of commitment. This may not be the case. Depression is rampant among law students, and the pandemic only increases the possibility that mental health issues are at play. Law professors are not therapists, of course, but we *are* in relationship with our students as part of a learning community. If we notice a student struggling, we can reach out. And yes, our students are adults and should be expected to contact us or the dean of students *as detailed in every syllabus ever written*. But when students are overwhelmed, it can be challenging to even send an email—receiving one from the professor can feel like a life-line.

Alternatively, a student might be emotionally checked-out because of a poorly handled traumatic experience in the classroom. The bare minimum for a trauma-informed classroom is the proper use of trigger warnings. Placing them in a 20-page syllabus is a first step, but students can easily miss such a warning. It is essential to re-issue the warning at least a week before the material is discussed. Trigger warnings are not proof that students are too fragile for the practice. They are a coping mechanism for trauma. Students are asking for the information so they might prepare themselves to participate in the face of their trauma—or to practice self-care by absenting themselves. Refusing to issue those warnings based on a misguided notion that students need to "grow a tougher skin" is needlessly retraumatizing.

2. *Assume that students have been traumatized.*

As professors, we have no idea of the range of experiences our students have lived—nor should we. A trauma-informed classroom does not require full disclosure of students' past trauma. But we can start from the presumption that any traumatic experience we might read about in a casebook has likely happened to at least one of our students. Rape is an epidemic in this country. Elementary school students participate in active shooter drills. Our students may have firsthand, lived experience with the criminal justice system or mental health or juvenile justice. Yet, students report that professors sometimes teach these cases as if they are anomalies. Students feel embarrassed and angry when their lived experience becomes the butt of jokes.

It can be easy to presume that "we" share a common experience with students that excludes these kinds of traumatic events. I can still remember when I made that mistake. It was more than 15 years ago, and I was in my second year of teaching contracts. A student and I were analyzing a legal capacity issue involving a plaintiff who had been committed to a mental institution. The student used the word "crazy," and a titter of laughter filled the room. I could have corrected the student. I could have used a more appropriate term. Instead, I repeated the word. It felt like "we" were sharing a forbidden joke about someone outside of our little circle. I cringe at my ignorance. But more importantly, I regret the pain I caused. No one ever raised the issue, but I *knew* that in that room of almost 90 students, I had cut someone to the bone.

   3.   *Learn to handle difficult conversations.*
Race, gender, disability, sexual orientation, and other "hot-button" issues routinely find their way into discussions in the law school classroom. These discussions are often rife with stereotypes and offensive assumptions—from professors as well as other students. When left unchallenged, these conversations are deeply traumatic.

Legal academics are not trained in the art of having difficult conversations, and the mere suggestion that such training is necessary raises Kingsfield's ghost all over again: Why are students so sensitive? Why can't they grow a thicker skin? Law students are graduating into a workplace that demands the ability to work in diverse teams and across borders. Students need training in bias, cultural competence, and anti-racism as part of a toolkit of essential skills for legal professionals in the 21st century. The majority of law professors simply do not have the requisite training to teach their students. Obtaining that training will go a long way toward helping professors frame these difficult conversations as intellectual discussions rather than traumatic experiences.

   4.   *Expand the canon.*
In the first year of law school students read a dizzying number of cases, many of which are the same ones I read in law school in the 1990s. Longevity is not, in itself, an argument for change. But the canon still mostly centers on white people, except in "designated areas" like criminal and constitutional law. We must expand the canon to include discussions of race, class, gender, disability, sexual orientation, and other differences throughout the first-year curriculum (and beyond).

When students fail to see themselves represented in the curriculum it can be easy to imagine that the law is not about them—except when it is being used *against* them. There is no reason to confine discussion of Mexican Americans to immigration law, while criminal law discusses race, and mental health law focuses on the neurodivergent. Nor does expanding the canon mean that students should be given even more cases to read.

I taught the first year contracts class for a decade, but these days I teach contracts as a three-week introductory course for international students. In this short span of time, I introduce students to the case method, Socratic method, *and* give them a birds-eye view of U.S. contract law. My readings must serve double and triple duty for students whose native language is not English. For a discussion on contract interpretation; Mexican culinary traditions; and the ways in which race, class, and culture have shaped contract law, I use *White City Shopping Center v. PR Restaurants, LLC*,[4] a Massachusetts case where, despite competing dictionary definitions, the judge relied on "common sense" to conclude that burritos could not be defined as sandwiches.

For discussions on freedom of contract, legal capacity, the doctrine of coverture, feminism, and public policy, I use a case, a myth, and Shakespeare: In *Borelli v. Brusseau*,[5] a wife sues her estranged husband's estate to enforce his promise to leave her certain property if she personally took care of him at home until his death. The court found she had offered no consideration for the promise because, under the state-imposed marital contract, she had a preexisting duty to personally tend to her estranged husband.[6] *The Handless Maiden,* a German folktale about a father who mistakenly sells his daughter into marriage with the devil, raises the doctrine of coverture. My students and I discuss the once prevalent notion that women had no legal capacity to contract because they were "covered" by their fathers and husbands. And the casket scene in Shakespeare's *Merchant of Venice* raises countless issues on feminism, public policy, and honoring the promise of another. My rebellious, 21st-century students cannot understand why Portia would obey her deceased father's dictate that she marry the man who can solve the riddle of the casket. We talk about how the law both liberates and constrains its subjects.

Expanding the canon is about adopting counternarratives to challenge canonical text. It is about bringing the discussion on race, class, culture, and other differences into classes that are traditionally silent on the issues. It enriches students' understanding of the law while bringing a diversity of characters into the law school classroom.

---

[4] White City Shopping Center v. PR Restaurants, LLC, 21 Mass. L. Rptr. 565 (Mass. Super. Ct. 2006).

[5] Borelli v. Brusseau, 12 Cal. App. 4th 647 (1993).

[6] *Id.*

    5.   *Adapt trauma-informed techniques from legal clinics.*
Clinical law professors are at the vanguard of the movement to adopt trauma-informed practices in the law. Their experience is invaluable even if it would have to be adapted for the needs of podium classes. Classroom simulations, client counseling exercises, or in-class contract drafting exercises could all benefit from the best practices of clinical professors.

The Trauma-Informed Classroom: What Law Students Can Do

As adult learners, law students have a duty and the capacity to shape their experience in the classroom. The first step is to become trauma-informed, not just as a means to deal with future clients but as a way of understanding one's own response to the law school experience. This book provides knowledge and resources on trauma and self-regulation, which are essential tools for all law students. In addition, students may find the following suggestions beneficial:

    1.   *Begin with the presumption that what happens in the classroom is not personal.*
The Socratic classroom can feel like a personal attack. It spotlights one student in a very public duel of wits with a professor who has mastered the material—and controls the questions. As I like to tell my students, the reward for a good answer is another, more difficult, question. Even when professors use "kinder, gentler" forms of the Socratic method—including the use of volunteers or panels—the experience can be overwhelming.

    Socratic questioning is a time-honored tradition unlikely to disappear from the law school classroom. The task for students is to manage their relationship to the experience. While the professor's stance may seem confrontational and aggressive, it is usually not personal—Kingsfield is long dead in most law school classrooms. How you choose to respond will help frame your experience. Anger and defensiveness are unlikely to be helpful, but learning a few self-regulation techniques can make a difference. "Take a deep breath" might seem simplistic, but breathwork is the foundation of many self-regulation techniques. You can also learn about tapping and other stress-release modalities to use in the moment.

    It is impossible to claim that personal attacks never find their way to the law school classroom, and I am not suggesting that students ignore that possibility. Later on in this chapter, we explore strategies for dealing with some of those issues.

    2.   *Imposter syndrome exists, as does structural and systemic barriers.*
It never fails to surprise me when some of my brightest women and minority students confess to not feeling smart enough. They tell me that law school only exacerbates their feelings of inadequacy. By now, most of them have heard the term "imposter syndrome" and readily identify with the phenomenon. Developed by psychologists Pauline Rose Clance and Suzanne Imes, "imposter syndrome" is said

to afflict many high-achieving women who, despite all evidence to the contrary, doubt their academic and professional accomplishments.

Imposter syndrome puts a name to a phenomenon experienced by many. In practice, however, it seems to encourage women to pathologize ordinary feelings of anxiety and stress while ignoring structural and systemic barriers. In an article published by *The Harvard Business Review*, Ruchika Tulshyan and Jodi-Ann Burey examine how women in the workplace confront gender and racial barriers to success that are reframed as personal failings and imposter syndrome.[7] Similarly, the law school classroom—and the legal system—has its own gender and racial barriers for students to navigate. Often, these barriers are couched in terms of the psychological, while ignoring structural issues concerning bias, racism, and misogyny. Tulshyan and Burey argue that we should stop telling women they have imposter syndrome and focus on changing the system. While this is undoubtedly a worthy long-term objective, it does not address the here and now. Nor does it take into account just how deeply some have internalized the message that they are not good enough.

When students share their fears with me, I honor their feelings even as I challenge them to examine the source. I tell them that the task is to make the invisible visible—to explore their internal scripts and to ask themselves where those messages might have come from. We discuss psychologist Carol Dweck's work in mindset theory, and talk about their goals and how they measure success. Most importantly, I share with them just how often I have these conversations with other smart and successful law students to reinforce the message that they are not alone. I do not imagine these conversations eradicate my students' imposter syndrome, but I know that talking about the issue dispels some of the charge.

3.   *Seek out assistance to work through personal trauma.*
I come from a Haitian family that values success. When I worried about doing well in class, my father would remind me that our ancestors staged the only successful slave uprising in modern history. Getting a perfect score on an exam was hardly a challenge by comparison! Needless to say, my upbringing encouraged all sorts of neurotic behavior. In law school, I would not have dreamed of calling any of my experiences "trauma" or to seek out assistance. My only tool for dealing with difficulties was to grit my teeth and bear it. There are better methods.

As a professor, I encounter students with significant untreated trauma that impacts their ability to function. Often, these students have never considered therapy or other forms of assistance. There is simply no good reason to suffer in silence. I urge students who need it to seek out professional care in order to heal from trauma.

---

[7] Ruchika Tulshyan & Jodi-Ann Burey, *Stop Telling Women They Have Imposter Syndrome*, Harv. Bus. Rev. (Feb. 11, 2021), https://hbr.org/2021/02/stop-telling-women-they-have-imposter-syndrome.

Some Trauma-Informed Frameworks for Legal Education: Including Trauma in Curriculum, Vicarious Trauma, and the Trauma of Marginalization and Racism

Educating Law Students about Trauma

Barbara A. Babb[8]

In August 2000, the University of Baltimore launched the Sayra and Neil Meyerhoff Center for Families, Children and the Courts (CFCC). CFCC's mission is to improve the practice of family law and to reform the family justice system in ways that better serve the complex needs of today's families, children, and communities. Two theoretical paradigms undergird our work: therapeutic jurisprudence and the ecology of human development. Therapeutic jurisprudence recognizes the power of the law and the behavior of legal actors to produce positive (helpful) or negative (harmful) consequences. The ecology of human development is a social science systems perspective that emphasizes a holistic approach to understand and resolve families' and children's problems.

One important component of our program is the CFCC Student Fellows Program. It is designed to teach second- and third-year law students about CFCC's underpinnings and cutting-edge family law issues, as well as related doctrines, such as preventive lawyering, restorative justice, and an ethic of care. Additionally, the program incorporates an experiential component, which requires students to participate in one of CFCC's projects.

During the doctrinal aspect of the program, law students learn about trauma, particularly within the context of family law. They learn how trauma may manifest; how they as future lawyers can begin to recognize it; and how they can employ various strategies and techniques to respond to trauma experienced by their clients, other family justice system professionals, and themselves. Often during class discussions, students reveal their own trauma experiences within and prior to law school.

Almost universally, students reveal that the first year of law school made them question their decision to attend because the first-year curriculum did not reflect their goals and values. At the conclusion of the program many students report that CFCC reminded them why they went to law school. Years after graduating, CFCC alumni continue to incorporate what they learned from the program into their legal practice. The education about trauma and its impact helps law students understand how to practice as caring attorneys.

---

[8] Emerita Professor Barbara Babb is former director of the post-JD certificate in family law and founder and founding director of the Sayra and Neil Meyerhoff Center for Families, Children and the Courts at the University of Baltimore Law School.

Why Law Schools Must Teach Trauma-Informed Lawyering

Victoria Craig and Hannah van Mook[9]

Legal work is inherently relational—one would be hard-pressed to find a lawyer who doesn't interact with other people. Ethical practice involves sensitivity to clients' emotions, personalities, motivations, beliefs, and values, which are all areas influenced by trauma.[10] Lawyers who fail to understand the feelings, responses, and behaviors of their clients are more likely to interact inappropriately with them.[11] This heightens the risk of retraumatization of the client and the vicarious traumatization of the lawyer and their colleagues.[12] To act ethically, lawyers must practice from a trauma-informed perspective. Essentially, trauma-informed legal practice is ethical practice.

Lawyers are trained not to be emotional in their relationships with their clients.[13] Traditionally the role of lawyers has been one of stoicism, with an exclusive focus on the legal principles and doctrines that are relevant to cases. Law school curriculums lack interpersonal and intrapersonal work. This effectively desensitizes students to personal and structural concerns of the people they interact with in a professional capacity.[14] In the first year of law school, professors tend to control the dialogue in a way that pulls students away from the humanity involved in the cases, focusing instead on substantive and procedural sources of authority.[15] This is not inherently problematic on its own, but more interpersonal communication is needed to prepare lawyers for effective future practice. Beyond mooting and oral advocacy, communication skills are rarely expressly taught in law schools.

It is undeniable that the legal profession is filled with emotion: business clients stress over mergers and acquisitions. Tax clients struggle to meet the demands of collection agencies. Indigenous communities continue to negotiate for recognition. Families break apart when loved ones are sent to prison, and

---

[9] Victoria Craig completed her undergraduate degree in social work at Western University. She completed her law degree and master's degree in public administration at the University of Victoria. Hannah van Mook completed a BA in biopsychology and an MA in cognition and brain sciences at the University of Victoria. She completed her law degree at the University of Victoria in 2021, where she volunteered with wellness initiatives. Both Victoria and Hannah are strong believers in the trauma-informed practice and look forward to bringing it into their legal practices.

[10] A.O. Burton, *Cultivating Ethical, Socially Responsible Lawyer Judgment: Introducing the Multiple Lawyering Intelligences Paradigm into the Clinical Setting*, 11(1) CLINICAL L. REV. 15 (2004).

[11] H. Brayne, *A Case for Getting Law Students Engaged in the Real Thing—The Challenge to the Saber-tooth Curriculum*, 34(1) THE LAW TEACHER 17–39 (2000), doi:10.1 080/03069400.2000.9993045.

[12] Burton, *supra* note 10.

[13] M.L. Jenkins, *Teaching Law Students: Lessening the Potential Effects of Vicarious Trauma*, 398 MANITOBA L.J., 399–418 (2013).

[14] Burton, *supra* note 10.

[15] *Id.*

children are thrown into custody battles. Lawyers must have the tools to navigate these difficult conversations with their clients.

Trauma-informed practice skills should be integrated into all courses but may also be well-suited to a more in-depth exploration within the required ethics course. Teaching trauma-informed legal practice in law schools has a practical benefit, because all future lawyers must attend law school. Teaching trauma-informed practice in law schools ensures that all practitioners consistently receive this critical training. Jenkins argues that "training law students on how to mitigate the effects of vicarious trauma is not only beneficial, it is essential."[16] Law school is where legal professionals develop the analytical skills and knowledge required to solve their clients' legal issues. It should also be where law students develop the tools for mitigating the effects of vicarious trauma on themselves and their clients.[17]

In addition, Meier argues that cultivating personal reflection skills and personal awareness are as fundamental for lawyers as learning to draft a brief.[18] Effectively stated by Kronman: "A lawyer's professional life begins the day he or she starts law school. It is as students that their professional habits first take shape."[19] Some learning, including trauma-informed practice, is so essential that it should not be left to learning "on the job." Jenkins provides us with four goals that trauma-informed education in law school should aim to achieve.[20]

1. *Help students develop the skills required to respond to emotions, reactions, and responses of traumatized clients.*

In order to respond to trauma, students must first understand what trauma is. Students need to become familiar with the definitions of trauma and understand the impact that trauma has on relevant practice areas.[21] Jenkins introduces students to the Diagnostic and Statistical Manual of Mental Disorders, which outlines a number of signs and symptoms that are consistent with trauma and related psychiatric disorders, such as PTSD.[22]

Instructors can teach students the psychology behind trauma, either through stand-alone courses or integration into existing courses (Sternlight & Robbennolt, 2015, & Brayne, 2000).[23] Equipping lawyers with the skills to

---

[16] Jenkins, *supra* note 13, at 401.

[17] Jenkins, *supra* note 13.

[18] J. Meier, *Teaching Lawyering with Heart in the George Washington University Law School Domestic Violence Project*, 22(12) Violence Against Women 1484–95 (2016).

[19] Kronman (as cited in Brayne, *supra* note 11).

[20] Jenkins, *supra* note 13.

[21] T. Kraemer & E. Patten, *Establishing a Trauma-Informed Lawyer-Client Relationship (Part One)*, 33(10) ABA Child Law Practice 197–202 (2014).

[22] Jenkins, *supra* note 13.

[23] J.R. Sternlight & J.K. Robbennolt, *Psychology and Effective Lawyering: Insights for Legal Educators*, 64(3) J. Legal Educ. 365–84, (2015); Brayne, *supra* note 11.

predict, manage, and use their emotions and the emotions of their clients or adversaries is integral to their legal practice.[24] Legal professionals trained to be trauma informed are able to recognize the signs of trauma in themselves and their clients and respond effectively and appropriately.[25] Kraemer and Patten introduce a number of important steps for creating positive relationships with clients with histories of trauma.[26]

2. *Help students develop coping mechanisms for their own emotions, reactions, and responses.*

Lawyers must learn how to manage their own emotions when working with clients with trauma. For example, a common behavior of traumatized clients is missing appointments, which can be irritating and frustrating. Knowledge and awareness of trauma and the effect of trauma on clients can increase understanding and patience, and ultimately lead to an overall more positive experience for traumatized clients. However, it is also important for lawyers to maintain professional boundaries. While it can be tempting to spend time with clients outside of work hours, this can blur the lines of the professional relationship. Lawyers and other professionals may become emotionally invested in the lives of their clients. Jenkins discusses how a lack of clearly defined emotional boundaries can result in job dissatisfaction and a higher turnover rate in the legal profession.[27] Law students must be trained on how to achieve a balance between professional boundaries and the empathy and patience that is required to work with traumatized clients. Many authors suggest that this can be achieved through clinical or experiential learning opportunities.[28]

While the case law method of teaching is the most common method implemented in law schools, the curriculum should include practice experience.[29] Experiential learning opportunities should not be limited to hard skills such as interviewing and examination; morals and values should also be addressed. Simply discussing values is not sufficient—students should be provided opportunities to explore their personal and professional values with the aid of a practitioner or professor's moral compass.[30] Some options for experiential learning within the traditional classroom include:

---

[24] Sternlight & Robbennolt, *supra* note 23.

[25] Jenkins, *supra* note 13.

[26] Kraemer & Patten, *supra* note 21.

[27] Jenkins, *supra* note 13.

[28] T. Biviano, *Practical Lawyering: Intervention in Law School Curriculum Requirements to Prepare New Lawyers for Ethically Competent Practice*, 30(4) GEO. J. LEGAL ETHICS 619, (2017); C.D. Cunningham, *How Can We Give Up Our Child?" A Practice-based Approach to Teaching Legal Ethics*, 42(3) THE LAW TEACHER 312–28 (2008), doi: 10.1080/03069400.2008.9959791; Meier, *supra* note 18; Sternlight & Robbennolt, *supra* note 23; Brayne, *supra* note 11.

[29] Biviano, *supra* note 28.

[30] Cunningham, *supra* note 28.

- ◆ Live client simulations can focus on a specific case/fact pattern, or client issues like confidentiality, conflict of interest, division of control, and so on.
- ◆ Role playing in which students can act out all characters, not just the lawyer.
- ◆ Watching videos of client interviews/ depositions.
- ◆ Small group exercises.

Experiential opportunities should be followed with a formal debrief to discuss the simulations. Feedback from lawyers with practice experience (including professors) is fundamental to learning from the opportunity.[31] Additionally, instructors can pair simulations with real-life stories. Students can be asked to compare their choices and actions in the scenario exercise with those of the attorney on the actual case, weighing the pros and cons of both. Clinical and experiential learning allows students to make mistakes in a controlled environment where they do not face the risk of harming themselves or their clients.[32]

When experiential opportunities are not feasible, students can be asked to engage in self-reflection papers, journaling assignments, or respond to hypothetical situations.[33] This type of activity can help students engage more deeply with course content.

3.   Develop an action plan for vicarious trauma.

An incorrect approach to trauma-informed practice poses the risk of retraumatizing students. Sanders highlights a number of things that should be avoided.[34] This includes fully immersing students in traumatic material, as this is ultimately destabilizing and counterproductive. It is also important to keep in mind that the threshold for retraumatization varies among students. Providing adequate notice or "trigger warnings" for students, monitoring student progress, and managing the amount of traumatic material presented in class are all steps that can be taken when educating students on vicarious trauma. Sanders also presents seven basic principles that educators can follow:[35]

- ◆ Prioritize learning and student safety.
- ◆ Recognize the vulnerability of students with traumatic histories.
- ◆ Be prepared with referrals.
- ◆ Recognize that trauma can impact performance.

---

[31] *Id.*

[32] Brayne, *supra* note 11.

[33] Meier, *supra* note 18; Sternlight & Robbennolt, *supra* note 23.

[34] J.E. Sanders, *Teaching Note—Trauma Informed Teaching in Social Work Education*, J. Soc. Work Educ. (2019), doi: 10.1080/10437797.2019.1661923.

[35] *Id.*

◆ Be aware of countertransference and personal reactions to traumatic material.

◆ Continue to critically evaluate the research on vicarious trauma.

◆ Do not assume that trauma is good or productive.

4. *Help students recognize how destabilizing the role of a lawyer can be and ways to mitigate the inevitable emotional impacts of the job.*

"When we open our hearts to hear someone's story of devastation and betrayal, our cherished beliefs are challenged and we are changed."[36] If we give students the tools needed to manage and mitigate vicarious trauma, we must also teach them about the destabilizing effects of vicarious trauma. While burnout is often discussed as a result of overworking in most professions, countertransference and vicarious trauma are more unique to "helping" professions, such as counseling, social work, and law.

Countertransference occurs when a person reacts emotionally to a client's situation because of similar experiences, and it can become vicarious trauma. Countertransference can occur even if a person does not have a history of trauma. Discussions with a client might simply bring up subconscious memories of something impactful from the practitioner's past. Jenkins noted that, while burnout is avoidable, vicarious trauma is often inevitable for people who work in helping professions.[37] Furthermore, perfectionists and overachievers, two personality types common in the legal profession, have a higher likelihood of developing vicarious trauma. Law students must be made aware of their susceptibility to vicarious trauma and the ways in which effects can be mitigated. Jenkins (2013) proposed that the most important and impactful method of mitigating vicarious trauma is to become more knowledgeable and aware of its existence.

If a legal practitioner's school or workplace does not acknowledge the existence of vicarious trauma or have supports in place to mitigate the impacts of vicarious trauma, the risk of developing vicarious trauma increases. Workplaces have an obligation to protect their employees from harm. Legal professionals must be able to take care of themselves before they can support their clients. Lawyers have a professional responsibility to safeguard their mental health and the mental health of their clients. As Jenkins stated, ". . . knowing ourselves is a powerful antidote to vicarious trauma."[38] Developing knowledge and awareness of vicarious trauma and a toolkit for mitigating its effects will lead to more effective lawyering.

---

[36] Jenkins, *supra* note 13, at 404.

[37] Jenkins, *supra* note 13.

[38] Jenkins (2013) (p. 416).

The Trauma of Race and Marginalization in the Law School Classroom

Marjorie Florestal

Law students from racialized or marginalized communities experience unique forms of trauma in the law school classroom. A blatant example is the bias exhibited by some professors. Recently, an adjunct at Georgetown recorded and uploaded a video discussion with a colleague in which she lamented the poor quality of an African American student's performance, noting: "I end up having this angst every semester that a lot of my lower ones are Blacks, happens almost every semester."[39]

Racialized and marginalized students routinely confront a presumption of incompetence. This form of bias is a microaggression, defined as

> subtle verbal and non-verbal insults directed toward non-Whites, often done automatically and unconsciously. They are layered insults based on one's race, gender, class, sexuality, language, immigration status, phenotype, accent, or surname.[40]

Microaggressions are particularly difficult to address because they play into stereotypes that victims can sometimes internalize. A study exploring the impact of stereotype threat on women's cognitive abilities illustrates the point.[41] Beilock et al. tested women participants' ability to perform high-level math problems when reminded of stereotypes such as "boys are better than girls at math."[42] They found that women's cognitive abilities diminished because their concern over the stereotype co-opted their working memory—especially their verbal resources. The stereotype threat undermined women's performance not just in math but in other topics as well. Not surprisingly, those who did not receive the stereotype reminder performed better.

The impact of stereotype threat is not limited to women. African Americans experience the same effect when reminded of stereotypes based on racial differences.[43] Yet, professors in the law school classroom are often unaware of how their own biases impact student performance. In the Georgetown example, the professor taught negotiations, which is typically graded based on a

---

[39] Janhvi Bhojwani & Nicole Acevedo, *Georgetown Law Professor Resigns over "Insensitive Remarks" about Black Students*, NBC NEWS (Mar. 13, 2021), https://www.nbcnews.com/news/education/georgetown-law-professor-resigns-over-insensitive-remarks-about-black-students-n1261034.

[40] Solorzano et al., *Keeping Race in Place: Racial Microaggressions and Campus Racial Climate at the University of California, Berkeley*, 23 CHICANO-LATINO L. REV. 15, 17 (2002).

[41] Sian L. Beilock, Robert J. Rydell & Allen R. McConnell, *Stereotype Threat and Working Memory: Mechanisms, Alleviation, and Spillover*, 136(2) J. EXPERIMENTAL PSYCH., 256–76 (2007), DOI: 10.1037/0096-3445.136.2.256.

[42] Beilock et al.

[43] C.M. Steele, *A Threat in the Air: How Stereotypes Shape Intellectual Identity and Performance*, 52(6) AM. PSYCHOLOGIST 613–29 (1997), https://doi.org/10.1037/0003-066X.52.6.613.

combination of simulation exercises and writing assignments. It is not a course subject to blind grading. As a professor who also teaches negotiations, I am familiar with the mix of subjective and objective elements used to evaluate student performance. If a professor engages in the evaluation process with the supposition that "every semester a lot of my lower ones are Black," it becomes a self-fulfilling prophecy. Every Black student is evaluated with that lens in mind.

The Georgetown example is disturbing in several respects. It fits a false narrative about the capabilities of Black students. The fact that a student received a poor grade—even the worst grade—should not be news. It is news only because the professor suggests this performance has something to say about the capabilities of other Black students. Disputing this underlying assumption sounds defensive. After all, the professor's assessment must be "true" based on her experience. Claims of bias or stereotype threat are dismissed as excuses. In fact, the professor's colleague in the recorded conversation would later state that he disagreed with the professor's assertions. This message did not make any headlines.

Further, there was only a single African American student in the class. One can imagine the trauma he endured listening to professors describe his so-called deficiencies for classmates—and the world—to hear. But in an apology letter provided to *The New York Times*, the professor reduced this traumatic experience to "hurt feelings," and news reports characterized her words as "insensitive." As is often the case with microaggressions, the horror of the experience, and its impact on the victim as well as the marginalized community he or she inhabits, are minimized. When a Georgetown alumna was interviewed about the incident—a Black woman who clerked for the Supreme Court and now holds a senior position at Big Law while juggling a teaching role at Howard Law School—she could only express resignation. She had grown used to people doubting her abilities, and holding Black people to different standards than their White peers. "It also has an effect over time on our mental health," she noted. "You start to absorb and believe those lies."[44]

Microaggressions and racial trauma are not about hurt feelings. They are pernicious forms of collective trauma. Researchers have found that among a subset of individuals, racial trauma can rise to the level of PTSD. PTSD is a disorder characterized by hypervigilance and hyperarousal and feelings of hopelessness, anger, and shame. The disorder is more prevalent among African Americans than Whites—9.1 percent and 6.8 percent, respectively—and more

---

[44] Lauren Lumpkin, *Georgetown Law Professor Terminated after "Reprehensible" Comments about Black Students*, WASH. POST (Mar. 11, 2021, 6:44 PM), https://www.washingtonpost.com/local/education/georgetown-law -sandra-sellers-black-students/2021/03/11/c798eae0-827d-11eb-ac37-4383f7709abe_story.html.

debilitating; African Americans suffer higher levels of functional impairment, including difficulty in working and carrying out everyday activities.[45]

For African Americans, racial trauma is collective trauma. This is an experience that White people simply do not share. For example, in a nationally representative study of police killings of unarmed African Americans, Bor et al., found adverse effects on the mental health of Blacks in the general population that were not observed among White respondents.[46]

The Georgetown incident is a rare example of making the invisible—racism and bias—visible. The majority of law students will thankfully never have such an experience. But they can be traumatized by the incident nonetheless through an experience known as vicarious racism. The term is generally defined as a secondary form of racism brought on by observing or learning about the experience of others. Jackson et al. have found that racism vicariously experienced can have a direct impact on one's psychological as well as physical well-being.[47] Vicarious racism also helps to explain how challenging it can be for students to engage with case law involving racial trauma or to adopt a pretense of "business as usual" after well-publicized racial incidents on or off campus.

---

[45] Williams et al., https://www.mdpi.com/2076-328X/4/2/102; Metzger, Leins & DeLapp 2018, p. 243, https://psycnet.apa.org/buy/2018-37737-001; Himle et al., 2009, https://www.sciencedirect.com/science/article/abs/pii/S0887618509000036.

[46] Bor et al., 2018.

[47] Harrell, 2000; Jackson, James, Owens, & Bryan, 2017.

CHAPTER 8

Systems Change and Trauma: The Legal System and Systemic or Collective Trauma

Our legal structure discourages us from being aware or responsible for the systemic traumas—or any emotional or collective sense at all. In this section, we will highlight some of the systemic challenges and look at how systems change works.

The legal system as a whole is in need of palliative care. We're not going to fix everything that is wrong, but we're going to look at it with compassion and create awareness of opportunities to include trauma-informed resources, and that's the first step.

Systemic Racism and Systemic Barriers to Justice

Systemic Racism in the United States

Benjamin G. Davis[1]

Introduction

From K–12 through college and or graduate school, when was the first time that you had a Black teacher or professor? That question is one I have asked on occasion to think about when the proverbial board at the front was desegregated for

---

[1] Benjamin G. Davis is a retired professor of law, University of Toledo College of Law. He is the former chair, ABA Section of Dispute Resolution; former member, ABA ROLI Africa Council and ABA Standing Committee on Law and National Security; and a former board member, Society of American Law Teachers. He is the 2021 D'Alemberte/Raven Award Winner, the ABA Dispute Resolution Section's highest honor.

a person. Frequently, the answer I have gotten from white students has been that the first time they had a Black teacher or professor was me.

Given there are say five classes a day in K–12 for a total of 65 classes, around four classes a term for a total of 32 in college, and maybe another 24 or so for graduate school, we get to a total of roughly 120 classes over the potential educational lifetime of a person. If one were to imagine that teaching positions were randomly distributed so that 13.4 percent[2] of the teachers/professors would be Black, that would suggest that 16 or so of the classes' students had would have had a Black teacher/professor.

Does this artificial and rough estimate suggest that the entire educational system intends to exclude Black teachers/professors? That kind of intentional and purposive racial discrimination might be actionable. Or rather than looking for and proving individual practitioners were practicing intentional racial discrimination, can we approach this from another vantage point that is more results oriented. That results-oriented approach would say that whatever the rationales or rationalizations for the numbers, the effect is that the numbers are so low.

But, if the numbers are so low and we cannot identify let alone prove invidious racial discrimination by specific actors, are we just to conclude that this state of affairs is just "the way it is" or some kind of natural state of things? Almost seeing it as if it had been ordained by a deity.

Calling on God or at Least His Messenger on Earth

So, let us then start with God as manifested on Earth through a Pope in the mid-15th century.

> . . . Thence also **many Guineamen and other negroes, taken by force, and some by barter of unprohibited articles, or by other lawful contract of purchase, have been sent to the said kingdoms.**
> . . . **and to reduce their persons to perpetual slavery**, and to apply and appropriate to himself and his successors the kingdoms, dukedoms, counties, principalities, dominions, possessions, and goods, and to convert them to his and their use and profit. . . .[3]

Here is religious blessing for perpetual enslavement of Africans and putting in place its systems such as the Atlantic Slave Trade. The best way I found to capture this flow of humans and their labor out of Africa to the New World is in a short video entitled "Transatlantic Slave Trade in Two Minutes, 315 years,

---

[2] Quick Facts, Census, https://www.census.gov/quickfacts/fact/table/US/PST045219.

[3] Pope Nicholas 5, Romanus Pontifex 1455 translation available at http://caid.ca/Bull_Romanus_Pontifex_1455.pdf.

20,528 Voyages, Millions of Lives," which I encourage the reader to watch now before reading further.[4]

So, we see the complex system of the Transatlantic Slave Trade operating for hundreds of years as a system blessed by God's earthly representative. For it to operate, it required capital, labor, norms, laws, practices, acquiescence, enthusiasm, all the attributes of the various communities that lived under and thrived in that period. Fast forward to the end of the Civil War in 1865, the end of slavery, and the beginning of Jim Crow and segregation. Again, the manner in which the system was to work required capital, labor, norms, laws, practices, acquiescence, enthusiasm, all the attributes of the various communities that lived under and thrived in that period. In the South, the euphemism describing that period was the "Southern Way of Life."

So, in this construct, just how bad was it to be Black? While statistical analyses are eloquent on their own, the best expression of attitudes toward Blacks I have recently come across is from the early 1900 Report on Peonage of Charles Russell.[5] Russell detailed the luring of newly immigrated Italians, Germans, Jews, and other Europeans from the North to the South where they were subject to horrific conditions of peonage at the hands of the local public and private partnerships of oppression. Blacks were also documented to be in this horrific system. What I love is that when the report came out, the public shock was that these brutal conditions **were not only being done solely to Blacks—meaning that if the brutality were only done to Blacks it would not have bothered** the general public. This example shows how deep and engrained is this despising of Blacks.

The Burden on Us All

The most succinct expression of the burden of racism that was more than just some individuals with invidious views toward Blacks in the United States was put by Martin Luther King Jr. in his "Three Evils" speech in 1967, to wit:

> Racial injustice is still the Negro's burden and America's shame. And we must face the hard fact that many Americans would like to have a nation which is a democracy for white Americans but simultaneously a dictatorship over black Americans. We must face the fact that we still have much to do in the area of race relations.[6]

---

[4] Andrew Kahn & Jamelle Bouie, *Transatlantic Slave Trade in Two Minutes*, SLATE, June 25, 2015. http://www.slate.com/articles/life/the_history_of_american_slavery/2015/06/animated_interactive_of_the_history_of_the_atlantic_slave_trade.html and https://vimeo.com/259604054.

[5] Charles Wells Russell, Report on Peonage, U.S. Government Printing Office (1908).

[6] *Martin Luther King, Jr. Saw Three Evils in the World*, THE ATLANTIC, https://www.theatlantic.com/magazine/archive/2018/02/martin-luther-king-hungry-club-forum/552533/.

Having lived the first six years of my life outside the United States in Liberia and Tunisia, from age 12 to 15 in Switzerland and Nigeria, and from age 27 to 45 in France, I have gone in and out of this American system of racism. On occasion, in Paris, when I would run into white American families on vacation who looked a little lost in the subway I would try to be of assistance in helping them find the tourist sights. When I told them that I lived in Paris, inevitably at some point and in a bit of a nervous way, they would in a complex kind of assertion and questioning mode state that I must miss being back in the States. It happened so many times that I came up with a stock answer, which was that in France, because I was not French, I knew that for the French I was not civilized. However, I never doubted that the French considered me human. Back in the United States, I have walked into rooms or been in places where the reaction of whites to me had made me wonder whether these persons thought I was human. Of course, I knew I was human, but their reaction made me wonder what made them think such crazy thoughts that I was not human. When you know the history, you can see from where this all comes, back to the 15th century and the Pope.

The system morphs all the time—it is a moving target. The morphing with technology now reminds me of the anomie experienced in the Jacksonian period in the transition from agrarianism to market capitalism and how the "winners" of that time were seen and saw themselves.

> American merchants, planters and large landowners, along with the lawyers and clergymen who served them, were accorded the exalted status of "gentlemen." . . . Gentlefolk lived in elegant townhouses or country mansions furnished like those of British gentry and adorned with family portraits. Through indulgent affection and careful education, they shaped self-reliant children for venturesome enterprise, prudent hedonism, and dynastic marriage. They were waited upon by slaves and servants and vied with each other in ornateness of coaches and extravagance of entertainments. Above all they demanded deference from inferiors.[7]

This demanded deference from those who consider themselves superior from those who they consider inferiors (more prosaically referred to as "knowing one's place") is nothing new, and the levers of power are exerted to try to maintain that social and spatial distance. That this mechanism is effective—for white people at least—was most aptly described by former President Lyndon B. Johnson in his famous aphorism:

---

[7] *Id.* at 21.

> If you can convince the lowest white man he's better than the best colored man, he won't notice you're picking his pocket. Hell, give him somebody to look down on, and he'll empty his pockets for you.[8]

So, as part of that ongoing effort to reinforce that hierarchy, we now see ourselves in the post-1965 period where we note the move from Jim Crow to the New Jim Crow detailing the process of subjugation in the current period.[9] Much like at the time of peonage just described, that this Jim Crow is inflicted on Blacks is considered acceptable.

One weird aspect of our current period is the idea of color-blindness. For someone to say they do not see color is as insane as me saying I do not see gender. Yet, the bizarre assertion of color-blindness is a new morph of the old dance in the American legal and social body politic (I call this Lee Atwaterism, as it is the morphing of the hate into abstraction that masks the remaining hate.)

However, this discourse raises some weird dissonances. For example, in the face of the actual vote totals, how can one understand former President Trump asserting what is still remarkably believed by so many white Americans that he was robbed of his landslide victory in 2020? The answer is underlying white supremacism. Trump had a landslide victory *among white Americans*, winning 57 percent of their vote. Ergo, he was "robbed," because he won the only votes that matter under a white supremacist worldview.

Effects

The American White Rage we saw in the Capitol insurrection and what we are likely to see in the next days and months, appears to be drawn substantially from this sense of a loss of the entitlement of whiteness as being the only thing that makes one a true American in this view. That whiteness is almost like having a property right—as some authors have said—similar to the propertied white male voters back in the time of the Founders and Framers.

So, we are called to cast our eyes on the effects of this system of racism.

And as if perfectly timed, we experience another round of state governments working intensively to silence nonwhites by suppressing their vote.[10] Nonwhites who acquiesce to this white nationalist view are tolerated under the heading of "conservative"—so closer to whiteness, but still not white enough.

---

[8] https://www.snopes.com/fact-check/lbj-convince-the-lowest-white-man/.

[9] MICHELLE ALEXANDER, THE NEW JIM CROW, MASS INCARCERATION IN THE AGE OF COLOR BLINDNESS (The New Press 2020).

[10] Voting Laws Roundup: February 2021, The Brennan Center, https://www.brennancenter.org/our-work/research-reports/voting-laws-roundup-february-2021.

So, let us continue with the risk of Covid-19. That risk has fallen signifi-cantly on the old,[11] nonwhites, the poor and low income or low wealth.[12] All the inequities of discrimination come to bear in this time: in health care, housing, education, criminal justice, and finance, health care access and utilization due to the current situation and the dark history, occupation in essential work set-tings like all those workers at the nursing care facilities, educational, income and wealth gaps, and housing. And within these inequities we see the inequi-ties being faced by women in particular experiencing tremendous unemploy-ment increases in this period.[13] Even with the advent of the vaccine, we see the rates of vaccination continuing to reflect these underlying inequities, with the result that the most at risk remain the least likely to be vaccinated—even among the old.[14]

Beyond health, let us look at the problems in transportation policy and infrastructure.

> Racial and economic segregation in urban communities is often understood as a natural consequence of poor choices by individuals. In reality, racially and economically segregated cities are the result of many factors, includ-ing the nation's interstate highway system. In states around the country, highway construction displaced Black households and cut the heart and soul out of thriving Black communities as homes, churches, schools, and businesses were destroyed. In other communities, the highway system was a tool of a segregationist agenda, erecting a wall that separated White and Black communities and protected White people from Black migration.[15]

We can move from transportation to banking:[16]

---

[11] Older Adults At Greater Risk of Requiring Hospitalization or Dying if Diagnosed with COVID-19, Center for Disease Control, February 26, 2021, https://www.cdc.gov/coronavirus/2019-ncov/need-extra-precautions/older-adults.html.

[12] Health Equity Considerations and Racial and Ethnic Minority Groups, Center for Disease Control, February 12, 2021, https://www.cdc.gov/coronavirus/2019-ncov/community/health-equity/race-ethnicity.html.

[13] Rogelio Saenz & Corey Sparks, *The Inequities of Job Loss and Recovery Amid the COVID-19 Pandemic*, August 11, 2020, https://carsey.unh.edu/publication/inequities-job-loss-recovery-amid-COVID-pandemic.

[14] Ruqaiijah Yearby & Seema Mohapatra, *Systemic Racism, The Government's Pandemic Response, and Racial Inequi-ties in Covid-19*, EMORY LAW J. (Forthcoming); David R. Williams, Jourdyn A. Lawrence & Brigette A. Davis, *Racism and Health: Evidence and Needed Research*, 40 ANN. REV. PUB. HEALTH 105–25 (2019), file:///C:/Users/bdavis8/AppData/Local/Microsoft/Windows/INetCache/Content.Outlook/AWBE29Q3/williams%20annurev-publhealth-040218-043750.pdf; Ruqaiijah Yearby & Seema Mohapatra, *Essay: Law, Structural Racism, and the COVID-19 Pandemic*, J. LAW & BIOSCIENCES1–20, doi:10.1093/jlb/lsaa036, file:///C:/Users/bdavis8/AppData/Local/Microsoft/Windows/INetCache/Content.Outlook/AWBE29Q3/Final%20published%20Yearby%20and%20Mohapatra%20JLBS.pdf.

[15] Deborah Archer, *"White Men's Roads Through Black Men's Homes": Advancing Racial Equity Through Highway Reconstruction*, 73 VAND. L. REV. 1259 (2020), https://vanderbiltlawreview.org/lawreview/2020/10/white-mens-roads-through-black-mens-homes-advancing-racial-equity-through-highway-reconstruction/; Deborah Archer, *Transportation Policy and the Underdevelopment of Black Communities*, IOWA LAW REV. (Mar. 4, 2021).

[16] MEHRSA BARADARAN, HOW THE OTHER HALF BANKS (2018).

The answer to the implicit question contained in her title, "How the Other Half Banks," is simple: The "other half" hardly banks at all. Many families below the midline of income distribution in the United States rely heavily on check-cashing services, payday lenders and title vendors charging fees and interest higher than any chartered bank could legally impose. Financial deregulation enabled banks to slough off low-income customers even as it created new opportunities for storefront profit-taking.[17]

This financial apartheid is seen as a threat to democracy much in the same sense that the systemic racism decried by Martin Luther King Jr. sought democracy for whites, and dictatorship for Blacks.

The Birth of the New Is Morphed Old

We have to understand that what we see today as it morphs also cycles back so far in our history that most of us are blind to its source.[18] And we have to understand that a crucial aspect of what is going on today is the mapping out of the kinds of interrelationships to that history to help us not only sense but really see the systems in play, so that they can be changed. Thus, we see the kind of work is emerging, such as:

1. Research that examines the structural and cultural impediments to opportunity that limit full inclusion and block benefits derived from an equitable society.
2. Addressing complex and intertwined issues holistically, cultivating research contributions and collaboration across fields.
3. Research informed by understanding how structures and systems work across domains to produce exclusion and inequality, and inclusion and equality.[19]

This work includes documenting the pain of Black life—and this pain includes traumatic childhood experience.

Let me stop here listing the horribles, as I think I have brought together a sufficient number for the reader to grasp the systemic racism. Not one of these horribles requires a person who screams a racial epithet at a Black person. All it needs is the machine to go grinding on in its inimitable perverse way.

---

[17] Nancy Folbre, "How The Other Half Banks by Mehra Baradaran," New York Review of Books, Oct. 6, 2015, https://www.nytimes.com/2015/10/11/books/review/how-the-other-half-banks-by-mehrsa-baradaran.html#:~:text=Mehrsa Baradaran, a University of Georgia law professor, simple: The "other half" hardly banks at all. Mehra Baradaran: Mehra Baradarn, How the Other Half Banks: Exclusion, Exploitation, and the Threat to Democracy (Harvard University Press, 2015).

[18] *Plessy v. Ferguson and the Legacy of "Separate but Equal" after 125 Years*, 7(1) The Russell Sage Found. J. Social Sciences (Feb. 2021), DOI: https://doi.org/10.7758/RSF.2021.7.1.01.

[19] About Us, Other and Belonging Institute, University of California Berkeley, https://belonging.berkeley.edu/our-story.

What Is to Be Done?

After taking on an over 500-year journey in a few short pages, I have no real uplifting ending here. I feel inadequate that I have not been even able to scratch the surface of the systemic racism that Asian-Americans, Native-Americans, and Hispanic-Americans are experiencing or the religious systemic racism against Muslims. These are all streams of which we should be aware.

Knowledge we are taught is power. Whether knowledge translates into power in confronting this kind of systemic racism is uncertain. What scares me is the willingness of so many to accept the oppression of others so blithely with a kind of faux innocence about it all.

In fact, it is appalling.

* * *

We Just Call Her Bubba . . .

Nwabundo Enuma Ume-Nwagbo[20]

At the firm's monthly firm-wide meeting, all the first-year associates (over 40 of us) sat nervously on the left side of the room in Atlanta awaiting our turn to walk onto the podium and be introduced by our team leaders to the entire law firm. It was our first formal introduction to this well-regarded law firm.

I was nervous (I don't like crowds), but I knew I had to stand up quickly and walk to the podium next to Don, a senior partner and the leader for the Employee Benefits team. I knew he would butcher my name. I just knew it. Before I could take another breath, it was time for my introduction. I stood next to Don as he mispronounced my name horribly just like I knew he would. I did not recognize it as anything sounding like my name. But I did recognize and I am still revolted by what he said next—"We just call her Bubba." And with that, I was introduced to the associates and partners.

This happened about 18 years ago, but, today, it has been brought back to my mind, especially in these times of the deaths of George Floyd, Breonna Taylor, Ahmaud Arbery, and so many others reverberating across this country and the world and is causing (and in a lot of cases, forcing) the nation to finally begin to reckon with its long and sordid history of slavery, centuries of racial injustices against BIPOC (Black, Indigenous and People of Color), and how those injustices have translated in promoting, sustaining, perpetuating, and allowing white privilege to govern every aspect of our lives for these almost 500 years in this nation.

These sweeping changes are forcing corporations, institutions, magazines of all sizes (but especially Fortune 500 corporations) to rethink and reconsider

---

[20] Nwabundo Enuma Ume-Nwagbo lives and works in Atlanta, Georgia. She co-founded Smithers + Ume-Nwagbo, LLC, a law firm that focuses on all aspects of setting up and running businesses and nonprofit organizations.

how they have perpetuated, supported, and encouraged these racist inequalities to persist for as long as they have. But I have not seen such willingness and openness to discuss these issues within Big Law.

According to the American Bar Association's National Lawyer Population Survey for 2019, 64 percent of all lawyers are male and 36 percent are female. Black/African Americans comprise only 5 percent of lawyers, Asians are just a paltry 2 percent, and Hispanics comprise a mere 5 percent. White/Caucasians are a whopping 85 percent. These numbers have remained relatively unchanged for the last ten years.

I suffered through one indignity after another at that well-regarded law firm because I was determined not to be the "angry Black bitch" who can't get along with anyone. So, I watched as white associates (male and female) were introduced to senior partners (99.9 percent of them were white) and began receiving billable work. Meanwhile, I sat wondering how many times I would be called to work on a presentation for the partners (which meant non-billable work) and I wondered when I would finally get a chance to work on billable matters with some of these partners.

The next firm I worked at was not any better. The firm spent little time in actually exposing me to different areas of the law to which I expressed an interest. I am an employee benefits lawyer and I wanted to be exposed to executive compensation issues, 457(b) plans, and employee stock ownership plans. I mentioned this during each annual review, but I never was granted those opportunities. Instead, I sat in my office day after day as my colleagues (who were all 100 percent white) were assigned mentors who gladly took their prized mentees to client meetings and other outings, which are highly cherished among associates as ways to move forward in one's legal career.

I look back at the four and a half years I spent working as a senior associate with yet another Big Law firm's Charlotte office. In those four and a half years, the team leader never called me by name. Not once!! It was demoralizing every single day.

I have had time to reflect on the first time I finally stood up for myself, ten years into my Big Law career. I was talking on the telephone with a partner, and she started an argument with me about how to pronounce my name. She was certain that the pronunciation was "Wanda" and not "Nwa'ndo." The absolute and utter arrogance of this non-Nigerian woman trying to tell me how to pronounce my Nigerian name because she heard other non-Nigerian people call me "Wanda." I responded with every fiber of my being that *she* was one of the people who called me "Wanda," even though I repeatedly told her my name was "Nwa'ndo." I also reminded her that just because she had decided what she thought my name should be did not, in any way, make it acceptable for her to mispronounce my name.

It felt good. I finally stood up and told a partner at a major law firm exactly what I needed to say in that moment. But I also knew my time at Big Law was ending. I knew that sooner or later I would find myself out of Big Law (either because they decided to fire me or because I decided to quit).

And, on April 15, 2012, I gave my two-week notice. I moved back to Atlanta and two weeks later, on May 1, 2012, I started a law firm with two of my friends.

The decision to start my law firm with my friends forced me to wrestle with the thought of my very Nigerian name being front and center for the world to see. My partners did not hesitate for one minute to use my full last name. I was not so sure. I wanted to get the thoughts of my family. All four of them (parents and brothers) thought it was "career suicide" to place my name, our name, on the letterhead. But I also had to think about everything I had done and accomplished with my last name. I realized that with that name, I came back to this country, worked two jobs to get through college and made it through Duke University School of Law. I started my career at a prestigious law firm and moved on to two other prestigious law firms using that very Nigerian name. I was on the cusp of diving into entrepreneurship with the only thing that has remained constant my entire life—my name.

In that moment, I made a decision. I decided to embrace my full name in every possible way. I decided to use my last name on that letterhead. Today, I use my full name on the Georgia State Bar's website. I sign my letters with my full name. I no longer censor my name in any way. For people who have a problem with pronouncing my name and decide to call me "Wanda" or anything other than my name, tough! If they can pronounce the Eastern European names that start with four consonants, they can pronounce my name. If anyone asks, I simply say – my name is Nwabundo Enuma Ume-Nwagbo. My friends call me Nwa'ndo.

* * *

Still Writing at the Master's Table: Decolonizing Rhetoric in Legal Writing for a "Woke" Legal Academy[21]

Teri A. McMurtry-Chubb[22]

Woke (wōk): An awakening to racial and social injustices

As the trees adorned their leaves in brilliant, fiery, and bittersweet, fall semester plodded along definitively toward anxiety, taking infrequent rests in apathy. During one such rest, I called my Critical Race Theory/Critical Race Feminism class to order in a classroom located in the Deep South at a law school named for a vocal proponent of school segregation. Our presence in that space

---

[21] Originally published at 21 The Scholar 255 (2019). Reprinted with permission.

[22] Teri A. McMurtry-Chubb is an Associate Dean of Research and Faculty Development and Professor of Law at the University of Illinois Chicago School of Law. She researches, teaches and writes in the areas of critical and comparative rhetoric, discourse and genre analysis, and legal history.

at that particular time was nothing short of miraculous. The class was comprised primarily of African American students, taught by a tenured African American female law professor of legal writing, and offered at a law school that had graduated its first African American law student in 1972.

The week's lesson was about legal storytelling and narrative, and was designated by topic on the course syllabus as "History, Herstory, Our (Legal) Story?" The one and a half hour class session began with a discussion of counter-storytelling as a means to expose history as "story," to critique and tear down dominant normative universes as they exist in law, and to provide alternate analytical frameworks for addressing legal problems. My shock blazed brilliant, burned fiery, and cooled more bitter than sweet when an African American student raised her hand to state confidently, "There is no African American history or culture." Her remark proved the existence of a dominant normative universe birthed from a collision of white supremacy, patriarchy, capitalism, and imperialism.

My epiphany from this blunt exchange was that my student and her like-minded peers' mis-education would form a basis for their interpretation of the law, inform their reasoning as they built legal arguments as advocates, and reveal itself to damaging effect as they communicated that reasoning through writing. As a law professor of legal writing, teaching students the communication processes by which to replicate the power structures that marginalized them and maintained the legal academy, without a critique of those processes, was the price I paid for us all to write at the master's table.

This article focuses on how law professors of legal writing are forced to serve as handmaidens of hierarchy in the maintenance of the legal academy as an elite and closed discourse community. It considers how in teaching students to "do" law—employ legal reasoning and analysis through written communication—legal writing curricula provide for no critique of the colonized formal rhetorical structures in which critical thinking, reading, analysis, and writing skills are grounded.

Western Thought and Inventio and Dispositio as Barriers to Social Justice

As the first African American woman to win a seat in Congress and to seek a major party nomination for President of the United States, Shirley Chisholm was no stranger to the series of inhospitable tables to which she carried multiple folding chairs. For the "unbossed and unbought" Chisholm, the master's table was the hostile forum of U.S. politics. For law professors of legal writing, the master's table is the legal academy.

Legal analysis and writing as taught in the legal academy are based on the five canons of rhetoric—also known as "classical rhetoric"—as well as Aristotle's emotional appeals. The five canons of rhetoric are Inventio (invention or discovery), Dispositio (arrangement or organization), Elocutio (style), Memoria (memory), and Pronuntiatio (delivery). Of particular interest to the study of legal reasoning, analysis, and writing are the canons Inventio and Dispositio. Inventio concerns the sources for arguments, and the process by which advocates categorize and connect information in those sources to formulate arguments. Dispositio is the means of organizing arguments into communication forms that are appropriate and effective for their purpose.

Aristotle's persuasive appeals: logos (using evidence and Western-based epistemology to persuade), pathos (using acceptable Western-based modes of emotion to persuade), and ethos (using Western-based conceptions of character to persuade) are tools used to marshal arguments for maximum impact. Both the classical rhetorical canons and Aristotle's persuasive appeals operate within the nomos, or the normative universe in which they function. Although not always explicit in most legal writing curricula, these canons and persuasive appeals have become foundational to teaching the processes of communicating legal reasoning and analysis in written form

Classical rhetoric is rooted in Western/European epistemology and ontology, or Eurocentric ways of knowing and being. Critical rhetoricians have problematized the relationship between the two as they recreate dominant ideologies under the guise of neutrality, and erase marginalized epistemologies and ideologies. This relationship is particularly troublesome given that as language is used to describe an experience or reality, it also acts to create the experience or reality it seeks to describe—language is epistemic. This country began with Indigenous decimation, continued with African chattel slavery, and mythologized its existence as a nation of immigrants. A Western epistemological rhetorical canon that does not problematize the existence of White supremacy, patriarchy, capitalism, and imperialism serves as fertile ground for Inventio and Dispositio that perpetuate untruths, and seek to solidify them through legal argument as memorialized in American jurisprudence. The struggle [is] to resituate Inventio and Dispositio in something other than Eurocentricity, in [an] effort to liberate the oppressed.

From Canonicity to Centering Oppositional Rhetorics

Like the canonization of literary and historical texts, canonizing rhetorical processes of argumentation is an exercise in exclusion and reification. Each time a court makes a choice to accept some legal arguments over others, some histories over others, it makes a choice about which values it wishes to protect and which it denigrates. Each time a professor teaches a case and the reasoning processes that led to its outcome benignly, the professor fails to "[decenter] and disrupt the implicit and explicit narratives—like Eurocentrism, conflict-resolution through violence, gender stereotypes, and racism—that canonical texts can foster in contemporary classrooms." Formalistic and abstract legal reasoning are situated in the West. Relocating canons of rhetoric outside of the

West problematizes the structures by which reasoning takes place by offering oppositional rhetorics as alternatives.

African Diasporic Rhetoric

The African holocaust forced Black bodies from the continent of Africa and scattered them throughout the world through the vehicle of human trafficking. Africans endured, and our encounters with non-Africans throughout the Diaspora forced cultural syncretism from shared history. In their path-forging work, *Understanding African American Rhetoric: Classical Origins to Contemporary Innovation*, rhetoric scholars Ronald L. Jackson II and Elaine B. Richardson position African American rhetoric as a valid subject of study in the academy worthy of scholarly inquiry. The foreword by activist and critical rhetorician Orlando L. Taylor notes that this work is important because scholars of African Diasporic rhetoric who are African Diasporic people are its contributors, engaged in the enterprise of decolonizing the knowledge of the discipline and their place in it. He writes, "Volumes such as these interrogate the flawed singularity of truth telling in rhetorical studies not only by exposing the limitations of the European-centered literature's hegemonic intent, but also by centralizing and celebrating the uniqueness of another rhetorical tradition, that of African Americans."

Understanding African American Rhetoric moves us beyond an understanding of African American rhetoric as oratory to an introduction of its African Diasporic rhetorical practices and traditions. It challenges Western "classical" rhetorical frameworks as "culturally generic paradigms" inadequate to examine the cultural specificity of rhetorical strategies. Accordingly, Africology (the study of the histories and cultures of African peoples on the African continent) and Afrocentricity (an African centered worldview) are foundational to building the culturally specific paradigms and methods by which to study African Diasporic rhetorical practices.

African Diasporic rhetoric marks the Kemetic texts of ancient Egypt as a starting point. These texts are a conceptual departure from Greco-Roman rhetorical texts, in that the latter are connected to the marketplace while the former are not. Rather, the Kemetic texts are an expression of community, an exercise in community building, and a practice of safeguarding community well-being. African Diasporic rhetoric originates in an oral tradition, rather than a written one. Scholar Maulana Karenga grounds the African oral tradition in the Black nationalist Kawaida philosophy, described as "a cultural core that forms the central locus of our self-understanding and self-assertion in the world and which is mediated by constantly changing historical circumstances and an ongoing internal dialog of reassessment and continuous development[.]" Kawaida is a lens that guides the scholarly interpretation of ancient African rhetorical texts.

The Book of Ptahhotep, an Egyptian text and the oldest rhetorical text in existence, has two basic tenets: "rhetoric as eloquent and effective speech itself (mdt nfrt—medet neferet) and rhetoric as the rules or principles for eloquent and effective speech (tp-hsb n mdt nfrt—tep-heseb en medet neferet)." This idea of eloquence as unity is reflective of ethical speech as a tool for community building, an expression of the ancient Egyptian moral tenet of Maat or "rightness in the world." Maat has seven principles: "truth, justice, propriety, harmony, balance, reciprocity, and order," truth being the most important. Maat also affirms the value of all people, regardless of race, class, or gender, and stresses the partnership between rhetor and audience in community building. Instructions for the practice of African rhetoric are found in the Book of Khunanup, which considers the rhetor's use of Maat to argue for justice. Maat's loose parallels in the Western world are Aristotle's persuasive appeals (logos, pathos, and ethos).

The African nommo, or nummo, is the universe in which invocations for justice function. In the Malian creation story "the Creator, Amma, sends nommo, the word (in the collective sense of speech), to complete the spiritual and material reorganization of the world and to assist humans in the forward movement in history and society." The word *nommo* makes community building, safeguarding, and well-being possible; it is the space that gives Maat meaning and form to achieve good in the world.

As expressed in African American rhetoric, nommo is resistance to oppressive regimes that made it illegal for enslaved persons to read and write. As an import to the United States through the bodies of trafficked Africans, nommo persists as a weapon of cultural resistance and a testament to cultural retention. It embodies the ethics of speech found in the Book of Ptahhotep that unify African American rhetoric:

> [1] the dignity and rights of the human person; [2] the well-being and flourishing of community; [3] the integrity and value of the environment [to repair ecological, social, and ontological damage in the world resulting from acts of commission and omission]; and [4] the reciprocal solidarity and cooperation for mutual benefit of humanity ["speak truth, do justice"].

These tenets provide the source for petitions to justice, and guide their arrangement and the medium in which they are presented.

Classroom Exercises Utilizing African Diasporic Rhetoric for Oppositional Discourse

- ◆ Utilize nommo as an interpretive framework for litigation over the "zero tolerance" immigration policy that resulted in family separation at the border, and Presidential Executive Order 13841 Affording Congress an Opportunity to Address Family Separation.
- ◆ Use Ella's song *We Who Believe in Freedom Cannot Rest Until It Comes* by the Africana women recording artists Sweet Honey in the Rock as an

analytical framework and expression of Maat to draft an alternative to Presidential Executive Order 13769 Protecting the Nation from Foreign Terrorist Entry into the United States (a.k.a. the Muslim travel ban)

◆ Compare and contrast the FBI's intelligence assessment of "Black Identity Extremists" to policies on domestic terrorism to challenge the process of criminalization as a culturally generic paradigm.

◆ Compare and contrast the U.S. Constitution and Confederate Constitution as oppositional rhetorics to nommo.

* * *

Some Book Survey Responses Addressing Race

We surveyed lawyers, asking for their views on topics covered in this book. Here are two of the anonymous contributions we received addressing race, racism, and discrimination (including critical race theory (CRT) and responses to it such as the CRT scare and replacement theory).

> I was asked to second chair a civil action against my governmental employee which involved the death of two young people, one of them Black. 3 white young people were also injured. My only role was to cross-examine the African-American decedent's mother—in essence, to add color to the table so it wouldn't be an old white guy asking her questions. I was very brief and respectful with my questions of her.
>
> –Anonymous

> In law school, a professor inadvertently disclosed that our class placements were based on "expected success." Most of the African Americans were in the same class, and the professor was admonished for sharing the information.
>
> –Anonymous

We also reached out to friends, students, and colleagues with an invitation to participate in the survey or to write. We got several responses like this one:

> I've experienced racism my whole life. I've changed my hair and learned to speak with extreme grammar so I could fit in. I dress very conservatively. I've learned to be polite and that I'm never allowed to be angry. I keep my opinions to myself most of the time. I am clear that racism is built into the fabric of this society. I'm not sure it will ever change. I'm tired of trying to fit in and exhausted from the conversation about racism and whether it exists in this country. I can't march any more. I can't even talk about it. I have no hope that anything will be different.

Addressing Trauma at the Community Level

Trauma-Informed Lawyering for Asian Communities[23]

Jacqueline Louie[24]

Have you ever seen a psychologist or counselor? I've seen a few over the past several years, and one of the first things they ask is whether I'd like tea or water. They tell me to make myself comfortable on one of their office's chairs, or maybe they have a couch. Often, they'll ask me what my preferred name is. If I start to cry, they offer me tissues and we sit in silence for however long I need. If they take notes, they let me know why, and that everything we discuss is confidential with a few exceptions. They ask if I have questions.

Good service will make you feel seen and heard, whether it is in a counseling context or not. Did you have a teacher that did that for you? Do you choose which grocery store to shop at because one caters to your cultural needs? On the other hand, have you felt ignored or dismissed about an issue in your workplace? Or a health issue with a medical professional? Has an advisor or counselor glossed over your culturally-specific issues and needs?

As I think of these counseling practices, I am struck by the number of parallels between them and trauma-informed lawyering. A trauma-informed approach to legal practice is simple—recognize symptoms of trauma and use this knowledge in interactions with others, in order to avoid inflicting further trauma.

Addressing Trauma within Asian Communities

Different kinds of trauma can manifest from several sources—whether as the result of multiple microaggressions or major life events. Clients in any field of law may bring trauma with them that will impact how a lawyer will serve them. Additionally, trauma may visibly manifest in many different ways, or not at all. For this reason, recognizing trauma can be difficult in Asian clients. Within many Asian communities, trauma may be unspoken as a result of shame, but it exists.

Trauma runs through our migration histories. It remains present in our experiences of family separation, disconnection from cultures of our ancestry, and intergenerational trauma. It continues to manifest as a result of racism. With reported anti-Asian hate crimes having increased by 878 percent since the beginning of the Covid-19 pandemic, there is no question that our communities

---

[23] This is an edited version of an article originally published on Cold Tea Collective. Jacqueline Louie, *Trauma-Informed Lawyering for Asian Communities*, COLD TEA COLLECTIVE (27 Dec. 27. 2020), https://coldteacollective .com/trauma-informed-lawyering-for-asian-communities/. Reprinted with permission.

[24] Jacqueline Louie is an articling student at Victory Square Law Office LLP and a Federation of Asian Canadian Lawyers British Columbia (FACL BC) member.

continue to experience trauma today.[25] It is also clear that our communities would benefit from being served by trauma-informed lawyers.

When communicating with Asian clients and communities, integrating a trauma-informed approach may look different. Where in some cultures it is appropriate to make eye contact to communicate active listening, it may be more appropriate in others to avoid it. Where silence and long pauses are uncomfortable for some, an Asian client carrying trauma may need more space and time to communicate the details of their issue and answer questions. A trauma-informed approach also considers these often-subtle, culturally specific needs.

Taking Trauma-Informed Approaches beyond Law

If you are an Asian lawyer, or serve Asian clients, a trauma-informed approach should be the standard for high-quality service. Just as currents of trauma continue to inform the Asian experience, Asian clients deserve trauma-informed service.

But beyond the legal profession, we should be collectively asking how to be trauma-informed in all of our work. How can government services, policy, and grassroots organizing be trauma informed? How would your work be different if you did it in a way that centered trust and humility? If you were aware of the types of trauma Asian communities have and continue to face?

Learning about these histories and contexts can help us be trauma informed. Resources such as Project 1907 work to chronicle ongoing incidents of anti-Asian racism, while providing historical context for the traumas that affect these communities today.[26] Beyond that, we can diversify our sources of information to learn directly from members of marginalized communities about their lived experiences and needs. In addition, the Trauma-Informed Lawyer podcast and FACL BC's podcast provide opportunities to learn more about trauma-informed lawyering.[27]

I encourage you, in whatever field you work, to learn about the communities you serve, the traumas they may carry with them, and to implement a trauma-informed approach for your interactions with others.

---

[25] Alyse Kotyk, *Anti-Asian Hate Crime Incidents Rose by 878% Compared to Last Year, Vancouver Police Report Says*, CTV NEWS (Oct. 29, 2020), https://bc.ctvnews.ca/anti-asian-hate-crime-incidents-rose-by-878-compared-to -last-year-vancouver-police-report-says-1.5166754.

[26] "Project 1907" (2021), online: *Project 1907*, https://www.project1907.org/.

[27] "The Trauma-Informed Lawyer hosted by Myrna McCallum," online (podcast): https://thetraumainformed lawyer.simplecast.com/; "FACL BC," online (podcast): https://open.spotify.com/show/3wLEXIVTWwjUlr EN2Mj1kc.

Intersectionality

Of course, racism is not the only systemic trauma. Besides racism, sexism, hetero-sexism, ageism, ableism, anti-Semitism, and binaryism are just some of the issues that shape a traumatizing system. All reflect that the history of law has been built in a time of white, straight, cis-gender male dominance. There are also issues of intersectionality where people are impacted by multiple forces. Kimberlé Crenshaw, who developed the theory of intersectionality, provides an approachable overview of it in her TED Talk.[28]

Now more than ever, it's important to look boldly at the reality of race and gender bias—and understand how the two can combine to create even more harm. Kimberlé Crenshaw uses the term *intersectionality* to describe this phenomenon; as she says, if you're standing in the path of multiple forms of exclusion, you're likely to get hit by both. In this moving TED Talk, she calls on us to bear witness to this reality and speak up for victims of prejudice.[29]

Now, you might ask, why does a frame matter? I mean, after all, an issue that affects Black people and an issue that affects women, wouldn't that necessarily include Black people who are women and women who are Black people? Well, the simple answer is that this is a trickle-down approach to social justice, and many times it just doesn't work. Without frames that allow us to see how social problems impact all the members of a targeted group, many will fall through the cracks of our movements, left to suffer in virtual isolation. But it doesn't have to be this way.

Many years ago, I began to use the term "intersectionality" to deal with the fact that many of our social justice problems like racism and sexism are often overlapping, creating multiple levels of social injustice.[30]

Inviting the Whole Self to Legal Practice

River Shannon[31]

The traditional model of legal practice can be an uncomfortable fit for Indigenous people, people of color, working class people, women, LGBTQ2S+ folks, and others for whom the unspoken "ideal" of the lawyer does not match the identities they bring with them into that first day of law school.

---

[28] https://www.ted.com/talks/kimberle_crenshaw_the_urgency_of_intersectionality.

[29] From the introduction to the TED Talk.

[30] A quote from the TED Talk by Kimberle Crenshaw, https://www.ted.com/talks/kimberle_crenshaw_the _urgency_of_intersectionality.

[31] River Shannon's professional passion is for legal and social justice education. They interned at legal clinics in Montreal and with the Children's Legal & Educational Resource Centre in Calgary. During law school, River held the position of associate managing editor with the McGill International Journal of Sustainable Law, Development and Policy. River has lectured on legal issues in environmentalism at the Department of Geography, University of Ottawa. River currently serves as Staff Lawyer of the YWCA Metro Vancouver Legal Education Program, where they assist women survivors of intimate partner violence.

As a genderqueer, nonbinary lawyer, I am familiar with the discomfort of squeezing into a professional identity that does not match my life outside the courtroom. When I started in legal practice, I wasn't complaining. The role of a lawyer felt like a promising means of running away from my feelings of self-hatred and inadequacy. I also thought it would afford me the respect and dignity I and those like me are so often denied. And so, I threw myself into the practice, believing that my being queer had nothing to do with being a competent lawyer.

The fact that I was miserable also felt like a private concern, separate from my service to clients, the court, and my community.

In taking up trauma awareness and cultural humility as the guiding lights of my practice, it has become clear to me that this was the wrong perspective.

I would like you to know, colleague, that your well-being and thriving are key elements of trauma-informed legal practice. Not as afterthoughts, some things to address on the way to serving clients—rather than harming them—but as integral components of a holistic perspective that includes not only the client's dignity, humanity, and well-being but also your own. Who you are beyond legal practice is not just invited to this work—it is welcomed and included.

To illustrate, I would like to relate the experience of including my pronouns (they and them) when I introduce myself to the court. In December 2020, British Columbia courts issued practice directions asking people to state their name, title (sometimes called "salutation"), and pronouns, and for lawyers to provide this information for their clients.

For example, when introducing myself to the court, I would say "Good morning your Honor, my name for the record is Mx. River Shannon—S H A N N O N—first initial 'R' and I use they/them pronouns. I appear this morning on behalf of the applicant, Ms. Jane Doe, who uses she/her pronouns."

The Sexual Orientation and Gender Identity Community Section of the Canadian Bar Association's B.C. branch was instrumental in bringing about these directions, and I am deeply grateful to them for their work on this.

At the time these changes came about, they were a welcome surprise. Earlier in 2020, I had struggled to have my chosen name recognized by my Law Society. I have regularly dealt with colleagues and the court taking me for either a woman or a man, particularly during pandemic telephone appearances.

To be clear, I have the privilege of knowing many lawyers and legal professionals who celebrate their trans and gender diverse colleagues. But our profession is slow to change and the cost of speaking out can be high—reputation means a great deal. And the reputation of a transgender lawyer, or an Indigenous lawyer, or a woman lawyer is inevitably more delicate than those of their counterparts.

Brad Regehr, president of the Canadian Bar Association, and Jennifer Brun, president of our B.C. branch, wisely pointed out in their defense of the practice directions that transgender and nonbinary lawyers are often placed in a double bind when they face misgendering or mistreatment by the courts or colleagues. They might ignore the misgendering, and suffer indignity and distress, or they might speak out and risk detracting from their client's matter.[32]

I can confirm this experience. I have rarely corrected misgendering at work. I have often felt that doing so would damage my relationship with my client, the court, or my colleagues. I have attempted, proactively, to communicate my pronouns and name, and to hope for the best. At times it has been stifling. And when, inevitably, I have been misgendered, I have smiled and shrugged it off. But it has hurt. Perhaps more insidiously, each time it has happened, the identity of "lawyer" fits a little less.

This new practice direction has opened a space of ease for me in my work. I no longer feel like a troublemaker or nuisance when I communicate my pronouns to the court. Instead, I feel that the courts and my colleagues have intentionally acknowledged my existence and have thereby allowed me to bring my full self into the courtroom with me. Moreover, by setting a new norm, they have made it easier for me to have conversations with my clients around my pronouns and gender.

After December 2020, it became a little easier to be a lawyer, for my identities as a lawyer and a nonbinary person to cohabit harmoniously in my life.

I would like readers to consider two things. First, which identities are important to you? If you are a person of color, do you find that there's an expectation, unspoken or otherwise, to leave aspects of that identity outside the courtroom or law firm? How often do you keep silent for your reputation or your client, at the risk of your dignity and well-being? Even if you are white and otherwise privileged, I would invite you to consider, if you are a parent or grandparent, is there space for that in your practice? What about your faith, tradition, or culture?

Second, when we talk about diversity in the profession, what do we mean? Certainly, one important step we can take to promote diversity is to ensure that marginalized folks are sitting on our benches, serving in our courtrooms, and leading our firms.

Trauma-informed practice and cultural humility ask that we do more than simply foster diversity of representation. They require us to investigate how we can actively make marginalized people feel welcome in our profession.

[32] Brad Regehr & Jennifer Brun, *In Defence of B.C.'s Pronoun Practice Directives*, THE LAWYER'S DAILY (Mar. 03, 2021), https://www.thelawyersdaily.ca/articles/25077/in-defence-of-b-c-s-pronoun-practice-directives-brad-regehr-and-jennifer-brun.

These new practice directions around pronouns have made a tangible, positive impact on my life and career. In turn, I must ask how I can advocate for the comfort, dignity, and inclusion of colleagues with different life experiences and identities than my own.

Beyond questions of diversity and wellness, I want to emphasize the importance of bringing the whole person into the practice of law. Not just for the well-being of the professional, but because it will make us better lawyers, better human beings, and help us create a better justice system.

As you consider trauma aware and informed practice, and how best to integrate its principles into your work and life, I would like you to practice with two compass points. First, how can you make your office, courtroom, and communities welcoming places for marginalized colleagues and clients? Second, what is it that you need to bring your whole person into your practice?

You may think that these two questions are quite different, sometimes even opposed. I certainly did for many years. But I would like to challenge that. I have come to recognize that when judges and lawyers are permitted to bring their full humanity—in all its diversity—to play in their practice, they are not only happier and healthier but more competent and compassionate as well.

I hope that, as we continue to explore and implement trauma-informed strategies and perspectives in our legal community, an attitude of active inclusion will become the foundation of a profession we can all call home.

Trauma Aware yet Not Trauma Defined

Annabelle Berrios[33]

What would it be like to be trauma aware and not trauma defined? What possibilities might open for myself and others in that space?

Trauma aware . . .

As a restorative justice practitioner, I feel excited about spaces where truth telling, accountability and compassion coexist. Our legal systems, in my experience, incentivize lying. In law school, I was taught CYA ("cover your ass") strategies from day one. Self-protection does not encourage responsibility; it only breeds adversaries. It starts out as an inside job, where guilt, shame, or fear disincentivize us to tell the truth to ourselves.

For example, maybe you have said to yourself something along the lines of:

I didn't do anything wrong—I'm a good person. I've been working for this cause my whole life.

---

[33] Annabelle Berríos, raised in San Juan, Puerto Rico, practiced law for 13 years, mostly in the criminal field. She has a JD from Boston College Law School and an MA in East West psychology from the California Institute for Integral Studies. She is a social impact consultant who partners with leaders willing to compost the silo of identity politics to unleash collective potentials for social justice. Her website is: www.umbralconsulting.com.

The thing is, it is legitimate—and well advised—to self-protect in an adversarial system, where winning presupposes that someone else has to lose. I prefer to think of truth telling as the practice of authenticity, because the root of the word is "author" and those who create conditions for safety in truth telling get to co-author relationships of care and respect.

This truth telling, generative "co-authoring" can only go well if compassion is practiced alongside it, starting with self-compassion. I invite you to consider self-compassion as a way to practice humility. I define humility as the acknowledgment that I am seeing things from a limited perspective—a perspective likely focused on my own experience—which may be making me blind to other, insight-offering perspectives. When I practice self-compassion, I am open to noticing my limits without judgment, to admit to what I don't know and consider how what I say out of my not-knowing could impact someone. This offers opportunities for learning, choice, and self-accountability.

For some of us, increased visibility of systemic inequity is an exciting opportunity creating new avenues for change. For those of us to whom these inequities have always been apparent and the harm is ongoing, it may hurt to see how societal inequities have shielded fellow citizens from seeing or experiencing that harm. There are multiple possible perspectives in-between those two binaries.

I think of this as a spectrum of proximity to systemic harm, where individuals are differently situated in relationship to that harm based on their privilege. For example, while someone could approach discussions on racialized violence from an intellectual or ideological stance, able to feel righteous anger without experiencing a trauma response, the person next to them could be struggling with trauma activation in that same conversation. As a Latina ex-lawyer, I may feel comfortable taking on a warrior stance to discuss racial disparities in mass incarceration, emphasizing the impact on Black men. However, I am not a Black man living the ongoing threat of violence that Black men face day-to-day in the United States, nor can I ever understand the cost of confronting this reality with others who are not directly experiencing it.

Trauma awareness means considering that good intentions do not protect us from having an unintended harmful impact on another. This is not about getting it right. A focus on getting it right kills humility, and brings out defensiveness. It blocks learning, growth, and real connection. It might feel risky or scary. Yes, it feels vulnerable. It may even hurt. Yet, what if the practice of self-compassion and humility builds capacity to be in true solidarity with others, in ways that build trust and open new creative possibilities?

. . . yet not trauma defined

Restorative practices open a portal sourced in Indigenous worldviews that inherently recognize our interdependence—well-being that is linked to one another's well-being. A restorative lens invites us to move past labels, presupposing that individuals are whole people, capable of growth and change.

What could it be to regard myself as a whole person, aware of trauma without being defined by it? I'll share an example from my own life of how I am living into that question.

When I was 19, I was held up at gunpoint by someone who looked no older than 13 years old. I remember how my friends and I were asked to stand side-by-side, forming a straight line, while this youth stood in front of each of my friends to take their money and jewelry. I was standing at the end of the line. At first, I was not looking at the youth. My eyes focused on the gun he was holding. When he stood in front of me, I noticed that the hand holding the gun was shaking. I managed somehow to look past the gun and saw the youth's face. We locked eyes. Tears were coming down his face. My eyes felt wet, too. I saw him look over his shoulder, and I followed his gaze. There was an adult looking over at us from a yellow car parked a short distance away. The youth looked back at me and said: "I'm sorry," tearing up further as he said it. I tear up now remembering it. That was a defining moment for me. He became a real person for me then—a human being who was likely coerced to do this, a young person with a sense that this action was wrong. I also connected to my own humanity, touched by empathy and standing taller in my own dignity, eerily calmer. We were two people experiencing a traumatic event that neither defined who we were nor precluded who we could grow to become. I like to think that this moment planted in me a seed for future exploration of how justice could promote healing instead of perpetuate harm.

When I last visited El Yunque, Puerto Rico's Tropical Rainforest, I noticed how the roots of some trees—which rose above the ground—appeared to be swollen like bulging veins. I was told that the trees do this to gain strength in advance of an oncoming storm. Sometimes, the roots of one tree entangle with the roots of another, building collective strength for the benefit of the larger ecosystem. It settles me to remember that a human being's inherent dignity—as a source of inner strength—exists beyond the storm of circumstances or limiting social identities, and that we can uplift one another in our strength. In truth, the human spirit in all its daring, rebellious joyfulness cannot be obliterated. In Puerto Rico, we have a saying *"tiene la musica por dentro"*—they have/hear the music within—which to me is a way of remembering that there is an existence beyond trauma, beyond fixed identities and adversaries, from where powerful, creative responses can be sourced for co-authoring care and responsibility. A space that neither denies trauma nor places trauma at the center, where the wisdom of wholeness can lead change.

* * *

Some Trauma-Informed Frameworks for Systems Change: Change Makers, Designing Systems and Cultural Organizing

What Is a System (and How Can We Change It)?

J. Kim Wright

If we're going to change the legal system or our larger systems, it is helpful to know something about systems theory and systems thinking.

My shorthand description of systems thinking is now this: everything is connected to everything else. We live in an interconnected, interdependent universe.

A systems thinking approach sees how things are connected and influence each other. For example, in the human body, we have many nested systems: respiratory, circulatory, digestive, and so on. Each can be studied separately, but they are interrelated and affect each other.

Another often shared mythical story talks about a village next to a river. One day, a baby washes up on the bank of the river. The villagers rush to rescue the baby only to find that another baby washes up a few minutes later. Eventually, hundreds of babies are washing up on the bank, each rescued and helped by the villagers. Finally, someone says, "Let's go up river and see where the babies are coming from!" That is the shift to systems thinking.

In the legal systems, lawyers valiantly defend clients accused of crimes that grew from systemic problems. The government builds more prisons. The bar associations create commissions to study lawyer well-being and make recommendations for self-care. We wear ourselves out with efforts that are akin to pulling babies out of the water, rather than changing the system that creates the conditions that have babies washing up on river banks. It isn't our lack of commitment or compassion that keeps us down the river. The work we do makes a difference for the ones we serve, but it doesn't stop the stream of cases that seem to never end.

So how do we make the changes that need to be made, to stop the flow of cases and create the society we want to create?

Systems theory tells us that systems are cyclical. They are born and they die. Societies rise and fall. Ideas ebb and flow. Scholars have studied historical patterns and we're in one of those times and their measures make a pretty compelling case that we are in the systems dying phase of a lot of our Western cultural and governmental systems. Those old dominant systems are beginning to be replaced—not reformed, but actually replaced—with new systems based on a different set of values and knowledge.

For some 25 years, I have been studying the emerging legal models. I find most hope in the integrative law movement. This book is an example of the thinking that comes from that movement. I've written two more with specific models, approaches, ideas, and examples. Approaches like Collaborative Practice (in divorce and civil matters), some forms of Mediation, Restorative Justice, Problem-Solving Courts, Holistic Law, Values-Based Contracts, and many more are examples of practice areas that incorporate a broader systems design perspective and offer role models for what's possible.

Roles for Change Makers

I am a student of the work of Margaret Wheatley, an author, systems thinker, and one of the founders of the Berkana Institute. Berkana has a theory, The Two Loops Theory, that explains how systems rise and fall. The model shows that as the old dominant system begins to fail, new ways start to emerge. The new ways are the beginnings of a new system and there are many roles that stakeholders assume during the shift.

I have expanded and adapted Berkana's ideas and have identified several roles in the transition between the old (dominant) legal system and the emerging system:

- ◆ Defenders of the dominant system. They think the legal system is fine the way it is and push back at any attempts toward change. I don't need to give you examples of who these people are. You meet them in law schools, courtrooms, and bar association meetings all the time. They push back against all changes and attempt to block change.

- ◆ Reformers of the dominant system. They think the system is basically sound and just needs a few tweaks to work better. They're the folks who just want to change a few rules, tweak a few things here and there, but believe that the system is working just fine for most people.

- ◆ Hospice workers. They bring aid and comfort to those who are suffering in the dominant system. The lawyers assistance programs, lawyer wellness programs, victim advocates, and your therapist fall in this category.

- ◆ Trailblazers and pioneers of the new system. Trailblazers have the ideas and pioneers put them into action. These include many integrative lawyers, organizations like the Center for Court Innovation, and the early trauma-informed courts. Trailblazers and pioneers can be local or global. Stu Webb who created the Collaborative Law model was a trailblazer who saw the pain caused by divorce litigation and offered an alternative model. The more than 50,000 lawyers who have been trained in the model could be considered pioneers in their communities.

- ◆ Protectors, supporters, and cheerleaders of the emerging system are individuals who are in the dominant system but they see the emerging system and share ideas, credibility, and even resources (such as grant funds) to help nourish those in the emerging system. This role is very important since we tend to look to leaders in the old system for guidance about where to go next. And the emerging systems may not yet have the resources or fortitude to continue without that support or credibility.

◆ Bridge builders help to connect people in the old dominant system with the emerging system. They help them transition from one system to another. They make connections. They showcase new approaches and encourage people to try something different. Bridge builders say, "Hey look! There is something cool going on over there! Let's check it out!" Bridges can be built by writing books and articles, by teaching, or by talking about new ideas.

◆ And finally, we have the designers who are the thought leaders who are working on making sure the new system is actually better and more workable than the old one.

These roles provide a path of action for lawyers who want to be change makers, no matter where they are in the system.

The common law system is based on precedent and therefore lawyers tend to be defenders of the status quo. Human beings, in general, but lawyers in particular are resistant to change. Our brains sort for exceptions to our comfort zones and try to avoid discomfort. But what can we do when the dominant system is dying, when the existing system is based on trauma and perpetuates it?

Designing a System

In the last few years, I have come to be a fan of design thinking as a tool for systems design. This area of study has led me down many interesting and fruitful paths and I've been introduced to many teachers and ideas. The design approach has made its way into progressive law schools and is a global phenomenon.

Legal design is human centered rather than centered on the old legal system. It is about effective communication, empathy, and creativity. Legal designers experiment to see what works, often creating prototypes of projects that might work and experimenting with them in action. They can design from a policy perspective or from a more local perspective. One of the things I love about this design perspective is that it recognizes that everyone can play a part in systems design—because we are all playing a part in keeping the old system in place.

There is growing attention for legal design in court processes, self-help information etc. The focus is on accessibility and user experience. See for example these guidelines: https://iaals.du .edu/publications/guidelines-creating-effective-self-help-in formation.

-Susanne van der Meer, legal information designer and
self-help coordinator at rural Colorado court

Cultural Organizing: A Tool for Creating Trauma-Informed Law and Policy

Danya Sherman, with contributions from Dan Jackson and Jules Rochielle Sievert[34]
Cultural organizing means "placing culture at the center of an organizing strategy." Stable Ground is an innovative program housed at Northeastern University School of Law (NUSL) that is deploying cultural organizing to create more trauma-informed local municipal housing law, policy, and programs. This chapter summarizes how we are deploying cultural organizing for this purpose, what's unique about our efforts, and what we've learned in terms of program impact in the first phase, which ran from 2017 to 2019.

Funded by the Kresge Foundation's Arts and Culture program, Stable Ground brings together the City of Boston, local artists, community-based organizations, legal experts, and trauma experts in order to (1) inform and impact the city's housing policy to be more trauma informed, (2) support community-based cultural organizing around affordable housing in Dorchester and beyond, and (3) learn how to support lawyers' approaches to working with and alongside impacted communities.

Stable Ground as Cultural Organizing

While communities have been using creative and cultural approaches to organize and demand tangible change for centuries, the recent proliferation of self-titled creative community development/creative place making work often does not focus on policy or systems-level impact. Projects tend to focus on the production of artistic work, the creation of tangible place-level impacts (such as affordable housing, or increased investment in historically and structurally disinvested neighborhoods), or relationship and community building and strengthening.

Given these trends, the Stable Ground program is unique as cultural organizing in several ways. First, it directly supports the leadership of artists that are from or already embedded in the communities they wished to engage, and who approached their work from a community and cultural organizing perspective. The financial support provided by the Kresge grant is directed to fund work that is already in motion and in process with communities directly impacted by displacement, rather than require artists or communities to create a new project. The program is also unique in that it intends to impact internal change at the City of Boston through direct partnership with one of its offices—the Office of Housing Stability (OHS), which is the first of its kind. The program is

---

[34] Danya Sherman is the founder of Sherman Cultural Strategies, a Boston-based consulting firm that works locally and nationally at the intersection of community development, the arts and social justice. Dan Jackson is the executive director of the NuLawLab at Northeastern University School of Law. Jules Rochielle Sievert is an Ambassador of Health Equity at PolicyLink and the creative director at the NuLawLab.

the only one we are aware of that is based at a law school, approaching arts and housing work from the valuable perspective of its legal implications. Lastly, the program focuses on understanding and calling attention to the human impact of the housing crisis—and its traumatic impacts—as opposed to the traditional focus on statistics, real estate, and units.

Stable Ground included a wide array of activities. The program's core areas of work emerged organically through ongoing conversation among Dan Jackson (executive director) and Jules Rochielle Sievert (creative director) at the NuLawLab, the artists-in-residence Ngoc-Tran Vu, L'Merchie Frazier, and Anna Myer, Mary Harvey, and Barbara Hamm at Violence Transformed, and Margo Lindauer at the Domestic Violence Institute at Northeastern University School of Law. The project's emergent style allowed partnerships to develop at the pace of trust, and activities to take shape according to participant and community desires and needs. The three core areas included artist residencies with grassroots organizations, partnership with the city of Boston, and legal innovation work led by Northeastern law students.

Specific activities included law student research, legal student arts partnerships, trauma workshops, poetry workshops, the City Life Vida Urbana 45th Anniversary Celebration, storytelling events, marching in a popular parade, housing agency community meetings, and a culminating block party featuring a dance performance and community dialogue.

Stable Ground Program Successes

Our evaluation of the first phase found that Stable Ground moved the needle with respect to its primary goals of informing and impacting the city's housing policy and programming to be more trauma informed, supporting under-resourced community-based cultural organizing around affordable housing that is already happening in Dorchester and surrounding neighborhoods, and learning how to support a lawyer's approach to working with and alongside impacted communities. While the work of dismantling an oppressive housing system is far from done, Stable Ground—through its inventive program structure, focus on direct support for cultural organizers and organizations already doing the work, and reflection on legal structure—made important strides and confirmed participants' instincts regarding the value of trauma-informed and culturally resonant practice.

We identified three key impacts from the program:

IMPACT #1: STRENGTHENING TRAUMA-INFORMED HOUSING ADVOCACY

The clearest impact found to date is the project's ability to support and strengthen advocacy for more equitable housing policy and practice among residents, the city, community organizations, artists, and law students. The project did this by assembling a unique and varied set of actors who interact with the housing field in different ways and do not often come together. Stable Ground leveraged the power of arts and organizing to engage participants in a more holistic look at displacement than is the norm, and contributed to building a powerful network across silos and boundaries. In particular, the inclusion of the city of Boston itself as a partner was noted by many participants as a unique and powerful element of Stable Ground. The dialogue among city officials, artist-organizers, and community-based advocates throughout the program helped to lay the groundwork for more trust and knowledge of each other's goals and constraints.

IMPACT #2: HEALING THE TRAUMA OF DISPLACEMENT
The artistic events and activities of phase one provided space for residents who are dealing with the extraordinarily exhausting, dehumanizing, and unspeakably difficult process of eviction proceedings, rent and property tax increases, loss of cultural and business community, and more to find their voice, connect with each other, and process emotions. The work also helped to elevate and center the voices of those impacted by the housing crisis, providing additional healing by reclaiming the narrative around the crisis. Providing the opportunity to participate in arts-oriented activities helped residents feel safer to share their trauma and make space for healing, without doing so in the formal context of a city meeting or hearing.

IMPACT #3: INTENSIFYING THE URGENT CALL FOR POLICY CHANGE
Finally, a vital impact of the program is its contribution to calling attention to the depth of trauma involved in the housing crisis. The program is educating people at various points in the housing system about housing policy and trauma caused by housing instability. A key piece of this impact is also elevating the power of art to support activism—by supporting artists embedded in organizing work, this program reinforced artists' expertise and arts activism through association with a large and powerful institution. As several city staff noted, this program's unique collection of attributes helped to unify disparate groups around a common goal.

Putting Trauma-Informed Lawyering into Practice: What Will We Do Now That We Know?

"The public deserves outcomes that do no further harm and inspires confidence in a system that is severely lacking. No one should leave our meeting rooms, hearing rooms or courtrooms feeling more traumatized, victimized, marginalized or dehumanized than when they entered. We have an obligation and an opportunity to empower the public when they come to us seeking justice, protection, or resolution. Trauma-informed practice is the only sustainable and practical way forward for the legal profession and it is the only way to promote and prioritize meaningful safety, resilience, healing, and rehabilitation for everyone who finds themselves engaging or working within our legal systems."

-from the Trauma-Informed Toolkit for Legal Professionals, by Myrna McCallum

The conclusion of a book is the place where authors often propose solutions to the problems they've presented. Unfortunately, it isn't that simple here as there.

There are several crises in the legal profession. Equal justice (which as Bryan Stevenson points out should be accessible across the legal system), court backlogs, systemic racism (including over-incarceration and underrepresentation of people affected by racism in the legal profession), lawyer well-being, and many more.

These crises create and perpetuate trauma in the legal system and among its stakeholders. Some of these crises are being partially addressed by legal technology and process improvements. However, none of these crises can be addressed either by technology alone or without a trauma-informed approach. Without TIL we will continue to have unwell lawyers and unjustly treated clients, with little or nothing to bridge the gap between them that requires more effective advocacy from lawyers in a profession already facing a continuously serious health crisis.

The first step in changing the system is being aware. What will we do now that we know the impact of trauma can affect the quality of our legal services, the capacity of clients to engage in the legal system, lawyer well-being and even access to justice, especially for clients who have experienced the legal system as harmful and not helpful? Attorney and activist Sherri Mitchell from the Penobscot Nation encourages the acknowledgment of the pain or "soul wound"[1] of collective trauma carried individually and collectively, instead of allowing it to persist silently within people and groups.

This book aims to give lawyers awareness of the TIL's benefits of TIL for all stakeholders and every level of the legal system: increased client satisfaction, better legal process design (and perhaps even better legal outcomes), improved lawyer wellbeing and increased access to justice and legal services by addressing trauma as a barrier to justice. The costs of not adopting TIL or treating it as a "nice to have" checkbox item instead of a "must have" are accepting the alarming status quo that continuously erodes confidence both in the legal profession and the legal system. The unacceptable status quo without TIL includes dissatisfied clients who find the legal system more harmful than helpful, processes and outcomes that either invite or ignore injustice (whether systematically or systemically), a worsening lawyer health crisis which does not contribute to access to justice, and allowing trauma to prevent stakeholders from accessing the justice or legal services they deserve.

The second step in changing the system is being willing to engage in change. For example, Gabor Maté calls upon us to envision systems that are rooted in humane approaches to the law such as rethinking what "correctional" means and replacing the essentially punitive measures that characterize our "trauma-punishing-and-inducing-system" with rehabilitative ones.[2] Maté asks:

> Can we next imagine a trauma-informed legal apparatus, one that could earn its title of "correctional system"? Such a system would have to dedicate itself to actually correcting things in a humane way, a far cry from what we have now. . . . A trauma-informed legal system would not justify or excuse harmful

---

[1] Sherri Mitchell, Sacred Instructions: Indigenous Wisdom for Living Spirit-Based Change (Berkeley, CA: North Atlantic Books, 2018).

[2] Gabor Maté with Daniel Maté, The Myth of Normal: Trauma, Illness and Healing in a Toxic Culture (New York, NY: Avery Publishing, 2022).

behavior. Rather, it would replace nakedly punitive measures with programs designed to rehabilitate people and not to further traumatize them."[3]

All transformative systems change begins with individuals. Each of us can start with willingness to engage with our clients, communities, systems, and even ourselves as lawyers differently, with TIL principles and tools alongside a renewed vision of the humanity that can accompany them.

While trauma isn't a comfortable topic, trauma-informed tools also allow us to deal humanely with the discomfort that Bryan Stevenson points out is an integral part of the pursuit of justice in an already difficult process.

> We have to be willing to do things that are uncomfortable and inconvenient, because justice doesn't come when you only do the things that are comfortable and convenient. . . . We advance justice only when we're willing to do things that are uncomfortable.[4]

We can apply our knowledge of trauma, to, as Bryan Stevenson has also suggested, gain *proximity* to a client's situation (which may be at the margins instead of at the center of society) in order to better represent them, and to bear both discomfort and inconvenience in service of justice.

Rather than being irrelevant and uncomfortable, as lawyers can be prone to assume, facing the trauma in a situation might actually be key to the capacity to pursue justice. International human rights lawyer Philippe Sands has discussed how the pursuit of justice can potentially support the well-being of clients affected by trauma. In his interview with trauma psychologist Jan Kizilhan, who works with people affected by war (including genocide), Philippe Sands writes "Kizilhan sees a connection between the possibility of justice and the future wellbeing of victims. . . . The law can help, as a way of dealing with past wrongs and present traumas, reinforcing memory."

We know many lawyers to be courageous professionals who want to provide better legal processes and outcomes for their clients, and a healthier profession for students, colleagues, and themselves. Now that we know the prevalence and impact of trauma on clients, legal professionals, and the justice system, what will happen if we choose to continue to ignore trauma, as we largely have? Will women continue to leave the profession? For how long will over-incarceration continue? Will young lawyers increasingly burn out or face unaddressed health challenges from their work amid collective silence?

As lawyers (individually) and as the legal profession (collectively) we have a choice—to courageously acknowledge and turn toward trauma with trauma-informed lawyering as a critical competency and skill under continuous

---

[3] *Id.*

[4] Bryan Stevenson, ABA Medal Acceptance Speech, Aug. 4, 2018, https://www.americanbar.org/news/aba news/aba-news-archives/2018/08/social_justice_activ/.

development. Or we can turn away from trauma, knowing that the next generation of students, lawyers, and clients are fated to deal with these same cycles of trauma impact. If we care about our systems and the people in them, we cannot allow it to remain stuck in the revolving doors of lawyer well-being epidemics and lack of justice access that plagues clients affected by trauma.

This primer provides an initial step for putting trauma-informed lawyering into practice across practice areas, across jurisdictions, across schools and courts and legal offices everywhere in order to better meet the needs of the people we serve. We invite you to take that step by learning more and sharing this book, including it in your work, the curriculum at your law school, professional development, community events, and conversations. Applying the principles and tools of trauma-informed lawyering in your own life and work can begin now, in your next meeting, if you are willing to turn toward awareness of and change in response to trauma instead of remaining in our collective legal comfort zones. We can courageously learn to be trauma-informed professionals and implement our professional skills for bringing justice, well-being, and healing to ourselves and communities.

The alternative is for we lawyers to remain haunted by the unbroken transmission of trauma across generations. Given the benefits and the costs of trauma-informed change, what steps are you willing to take outside your comfort zone to create legal system changes that work for everyone, and gain skills that can make you a better (and even a happier) lawyer in the process?

Index

legal systems, 151–154, 210–212
lens-based practice, 64
Levine, Peter, 25, 36, 52–53
limbic brain, 28, 30, 33, 34, 52
limitations, relationship, 56–57
loss, 2, 3, 19, 31, 34, 53, 59, 61, 66, 67, 68, 72, 75,
    79, 94, 108, 126, 134, 137, 145, 146, 156,
    192, 215. *See also* grief
Louie, Jacqueline, 202–203, 202n24

M

Maki, Helgi, 3–4, 28, 63–64, 79–82, 90–93,
    99–101, 122–123, 129–131, 145
Mandela, Nelson, 122
marginalization, 184–186
Maté, Gabor, 156, 218–219
Mayer, Victoria, 118
MBSR. *See* Mindfulness-Based Stress Reduction
    (MBSR)
McCallum, Myrna, 4, 5, 8–9, 22, 121–122, 153,
    155–163, 217
McGrath, Kelly, 66n6
McLachlan, Katherine J., 168–170, 168n7
McMurtry-Chubb, Teri A., 196–201, 196n22
Mead, Margaret, 58
meaning-making, 79–82
medicalization, 1
meditation, 76, 97, 123, 145. *See also* mindfulness
Mehl-Madrona, Lewis, 7
Meinster, Ann Gail, 106
memory, 14, 15, 28, 33, 34, 43, 51, 62, 88, 91–92,
    105, 148, 153, 158, 184, 219
Menakem, Resmaa, 122
mental health, 10, 12, 34, 35, 40, 58, 100, 108, 109,
    129–131, 158–165, 173–175, 183, 185–186
mental well-being practices, 129–144
mentors, 78
microaggression, 184, 185, 202. *See also* racism
Milkwood, 118–119
mind-body practices, 126–129
mindfulness, 41, 50, 51, 123, 129, 143, 145, 161,
    162. *See also* meditation
Mindfulness-Based Stress Reduction
    (MBSR), 123
mirror neurons, 101
Mitchell, Sherri, 153
Model Rules of Professional Conduct, 76–77
Moghadami, Nazanin, 133–134, 133n52
moral injury, 79–82
Moreland-Capuia, Alisha, 33
motivational interviewing, 105, 106
movement and movement practices, 44, 122,
    123, 125, 128, 145
multidisciplinary approaches, 39–57, 118–119
multiplicity, 46–47
Murray-Garcia, Jann, 121
Muslim people, 194, 201
myths, trauma, 25–26

N

narrative(s), 6–7, 14, 32–34, 40, 41, 73, 91, 92,
    105, 185. *See also* story; storytelling
Näsström, Jens, 48n22
nervous system, 126–127
neurobiology of trauma, 29, 30, 33, 42, 91. *See
    also* amygdala; autonomic nervous
    system; hippocampus; limbic brain;
    mirror neurons; nervous system;
    parasympathetic nervous system;
    prefrontal cortex; polyvagal theory;
    sympathetic nervous system; vagus nerve
neurodivergent, 175
neuroscience, 6, 91
neuro-somatic approach, 42–45
nonbinary, 205, 206
nonjudgment, 101–102, 122–129
nonviolent communication (NVC), 119–122
NVC. *See* nonviolent communication (NVC)

O

oppositional rhetorics, 198–199
oppressive environment, 55–57
orienting, 125
Other Conversational Responses, 119–120
oxytocin, 6–7

P

parasympathetic nervous system, 28, 30, 34, 36,
    37, 43, 126, 127
parent orientation and education, 167
PCAs. *See* Primary Claims Advocates (PCAs)
Peck, M. Scott, 114
permission, 72
phenotype, 184
PNDC. *See* Powerful NonDefensive
    Communication (PNDC)
polyvagal theory, 36, 123
Porges, Stephen, 36
Porterfield, Kate, 15, 68–76, 68n7
positive childhood experiences (PACEs), 20
posttraumatic growth, 35, 42, 45–46, 58, 129,
    139, 143, 144
post-traumatic stress disorder (PTSD), 30–31,
    109, 185–186
poverty, 2, 21, 58, 87
power, subjectivity and, 47
Powerful NonDefensive Communication
    (PNDC), 121–122
practice areas, 82–97
prefrontal cortex, 33
presentness, 145
Primary Claims Advocates (PCAs), 107
probate law, 66–68
professional identity, 77–78
professional responsibility, 77–78
proprioception, 44
proximity, 219